'No issue divides neoclassical economics and its critics more than the treatment of time. In contrast to concepts like discounting, optimization, and the growth imperative, this volume offers novel and insightful perspectives on the economics of time and sustainability.'

John Gowdy, Rensselaer Polytechnic Institute, New York, USA

'The authors have taken on the demanding task of devising a strategy – or heuristic – for analyzing sustainability issues. Emphasizing the concepts of stocks, time and judgement, they build a heuristic emphasizing that sustainability analysis is a scholarly endeavor, while in the form of art. The book is interesting reading, pushing an important frontier forward.'

Arild Vatn, Norwegian University of Life Sciences, Norway

Sustainability and the Art of Long-Term Thinking

Dealing with time is intimately linked to sustainability, because sustainability, at its core, involves long-term ethical claims. To live up to them, decision- and policy-making has to consider long-term development of society, economy, and nature. However, dealing with time and such long-term development is a notoriously difficult subject, both in science and, in particular, practical decision and policy making.

Rooted in philosophical and scientific reasoning, this book explores how the concept of time can be incorporated into effective practical action. The book describes a system and uses case studies to help sustainability practitioners and researchers consider the long-term consequences of our actions in a methodical way. The system integrates scientific and practical knowledge about time and temporal developments to help break down the sometimes overwhelming complexity of sustainability issues.

Combining theoretical conceptual thinking and practical applications, this book will be of great interest to students and researchers of sustainability science, environmental sciences, sustainable development, environmental economics, political sciences, and practical philosophy.

Bernd Klauer is a senior scientist at Helmholtz Centre for Environmental Research, Leipzig and an Honorary Professor for Sustainability and Water Resources Management at University of Leipzig, Germany.

Reiner Manstetten has a Habilitation in Economics at the University of Heidelberg, Germany. He is currently a lecturer at the Philosophical Seminar of the University of Heidelberg.

Thomas Petersen has a Habilitation in Philosophy at the University of Heidelberg, Germany. He is currently a lecturer at the Pädagogische Hochschule (College of Education) Heidelberg.

Johannes Schiller is a senior scientist at the Helmholtz Centre for Environmental Research, Leipzig, Germany.

Routledge Studies in Sustainability

Critiquing Sustainability, Changing Philosophy
Jenneth Parker

Transdisciplinary Sustainability Studies
A Heuristic Approach
Katri Huutoniemi and Petri Tapio

Challenging Consumption
Pathways to a more sustainable future
Edited by Anna R. Davies, Frances Fahy and Henrike Rau

Democratic Sustainability in a New Era of Localism
John Stanton

Social Practices, Interventions and Sustainability
Beyond Behaviour Change
Edited by Yolande Strengers and Cecily Maller

The Politics of Sustainability
Philosophical perspectives
Edited by Dieter Birnbacher and May Thorseth

Promoting Sustainable Living
Sustainability as an Object of Desire
Justyna Karakiewicz, with contributions from Audrey Yue and Angela Paladino

Rethinking the Green State
Environmental governance towards climate and sustainability transitions
Edited by Karin Bäckstrand and Annica Kronsell

Energy and Transport in Green Transition
Perspectives on Ecomodernity
Edited by Atle Midttun and Nina Witoszek

Human Rights and Sustainability
Moral responsibilities for the future
Edited by Gerhard Bos and Marcus Düwell

Sustainability and the Art of Long-Term Thinking
Edited by Bernd Klauer, Reiner Manstetten, Thomas Petersen and Johannes Schiller

Sustainability and the Art of Long-Term Thinking

Bernd Klauer, Reiner Manstetten, Thomas Petersen, and Johannes Schiller

With contributions from
Beate Fischer, Frank Jöst, Mi-Yong Lee, and Konrad Ott

Translated by Kathleen Cross

First published 2017
by Routledge
2 Park Square, Milton Park, Abingdon, Oxon OX14 4RN

and by Routledge
711 Third Avenue, New York, NY 10017

First issued in paperback 2018

Routledge is an imprint of the Taylor & Francis Group, an informa business

Cover art: Paul Klee: Hauptwege und Nebenwege, 1929, oil on canvas, Museum Ludwig, Köln.
Cover photo: © Rheinisches Bildarchiv, rba_coo4581.

British Library Cataloguing-in-Publication Data
A catalogue record for this book is available from the British Library

Library of Congress Cataloging-in-Publication Data
A catalog record for this book has been requested

ISBN 13: 978-1-138-59742-6 (pbk)
ISBN 13: 978-1-138-68990-9 (hbk)

Typeset in Bembo
by diacriTech, Chennai

Contents

Figures

Tables

Preface

The saying 'Those who are late will be punished by life itself' came to be a well-known slogan of German unification. Contrary to popular belief it was not Mikhail Gorbachev but his foreign affairs spokesman, Gennadi Gerasimov, who inscribed this saying onto the pages of the history books, thereby expressing the attitude of the then Soviet government towards Erich Honecker on the fortieth anniversary of the founding of the German Democratic Republic (GDR). Clearly the old GDR government had failed to read the signs of the times. But what about us? Are we reading the signs of the times today when it comes to our grandchildren's well-being and the preservation of the natural environment on which all life depends? Long-term prescient thinking apparently does not come at all easily to any of us.

This book addresses the topic of 'time', a topic that is seldom placed at the centre of scholarly study – perhaps precisely because it is so fundamental and ever present. In fact, the same is true even of sustainability research, where thinking in long-term time horizons actually ought to be taken for granted. In academic studies time is generally dealt with (if at all) as a secondary issue or as merely implicit. The topic has no prominent place in present day philosophy either. In this book, however, we have placed this otherwise marginal topic firmly centre stage. Both as academics and philosophers we are keen to explore ways of acquiring the ability to think in long timescales. We seek to provide knowledge that serves as an orientation for practical political action in situations where it is crucial to adopt a long-term perspective.

We have been studying the topic of time for some time now. This is certainly due in large part to sharing an intellectual affinity to the former Chair of Economic Theory II, Emeritus Professor Malte Faber, at Heidelberg University, where most of us have our academic roots. It was here, during the 1970s, that we addressed time in the context of the so-called neo-Austrian theory of capital, an approach that enables long-term developments in the economy, such as the successive replacement of technologies, to be studied. Very soon after that we started looking at the time-related aspects of environmental issues, and since the publication of the Brundtland Report in 1986 research has been progressing on issues of sustainability and intergenerational justice. One specific feature of the study group was that it included not only economics scholars but also mathematicians, physicists and philosophers. The substance and style of the research along with the interdisciplinary dialogue that went on within the research group bore all the characteristics of a distinct school of research, described by some as the *Heidelberg School of Ecological Economics*. The present book can be situated squarely in the tradition of this school, whose main geographical locus shifted from Heidelberg to the Helmholtz Centre for Environmental Research – UFZ in Leipzig after Malte Faber became an Emeritus Professor.

The interdisciplinary style of study and research adopted by the author collective is reflected in the different styles of writing chosen for each of the different chapters. Chapters 5–8, for example, are written in a more philosophical style, whereas Chapter 4 contains elements of mathematical exposition. The empirical case studies in Chapters 9 and 10 are narrative in style, while the presentation of a heuristic in Chapter 11 is more descriptive and explanatory.

At this point we would like to offer the readers of this book a few suggestions for how to approach it. The key outcome of this book is a heuristic for a politics of sustainability. This is described in Chapter 11. The heuristic builds upon the core conceptual elements 'time', 'judgement' (the faculty of judgement) and 'stock', which are elaborated in Chapters 4–8. In order to enable the reader to skip more easily back and forth from one chapter to another, the main points from these chapters are summarised in a box at the end of each chapter. Chapter 6 contains an additional box at the end of Section 6.2.

For those who read with haste, we recommend the following approach:

- Chapter 1 motivates the reader to take a closer look at the topic of time.
- Section 2.5 names four aspects that are essential to sustainability as a normative model of political and individual action.
- Sections 4.1–4.3 as well as the summary boxes at the end of Chapters 5–8 describe the key concepts and terms 'material stock', 'institution', 'judgement' and 'time'.
- Chapter 11 also begins with a retrospective consideration of the core elements of the stocks framework and proceeds to link these together into a heuristic for sustainability.
- Finally, Chapter 13 describes the character of the stocks framework as a school in which it is possible to learn the art of thinking in long timescales.

Although the book is based on a long series of previous studies, key sections of it emerged out of the project 'The Conceptual Framework of Stocks as a Decision Making Resource for a Politics of Sustainability', funded by the German Federal Ministry of Education and Research (BMBF). All those who worked on that project are also the authors of this book. However, at the end of the funding period, the book was still an 'unfinished symphony'. It was completed in the course of the follow-on project, 'Structures of Responsibility as a Precondition for Sustainability: The Management of EU Water Resources' (likewise funded by the BMBF). Both projects were part of the priority research programme 'Economics for Sustainability', which in turn is part of the BMBF framework programme

'Research for Sustainable Development' (*Forschung für Nachhaltige Entwicklung*, FONA).

The authors of this book worked extremely closely together. Many ideas were developed collaboratively, then written down and presented again to the group. It was not uncommon for the first version of a passage of text to be formulated jointly by two authors. The texts were then edited several times by at least two other authors.

As a result, the book in its present form is a collaborative piece of work, even if the individual contributions towards it have varied. The main authors of the book are, in alphabetical order: Bernd Klauer, Reiner Manstetten, Thomas Petersen and Johannes Schiller. In addition to authoring specific chapters, they were responsible for the overall conceptual design of the book, for formulating its main lines of argument and for giving it its final form. Then there are other authors who contributed in key ways to various chapters of the book. These are, likewise in alphabetical order: Beate Fischer (Chapters 6, 10 and 11), Frank Jöst (Chapters 6 and 10), Mi-Yong Lee (Chapters 5 and 9) and Konrad Ott (Chapter 2). These authors are named as co-authors at the start of the relevant chapters. It should also be mentioned that the empirical studies on the issue of contaminated sites in Saxony-Anhalt (Chapter 9) were conducted mainly by Mi-Yong Lee and that the empirical studies on German land management policy (Chapter 10) in essence by Beate Fischer and Frank Jöst.

It is an honour and a duty to thank those people who supported us in many ways during the writing of this book. First and foremost we would like to express our heartfelt thanks to our friend and *spiritus rector* Malte Faber, who brought us together and inspired us to get to grips with time and stocks. He has provided ongoing support to our work as it has progressed, partly as a member of the Academic Advisory Council to the research programme 'Economics for Sustainability'. Not least, we thank him especially for his close reading of the entire manuscript and for his kind words in the Foreword.

Next we would like to thank the German Federal Ministry of Education and Research for its financial support and Thomas Schulz for his very helpful supervision of the project in terms of both administration and research guidance. We also thank the members of the Academic Advisory Council of the research programme 'Economics for Sustainability', especially Dieter Ewringmann and Wolfgang Buchholz, for their encouragement and support.

This book was originally written in German and published at Nomos-Verlag, Baden-Baden. The German title of the book is: Die Kunst langfristig zu denken: Wege zur Nachhaltigkeit; ISBN 978-3-8487-0070-7; Nomos Verlagsgesellschaft, Boden-Boden, Germany. We wish to express our appreciation to Kathleen Cross for her meticulous and thoughtful translation of the manuscript. We would also like to thank the team from Routledge for their professional support in the publication process of this book.

We are additionally grateful to all those with whom we have discussed our ideas and who have read, commented on and critiqued our texts or parts of the manuscript. In this regard we would like to mention Frauke Bathe, Stefan Baumgärtner, Sylvia Bittner, Sebastian Hartig, Wolfgang Köck, Martin Quaas, Peter Reichert,

Mario Schirmer, Nele Schuwirth, Andrew Stirling and Anne Wessner. We are indebted to Stefan Gunkel (BUND/Friends of the Earth) for giving us permission to use material from a text about inland waterways transport policy in Germany, written jointly with Bernd Klauer, in Chapter 12. Our thanks also go to those who participated in interviews and informal conversations for the two case studies on contamination management in Saxony-Anhalt and on land management policy in Germany, especially Vera Gäde-Butzlaff and Klaus Rehda.

Last but by no means least we extend our grateful thanks to both the directors and our colleagues at the Helmholtz Centre for Environmental Research for contributing towards making UFZ an excellent place to conduct creative work.

The Authors

Foreword

by Malte Faber

The conflict between theory and practice often seems hopelessly entrenched, with academics bemoaning the lack of attention politicians pay to their research results and politicians complaining that academics contribute too little towards solving their problems. With the advance of interdisciplinary research and systems analysis the two contrary positions have seen a degree of rapprochement, of course, but a fundamental and insurmountable chasm between academia and politics remains nonetheless. The authors of this book – economists, sociologists, political scientists, mathematicians, physicists and philosophers – make no attempt to overcome this opposition. Rather, by accepting it as given, they use it as a springboard to highlight ways of dealing constructively with it. Their conceptual framework of stocks, which takes certain ideas from the economic theory of capital, elaborates them further and has been tested in three case studies, is evidence of the extent to which they have succeeded in doing so. It is no exaggeration to claim that it constitutes a revolutionary method in research-based policy advice. Within 5 minutes flat – the amount of time politicians grant academics for an initial advisory session – advisers can present a diagnosis, analysis and potential remedies for complex long-term problems. Although the method has been developed on the basis of scholarly – especially philosophical – foundations it is not itself an academic discipline but rather an art: *the art of long-term thinking*.

This art is based on the conceptual framework of stocks, which has been elaborated in the course of years of research. Stocks are both material and immaterial in nature. In the former case they are things, such as machines, and in the latter institutions, such as habits and rules. By looking at stocks we are able to provide an initial description of the problem that is immediately and readily evident. If fundamental changes are to be made to transportation, an overview of stocks in terms of roads, cars, motor vehicle companies, traffic regulations, transportation plans, transportation volume and typical behaviour in traffic makes it plain straight away that such changes can only be made over the long term and only with political will coupled with patience and determination. Stocks – in German *Bestände* – draw attention to the fact that a particular thing that exists – *das Bestehende* – is by nature long lasting and inert, in other words, that it displays persistence through time – *Beständigkeit* – regardless of whether or not we wish it to continue. When dealing with stocks, the key is to develop a 'sense of time'. It is not only a matter of possessing patience and endurance: it is also a matter of recognising the right moment to act and doing so, much like Field Marshall Kutuzov in Tolstoy's *War and Peace* (cf. Section 8.4 in this book). The conventional means of decision support provided by the disciplines of economics and politics are not up to the task, and neither is rational choice theory or its successor theories. Making sound decisions requires more than just taking into account profits and costs determined on the basis of the present pricing system. It requires judgement refined by experience. In complex situations where decisions need to be taken and there is a lack of knowledge about many aspects of the potential options, the conceptual framework of stocks makes available to the decision maker's faculty of judgement a set of guidelines for creating order and making sense of all the different disciplinary expert knowledge available. At the same time, judgement provides appropriate space for creativity, intuition and feeling without being overly dominant. The focus on ways of looking at stocks ensures that the openness available for decision making does not tip over into arbitrariness.

The stocks framework is a path-breaking innovation in that it offers a way of generating clarity and – given patience and determination – providing practical leverage for politicians dealing with complex problems that demand far-reaching action. Now it is up to politicians to apply this method and, drawing on their own practical experience, to deal with research outcomes in a new and constructive way. If they do, it will become possible to solve complex long-term problems to an as yet unprecedented extent. Doing so requires *the art of long-term thinking.*

Malte Faber

Part I

Sustainability and time

1 Different approaches to sustainability policy

1.1 Time

How can we slow down global warming and how can people adapt to a changed climate? How can we ensure that everyone has access to enough clean drinking water and adequate food every day? How can we deal appropriately with an expanding world population on the one hand and with ageing populations in many industrialised societies on the other? How can global change be shaped and influenced? How can energy supplies be secured over the long term? What should be done to prevent the decline in biological diversity? How can the growth of megacities be kept within reasonable bounds? How can we preserve the beauty of our countryside landscapes? What can we ourselves do to solve these problems, and what is the role of policy makers? How can we create a decent and liveable future for our children? We might sum up these and many other questions by asking: what must we do to achieve *sustainable development*?

Sustainability has become a widely recognised normative model in which our concerns about the future find expression. While the current focus of the sustainability debate is on environmental and resource-related problems, issues of inter- and intragenerational justice are also being raised, doubts are surfacing about what technological progress can really achieve, and there is a debate about changes in environmental awareness and consumer behaviour. However, our impression is that one particularly crucial aspect is not being adequately addressed in the sustainability debate, and that is the dimension of *time*. This may seem paradoxical given that, after all, sustainability is about the rights of future generations and therefore about the future. Surely it is precisely this long-term perspective – the dimension of time – that sets sustainability policy apart from any other kind of policy. So what do we mean when we say that time is not being adequately addressed in the debate about sustainability?

Time is a word with several meanings. When we say that time is not given the attention it deserves in the sustainability debate we are not talking initially about the kind of time you can read on a clock or a calendar. Instead we are interested in two other meanings of time.

First, time can be talked about in terms of the *time inherent to things*. If we want to ask whether or not a specific type of development is sustainable or what sustainable development might mean in concrete terms, we need to look at the entire span of time over which certain things exist – things such as resources, contaminants, infrastructures, manufactured goods, landscapes, animal populations, laws, regulations and consumer habits, as well as other things that persist through time. Although these things are constantly changing as a result of circumstances either internal or external to them, they also display a certain inertia or persistence that becomes especially apparent when we wish to change something. A spent open pit lignite mine, for example, remains a huge hole in the landscape that can only gradually be filled with water, disused refrigerators are piled on refuse tips and rot down only slowly, and life without a car is inconceivable for many people who live in rural areas because mobility is an integral part of the way they imagine their life to be. Slow-moving processes of this kind are all too lightly glossed over in academic studies and policy discussions alike. Yet when it comes to dealing with global developments and the long-term well-being of humanity or when creeping changes to the environment threaten the very basis of survival for humans and animals, an analysis of slow-moving, persistent things and their 'inherent dynamic' may be the key to understanding what is going on. If the aim is to intervene and to steer change in a new direction, it is necessary to be aware of the inertia, persistence, durability and dynamics of things and to take them into account when conducting that intervention.

The other important meaning of time in the context of the sustainability debate can be described as the *time for action*. If we seek to change things, situations and structures in order to bring about lasting positive developments, it is necessary to identify the right moment – or, in current usage, to recognise a 'window of opportunity' and to make the most of it while it is still open. Taking action before the window opens means acting overhastily; acting after the window has closed means missing an opportunity.

It is probably not necessary to explain why time in both these senses is important for any sustainability policy. Nonetheless, time – especially if we are talking about more than just a chronological series of events – has proved to be difficult to handle when formulating theory. Time in the first sense of the 'time inherent to things' is indeed the object of study in various respects in the natural and social sciences and in cultural studies, depending on the research topic concerned, and yet the way each discipline approaches phenomena of persistence and dynamics varies greatly.

Academic advisers on sustainability policy and public policy makers alike need to consider the interplay among a range of factors – not just ecological but also economic, social and cultural; they are often at a loss when faced with research results from specific disciplines. Studies conducted by soil researchers, toxicologists, water researchers, ecologists, economists and sociologists are often so diverse in terms of their methodological approaches and the language they use that it is almost impossible to get an overall picture of the situation and of the dynamics of the things under consideration from the host of detailed information provided. There is no language available to express all the knowledge in the same terms and there is no way of establishing an overall view of it. Yet without a clear picture of the situation – its constraints and its possibilities – we know neither where we stand nor what we ought to do. In our view, the fact that there is no language (much less a method) for comprehending the time of things as a whole – beyond the separate disciplinary perspectives – is a major reason for the lack of clarity that threatens to obstruct policy action on sustainability.

By contrast, time in the second sense of 'time for action' is generally not regarded as a subject for theoretical debate at all; instead it is seen as a matter of the experience, intuition, gut feeling or instinct for power possessed by particularly gifted politicians. This means that something which is – literally – decisive for the success of any sustainability policy, namely, being able to do the right thing at the right moment in time, seems to be something irrational, something that exists not only outside the realm of scholarly theorising but is not even amenable to discourse or even to the careful weighing of lucid arguments. Because this is perceived to be the case, the notion of time for action does not command scholarly attention. We think this is a mistake, and it is one we seek to help rectify. As we will show, even if the time for action is not a discrete object of study in the individual disciplines, there are nonetheless ways of thinking rationally about this sense of time and of saying something meaningful about how it relates to sustainability policy.

In our view, sustainability policy all too often fails because politicians and their academic advisers have either not adequately understood the nature of time in relation to the things (including structures) to which their policies apply (one example of this is land use, which we examine in Chapter 10) or else they fail to recognise the time for action, missing the opportunity to act at the right moment or acting too quickly. Above all, there continues to be a lack of understanding regarding the interplay between the two senses of time[1]. However, if we attempt to grasp this interplay, then those who are able to perceive them will find that occasionally, 'in the course of things', certain *windows of opportunity* will present themselves for appropriate action. In fact, it even becomes possible to look for – or actively bring about – such windows of opportunity.

Our concern here is to develop a set of concepts and methods that facilitate an understanding of the phenomena of time – in both its senses and in their mutual interplay – in sustainability policy. Using terms such as persistence (*Beständigkeit*), stock (*Bestand*), the *inherent dynamic* (*Eigendynamik*) of things and the judgement (*Urteilskraft*) possessed by policy makers and advisers, we seek to render time comprehensible in terms of the ways its different aspects fit together.

1.2 Academia and sustainability policy

The terms mentioned above are set to play a key role as the contents of this book unfold; some brief introductory comments on them form part of this introductory chapter (Sections 1.3–1.5). First, though, we wish to mention one general concern embodied in this work. Our discussion of the topic of time in this book is not a matter of 'theory for theory's sake'. Instead – all discussion of fundamentals notwithstanding – it is always conducted with a view to practical utility.

In other words, all of us who have contributed to this book are keen to contribute towards the success of sustainability policy. To this end, we begin by elucidating the demands made on politicians dealing with sustainability before drawing conclusions from this regarding the underlying knowledge base and finally turning to the relationship between knowledge, or academia, and politics.

1.2.1 Demands made on politicians

The questions posed at the start of this introductory chapter about what needs to be done to achieve sustainable development in various situations contain challenges for society and for public policy in particular. Compared with a more traditional understanding of politics, the responsibility borne by policy makers facing sustainability issues is very much greater (Jonas 1984): their focus is no longer just regional or national but increasingly global as well, and it extends not only to the near future but to predicted medium - and long-term ecological and social processes and events[2].

In very general terms, good public policy requires a *normative orientation, adequate information* and the *capacity to act*. In other words, its objectives need to be reasonable (in the sense of achievable), existing circumstances and options for action need to be clear, and the relevant actors need to be in a position to carry out what they have identified to be the correct course of action. In the case of policies aimed at achieving sustainable development, these requirements are usually very hard to fulfil – indeed, they can often seem to be simply too much to handle. Normative issues need to be considered in relation to various ecological and socio-economic concerns whose relative merits are extremely difficult to calibrate. Information comes from different sources that do not communicate with one another; it comes with a considerable degree of uncertainty attached and is often heterogeneous or even contradictory so that its cumulative effect is one of numbing complexity. And since politics as a whole consists of many poorly coordinated regulatory systems, official bodies and individuals at different hierarchical levels whose efforts often have to be coordinated across country borders, the capacity of politicians to act on issues of sustainability is similarly constrained by all kinds of obstacles.

Some of these demands and stresses affect policy makers in particular, while others have an impact on all of a country's citizens. As far as the information base is concerned, it is not only practitioners' experiential knowledge that is required (and this should not be underestimated), but especially knowledge gained from academic or specifically scientific research.

1.2.2 Gaps in the knowledge base for sustainability policy

As scholars working on environmental and sustainability research we – the authors of this book – are keen to ensure that our understandings contribute towards successful sustainability policy. To this end, indeed, some of us are directly involved in policy advice processes. When we recall the many small and large research or consultancy projects and the national or international research programmes and funding calls with which we have been associated in some way or another in the course of our work and which claimed to be problem-based and relevant to practical concerns, we often ask ourselves: does the research community provide adequate support to politicians who seek to do justice to the challenges arising from the goal of sustainable development? Does it contribute all it is capable of contributing towards sustainability policy? Where are the gaps? What could it do better?

The various academic disciplines have certainly contributed a great deal towards sustainability policy: the array of knowledge that has been generated over the last few decades on issues relevant to sustainability in nature and society is impressive. It is true enough that there is uncertainty and considerable ignorance in almost all relevant areas, but the current generation cannot justify inaction on setting a policy direction or implementing measures by saying we do not yet know enough to do so. Uncertainty and lack of knowledge will never disappear completely, but even so in most cases we already possess enough knowledge to act – even if it would often be helpful to know more when it comes to the finer details. Despite this, many of us who work as advisers to policy makers dealing with sustainability issues have come to feel a certain sense of unease and perplexity. We believe the problem is mainly one of a lack of clarity and integration of the knowledge that is available.

Let us look at climate change and energy policy for example. It is widely known that fossil fuels are not a long-term viable basis for energy supplies anymore given that they are a major contributor to anthropogenic climate change and are finite. Similarly, there is also a consensus of opinion – in Germany, at least – that the resulting shortfall cannot be made up by nuclear energy. The resultant forceful, all-out push for bioenergy – especially biofuels – adopted by Germany and other countries is one response to this, albeit one that in turn leads to a whole host of further problems. The growing demand for biomass generates a strong incentive for farmers to use land for biomass production. Having used subsidies for many years to achieve a lower level of intensification in agriculture, Germany is now seeing a trend towards reclaiming marginal land – land whose yield is barely worth the effort to cultivate it – for agricultural production and again intensifying agriculture as a whole, with all the negative impacts this has on nature conservation and water resource management. This is happening all over the world and is evident, for example, in increasing pressures on tropical rainforests and the fact that the world market price for maize has risen sharply due to competition over food versus biomass production.

The bioenergy example gives an indication of how complex the task of implementing a *sustainable* energy policy is. What we are also seeing, though, is that policy making typically makes use of simple patterns of cause and effect, along the lines of 'there's the problem, here's the solution'. This can be illustrated by reference to a host of examples from different policy areas relating to sustainability – from the German Renewable Energy Sources Act (*Erneuerbare-Energien-Gesetz*, EEG) to the European ban on traditional light bulbs and the German policy of funding for transport infrastructure. One fundamental problem in all this has to do with the knowledge base: it is virtually impossible for any one person to have an overview of the host of knowledge available in the sciences, economics, the social sciences, law and the humanities that is relevant for making 'sound' sustainability policy in the broadest sense – much less to communicate it in a meaningful way. This means that decisions are often made on the basis of a more or less random selection of the knowledge that is available and most relevant. There is no means of integrating the knowledge gained from research into a clear general picture (Mieg 2005).

In our view the reasons for this shortcoming lie not least in the peculiarities of the current system of academic research. Researchers who publish their results are usually seeking either to contribute to the progress of knowledge within the scientific (or general academic) community or to facilitate the development of technical applications. The aim of passing on knowledge to policy makers or advisers in sustainability policy tends to be the exception. Generally speaking, knowledge is documented and communicated in a way that is hard for advisers and policy makers to understand. What is lacking are ways of presenting knowledge from the individual disciplines that make it accessible to interested non-experts without resorting to misleading simplifications. Conversely, all too often policy makers have not been able to access the knowledge relevant to the problem they need to tackle[3].

1.2.3 Academic research and sustainability policy: aims of this book

It is against this backdrop that we hope this book may help to make existing knowledge accessible to sustainability policy advisers and policy makers so that it can be put to practical use in solving specific problems. The book thus addresses the interface between knowledge and policy – albeit not primarily as an object of academic research but in a way that enables policy makers to acquire useful tools that will help them work towards possible solutions in the complex situations presented by many sustainability problems. We seek to contribute at three distinct levels:

- at the level of theory, by developing a conceptual scheme and a perspective that enables knowledge relating to sustainability – both academic knowledge and practical knowledge – to be structured clearly and thus to identify practical options for and constraints acting on advisers and policy makers;
- at the empirical level, by discussing real-world case studies in sustainability policy; and
- at a practical level, by presenting a heuristic that offers decision makers and advisers a procedural tool for unravelling and exploring sustainability problems, dividing them up into workable chunks and making them amenable to sensible solutions.

The ideas presented in this book hinge on the issue of *time*. Time is the factor that structures sustainability-related knowledge theoretically, but it is just as important for studying empirical cases and structuring a heuristic. The concepts of *stock* and *persistence* together with the faculty of *judgement* form the focal point of our theoretical study. Using time as a connecting factor, these terms are linked together and developed into a *heuristic for sustainability policy*. In situations where politicians are faced with a complex and confusing problem, the heuristic is designed to enable them to generate a rough overall picture of the situation and gain access to the relevant knowledge base; it enables them to get an idea of what needs to be done and to develop ideas for feasible options, and it helps to highlight appropriate windows of opportunity for implementing those options.

1.3 Persistence as an expression of the time inherent to things[4]

When we speak of stocks and persistence we mean things, circumstances and structures in existence that persist over long periods of time – regardless of whether their existence is desirable or undesirable. Here we offer a few illustrations:

- A river may flow for centuries, perhaps for millennia or longer. It changes its shape only slowly as it carves a path through the landscape. It carries boats, drives hydropower stations and sometimes floods fields and towns.
- Headframes are erected to bring coal to the surface; but when coal is no longer being mined they may 'stand around' for decades until they are demolished or preserved as industrial monuments.
- A population of wolves consists of several packs as well as lone individuals. A pack is made up of the parent animals, the wolf cubs and the juvenile wolves. From time to time a pack will disband because the parents have died, but new packs form at the same time and the population survives.
- The burning of coal, crude oil and natural gas produces CO_2. This initially goes more or less unnoticed until – in some cases much later – it affects the climate as part of the stock of CO_2 in the atmosphere.
- Crude oil can be used to make plastics. A plastic bag that is no longer used continues to exist as waste for a long time. Large amounts of this kind of waste are increasingly accumulating in the world's oceans.
- A nuclear power plant serves to generate energy for several decades. In addition to electricity it also generates radioactive waste. Once it is turned off the power plant continues to exist for centuries or even longer as a set of radioactive building components. The waste also continues to emit radiation over a period of centuries or even millennia.
- When laws are passed, they may help human beings to live alongside one another, and yet at the same time some clever observer may later say of them: 'Like an eternal, rank contagion, / Statutes and laws are inherited. / They drag from generation on to generation, / And stealthily from place to place they spread. / Reason to nonsense turns, blessings to curses' (Goethe 1912: 88).

These varied examples have one thing in common: they are all things that remain in existence for a long time and are also inert and resistant when it comes to enforced change. They have 'their time', as the Old Testament book of

Ecclesiastes (3, 1–11) puts it. In the present book this characteristic is referred to as the *persistence* (*Beständigkeit*) of a thing.

The long or short life span of a thing is not a positive or problematic characteristic *per se*. But it can turn into a problem if it becomes the object of human desires, worries or interests, or if it is a thing we want to reduce or remove or perhaps increase or prevent from disappearing. An area of marshland is initially simply there and will most probably remain there if no one interferes with it. It becomes a problem if someone wants to use the land for agriculture and attempts to drain it or if they want to preserve it over the long term as a nature conservation area, having realised that it is in danger of drying out as a result of climate change. Many things in nature, such as rivers or mountains, may come under the sway of human interests and be altered because of this – but not everything is possible. The appearance of the Alps may be shaped or disfigured by human intervention, the glaciers may melt, but the persistence of the mountain range itself is – considered on the timescale of human existence and regardless of how we would wish it to be – simply a fact that those concerned with land use or traffic planning or the tourist industry have to live with.

Unlike rivers and mountains, things that are made by people owe their existence to human desires, worries and interests. They are created for certain purposes and it may be hoped that they will continue to exist for as long as they fulfil their purpose. But should they no longer be capable of fulfilling this purpose, they (or a part of them) will often continue to exist nonetheless, in some cases long into the future. Then they are simply there – part of the landscape, as it were. In some cases – as, say, with a slag heap in a coal-mining area that is now covered with mixed woodland – this may not be a problem. Often, though, what remains is not harmless or irrelevant but rather dangerous, harmful or destructive. Waste matter, wastewater and spent air from current or past production processes, derelict production facilities, contaminated soils, and odds and ends left over from consumer goods and interventions in nature and the landscape often cause problems. Far from simply appearing as an inevitable part of the landscape, they remain objects of perennial worry and concern. However, the same applies to laws, rights, organisations and lifestyle habits which, at the time when they arose, appeared perfectly sensible: all too often they still make their presence felt long after they no longer make any sense and instead act as a hindrance to economic progress or human co-existence (as hinted at in Goethe's verses)[5]. Even in respect of these immaterial things there is a certain persistence that is hard to accept without holding on to the notion that it might yet be possible somehow to be rid of these institutions and customs once and for all.

The things described in the previous paragraph differ from purely natural things by virtue of their prior history. Their existence has its origins in people's intentions and is thus their responsibility. At the time when they were thought up and made a reality, not much thought (if any) was put into asking what use they might be once they have fulfilled their purpose and are no longer needed. It was not until the idea of sustainable development came along that many people came to see the importance of considering what impacts things have when they are no longer useful or fulfil a purpose – and incorporating these insights into their manufacture and mode of use[6].

To be able to implement a foresightful sustainability policy in a situation involving diffuse problems, it is crucial to recognise the persistence of things over time and to deal with it in an appropriate manner. There are many objects among those that persist over time whose existence and dynamics are relevant to sustainability policy – whether this is because they need to be preserved or strengthened or because they are obstacles that need to be removed or reduced. This book discusses groundwater resources, landscapes, rivers, lakes, raw materials deposits, accumulations of pollutants, plant and animal populations, the populations of cities and countries, machines and buildings, as well as organisations, corporate bodies, and indeed even laws, institutions and technologies in terms of their persistence through time. Our aim in doing so is to shed light on their temporal processes and dynamics, setting these against one another in order to reveal medium- and long-term options, or indeed constraints, for sustainability policy.

We are in possession of a great deal of knowledge and yet we have considerable difficulty exploiting it in the service of policies conducive to sustainability. Looking at things in terms of their persistence through time, however, can serve – like a spotlight in the dark – to throw into sharp relief the temporal aspects that are so important for sustainability issues. Doing so will prevent us from becoming lost in the detail of the specific problem formulations and approaches of individual disciplines and instead enable us to examine systematically the various disciplinary theories, methods and research results in terms of persistence through time, in order to uncover their particular contribution towards analysing and resolving sustainability problems.

The perspective of persistence through time is the common thread that runs throughout this book. In Chapters 3 and 4 the concept of stock (*Bestand*) is developed and elaborated in order to provide a detailed formulation of this perspective, to reflect on its theoretical and practical implications and to render it useful for those involved in sustainability policy action. The term 'stock' was used initially by Nicholas Georgescu-Roegen (1971: Sec. 3) to refer to the relationship between the economy and the environment and has subsequently been taken up in several strands of the literature[7]. The author sees 'stock' as a contrasting term to 'flow', both of which need to be considered to obtain a complete picture of an economic process.

The stocks perspective is not suitable as such to address purely normative aspects of sustainability policy and especially issues of justice. This need not be seen as a shortcoming, however; rather it can be regarded as an advantage because it is precisely by emphasising the descriptive aspects of a sustainability problem that it becomes easier to separate these from the normative ones.

1.4 The time for action: political judgement[8]

Another fundamental concept in this book is that of judgement (*Urteilskraft*), a term substantially defined and developed by Immanuel Kant (1855: 104f., 2001). Those who act are rarely able to do so merely by following certain routines or mechanically obeying predetermined norms, rules or formulas. Nor can academic analyses or research-based solutions ever be put directly into practice. Specific situations are always contingent: they embody specific characteristics, possibilities or difficulties which cannot be a part of pertinent norms, rules, formulas or research-based solutions because the latter are associated with the claim of universality. Being able to deal appropriately with universal precepts in specific circumstances – which may entail deviating from a norm or a rule according to circumstances – requires judgement.

Judgement refers to an individual's ability to do two things: first, to recognise how a set of general considerations, guidelines and rules can be applied in a specific case and conclusions drawn from them and, second, to understand what the overarching, universally valid considerations are in any particular case. In the context of policy action, judgement also encompasses an ability to wait for the right moment to implement an idea deemed to be the right one and to act resolutely when that time comes.

In relation to sustainability policy, judgement means assessing a given situation correctly. Doing so requires information suited to gaining an initial overview of the situation. What is needed is an ability to identify the key facts from the point of view of sustainability, to distinguish relevant knowledge (provided by researchers and practitioners) from non-relevant knowledge, and to make proper use of it.

The term 'judgement' points to a problem that is extremely hard for political theorists and policy advisers to resolve satisfactorily. Judgement highlights the fact that successful policy action and good policy advice are linked to certain personal skills. As with any skill, judgement requires both a certain natural talent as well as practice. As far as talent is concerned, generally speaking, a person either has it or they do not. When it comes to practice, there are certain guidelines and methods that can help a person to acquire it. Judgement differs from 'gut feeling' in that it is receptive to rational guidance and a structured approach. Strictly speaking it is not possible to say much about gut feeling, whereas it is perfectly feasible to apply certain rational rules of thumb when it comes to using judgement properly – even it if remains the case that any judgement leading to successful action is hard to imagine without a touch of intuition (a residual 'gut feeling').

Looking at situations and events through the lens of persistence through time enables us to develop guidelines for the faculty of judgement; these can offer orientation amidst the complexities and confusions involved in putting sustainability into practice. In particular, the concept of stock enables us to develop a methodical set of steps by which judgement can proceed. We show how it is possible to frame *specific* sustainability problems using *general* forms of knowledge and then to explore options for action. This set of steps was referred to above as a heuristic.[9]

1.5 The conceptual framework of stocks as a heuristic for sustainability policy: themes and structure of the book

In the present book we introduce a number of unfamiliar terms and in some cases develop them from scratch. Because the book is aimed at scholars from a variety of disciplines, experts with different educational backgrounds and interested lay people, we have done our best to avoid specialist jargon, to explain unfamiliar terms in detail and to use language that is broadly comprehensible. However, the book does not remain at the conceptual level: it attempts to apply the terms introduced to practical examples, not least in order to fulfil its purpose of offering not only theoretical ideas but also applied, practicable contributions to sustainability policy. It is thus fairly ambitious in its scope.

Before addressing the issue of how to devise sound sustainability policy and what academic researchers can contribute to this, we begin in Chapter 2 (which, together with this introduction, forms the first part of the book) by reflecting on the way politicians and academics use the term 'sustainability' and briefly outlining current debates around it.

The second part of the book, Chapters 3 to 8, is devoted to the basic concepts with which we are concerned. The key concept we examine in terms of its core meanings, its implications and its practical uses, is that of *stock*. This concept offers us a new perspective on sustainability problems. It refers to both material and non-material things and structures which display a certain durability or permanence, as illustrated by the examples given in Section 1.3 above. The duration, dynamics and resistance of things – as well as their fragility and impermanence – are brought conceptually into focus when we view them as a stock. Chapter 3 introduces the concept of stock in general terms. Chapter 4 looks at material stocks in greater detail, while Chapter 5 focuses on non-material stocks. One important aspect of non-material stocks, especially for sustainability policy, namely, the persistence of institutions, is addressed in Chapter 6. The final two chapters in this second part of the book deal with the other two basic concepts it addresses: *judgement* and *time*. Exactly what judgement is and what difficulties are involved in using the term is discussed in Chapter 7. Judgement enables us to apprehend the essentials of a given situation. The same goes for the temporal dynamics of a situation – here, a person needs a 'sense of time'. This is not the homogeneous time of classical physics but rather the right time to act. This and other conceptual distinctions between aspects of time are introduced and elucidated in Chapter 8. This chapter also serves to show how the faculty of judgement can embrace and develop this sense of time by adopting a perspective that views circumstances and situations in terms of stocks.

In the third section of the book we look at applications of the terms and concepts developed previously in relation to two practical areas of sustainability policy, testing the theoretical ideas in the context of two case studies. Chapter 9 looks at a successful example of sustainability policy, with a study of the gradual remediation of large-scale chemical contamination in Saxony-Anhalt after the peaceful revolution (leading to the reunification of East and West Germany) of 1989. One important aspect of this is an analysis of the broader circumstances and factors leading to the institutional change observed in this context. The study demonstrates how an 'all-round view' of the sustainability problem that includes the long term as an issue is in itself a major step towards a creative solution. The second case study, described in Chapter 10, is about German land management policy. In its sustainability strategy (German Federal Government 2002) the German government has formulated the goal of limiting the amount of new land designated for human settlements and transport infrastructure from its current level of around 100 hectares a day to just 30 hectares a day from the year 2020. An analysis of some of the material and non-material stocks involved illustrates that this goal is unrealistic but also shows where there is a need for action and what the practical options are.

In the fourth and final part of the book, the terms and concepts developed previously are brought together in order to suggest how they can be rendered fruitful for tackling practical policy issues in the field of sustainability. Chapter 11 evaluates the experiences gathered in the two case studies. It then relates the three core concepts of *time*, *stock* and *judgement* to one another and on this basis develops a heuristic capable of providing practical guidance for devising successful sustainability policies. The heuristic helps those who have a vague, diffuse sense that certain developments in politics, society, nature or business are not sustainable to shape this sense into a lucid description of the problem. This in turn makes it possible to formulate what needs to be done and, where appropriate, to identify existing options. The conceptual framework of stocks helps policy makers to gain a comprehensive and yet not overly complex picture of the problem and to generate a robust knowledge base for policy decisions and measures. The two case studies presented in Chapters 9 and 10 can be seen as preliminary studies for this heuristic.

In Chapter 12 the heuristic is applied to inland waterways policy in Germany and is thus put to the test, as it were. The example serves to demonstrate that the heuristic is genuinely suited to integrating available theoretical and practical knowledge into an overall picture and outlining the need for action in German inland waterways policy. The case study illustrates how the heuristic works and what kinds of information it can help to generate. The concluding chapter of the book, Chapter 13, reflects on what the conceptual framework of stocks and the heuristic arising from it can be used to achieve. It also attempts to identify the nature of the framework given its dual role in both theory and practice. The conclusion we reach is that when it comes to applying the framework of stocks in practice, we are dealing not so much with science or scholarship as with an art – *the art of long-term thinking*.

Notes

1 In a similar manner Held and Kümmerer (2004) call for a 'fundamental theory of time' so that the normative model of sustainable development can be effectively put into practice: 'Sustainable development requires the analytical foundation of a concept of time which makes it possible to systematically capture the phenomena of rhythms [...], of the interplay between different scales of space and time with the specific times belonging to their associated systems and individuals, differing speeds, periods of adaptation, continuously accumulating changes and those that occur within very short spaces of time, including genuine uncertainty. This is of fundamental importance, particularly for periods of transition and thus also for the transition from a non-sustainable form of economics to a sustainable one. But it is equally important for sustainability itself which – rather like an ecological state of equilibrium – is not static but rather must repeatedly develop onwards and anew' (Held and Kümmerer 2004: 143).

2 On the fundamental questions associated with this, see also Heidbrink (2003) and Petersen and Faber (2005).

3 For a detailed account of this problem, see Faber and Manstetten (2003: 23–26).
4 Stocks and persistence form the focus of Chapters 3 to 6.
5 For example, the system of guilds was a stabilising factor for class-based European societies during the Middle Ages, one which often served to make economic transactions possible in the first place. With the rise of the bourgeois society in the 18th century, however, the continuing rights of the guilds came to be branded as obstacles to free economic exchange by liberal thinkers such as Adam Smith (1977).
6 The problems that arise from the fact that the production of a desirable item always also involves generating by-products and waste are addressed in detail by Baumgärtner et al. (2006) under the heading of 'joint production'.
7 Important work previously undertaken on the concept of stocks as it is used in this book can be found in Schiller (2002), Faber et al. (2005a, b), Fischer et al. (2010, 2013) and Klauer et al. (2013).
8 Judgement in general and in relation to time in particular is addressed in Chapters 7 and 8.
9 Cf. on this Kant (2001), Wieland (2001) and Petersen (2005a, 2005b).

2 Sustainability

Theory and policy

with Konrad Ott

2.1 Sustainable development: nice sounding but meaningless or a sound strategy for future-oriented policy making?

Nowadays modern environmental policy is often considered essentially to be sustainability policy. In 2002, the German Advisory Council on the Environment stated: 'Since the adoption of Agenda 21 at the United Nations Conference on Environment and Development in Rio de Janeiro in 1992, the concept of sustainability has become a key component of international and national environmental policy making' (SRU 2002: 57). The prominence (indeed, almost dominance) of the concept, however, appears to be a rather two-edged sword in the quest for successful environmental policy. On the one hand it clearly attributes major importance to environmental concerns and yet, on the other hand, 'the debate [on sustainability] is characterised by a lack of clarity in terms of both conceptual orientation and content and is also increasingly being trivialised' (SRU 2002: 57)[1].

The Advisory Council's reservations regarding the term 'sustainability' are understandable: it has come to be used in an inflationary and arbitrary way. Reference is made, for example, to 'sustainable financial policy' – meaning consolidation of a state's budget – while major corporations have 'sustainability centres' whose raison d'être has less to do with environmental concerns than with the company's standing in global markets. The dangers entailed by this frequent, associative and conceptually free-floating use of the term are obvious: sustainability might come to be seen as nothing much more than a nice sounding but essentially meaningless concept. It is hard to prevent the term being emptied of its meaning (intension) by this wider and looser use (extension). All we can do is counter it by creating a convincing conceptual foundation and set of definitions.

The concept of sustainability plays an important role in current environmental policy. It addresses key problems associated with modern society – the threat posed to the natural environment by our way of life and our economic system, global change, the manifold complex and long-term impacts of human interventions in natural systems, concerns over the long-term well-being and indeed the very survival of humanity. Correspondingly, academic research and debate on these issues is wide ranging, one important aim being to clarify the meaning and implications of sustainability as a concept. Finally, various attempts have been undertaken to develop systems and operational approaches capable of linking the sophisticated theoretical conceptions with the practical demands of sustainability policy (see SRU 2002, 2004, 2008).

Rather than providing a comprehensive overview in this chapter, we seek instead to offer a few specific insights into different conceptions of sustainability in order to draw on them for our conceptual framework of stocks. To begin, we outline the origin and meaning of the term in the context of German, European and international politics (Section 2.2). This is followed by an introduction to some of the main theoretical conceptions of sustainability, looking especially at how they differ and what they have in common (Section 2.3). Since sustainability is, in and of itself, merely an abstract normative idea, we will discuss the need to operationalise the term so that it can serve as a guide for action in concrete situations (Section 2.4). Finally, we elaborate on a few aspects which, differences notwithstanding, the various conceptions of and practical approaches to sustainability have in common; we explore some of the shortcomings of the sustainability debate as conducted in the political and academic arenas, and we offer a preliminary indication of how the conceptual framework of stocks can contribute towards successful policy making (Section 2.5).

2.2 The origin of the concept of sustainability[2]

In Germany the late 1950s and the 1960s were characterised by optimism and economic growth. It was in this context that the oil crisis of 1973 – triggered by the oil embargo enacted by the petroleum exporting countries (OPEC) – hit society and the economy where it hurt. The crisis made people aware of the finiteness of fossil energy resources. The dangers posed to humans and the environment by economic activities came to be a much discussed issue in the media as a result of events such as the chemical accident in Seveso, Italy (1976) and the *Amoco Cadiz* oil tanker disaster (1978). Although public interest was initially focused on acute risks and current disasters, gradually the global extent of and interconnections between environmental, resource and population problems came to be recognised. The 'Report of the Club of Rome on the State of Humanity: The Limits to Growth' (Meadows et al. 1972) and 'The Global 2000 Report to the President of the U.S.' (Barney 1980) were important contributions in this regard. These reports raised grave doubts about whether resource and environmental problems could be solved by economic growth. Indeed striving to achieve permanently high economic growth was interpreted as being the key cause of the environmental crisis, as it was assumed that high economic growth implies steadily increasing consumption of natural resources.

With awareness of the problem having been raised during the 1970s, attempts were made during the 1980s to come up with constructive solutions. At its 38th meeting in autumn 1983 the United Nations General Assembly decided to establish a World Commission on Environment and Development (WCED), tasked with drawing up 'a global agenda for change' (WCED 1987: ix). The Commission presented its final report, entitled 'Our Common Future' (WCED 1987), to the 42nd meeting of the General Assembly in autumn 1987 (WCED 1987: 352). The report is widely known as the Brundtland Report, named after the Commission's chairperson, former Norwegian Prime Minister Gro Harlem Brundtland. One key building block in this report is the demand for *sustainable development*:

> Sustainable development is development that meets the needs of the present without compromising the ability of future generations to meet their own needs. It contains within it two key concepts:
>
> - the concept of 'needs', in particular the essential needs of the world's poor, to which overriding priority should be given; and
> - the idea of limitations imposed by the state of technology and social organization on the environment's ability to meet present and future needs (WCED 1987: 43).

Whenever policy makers or academics quote a source for the concept of sustainability, it is almost always this one (cf. Box 2.1)[3].

It is highly likely that the 'lack of clarity' and increasing trivialisation bemoaned by the German Advisory Council on the Environment (SRU 2002: 57) is due to the compromises contained in the Brundtland report's definition, which in turn reflect a range of divergent, antagonistic interests:

- those of many developing countries seeking to 'catch up' with industrialisation in order to achieve the same levels of prosperity as the industrialised countries and to make greater use of natural resources in order to do so (Ott and Döring 2008: 27); and
- those of concerned individuals and organisations – present-day advocates speaking on behalf of future generations – that seek to limit the consumption of natural resources in order to halt the advancing destruction of the environment by humans[4].

The element of compromise embodied by the Brundtland definition of sustainability may be responsible for a number of the difficulties entailed in putting sustainability into practice, i.e. specifying precisely what the term means in concrete terms and deriving from this a set of normative demands and management rules that offer practical guidance. At the same time this very compromise is what made it possible for the international community, at the UN Conference on Environment and Development held in Rio de Janeiro in 1992, to adopt a declaration in which 172 countries pledged to pursue the ideal of 'sustainable development' as a binding obligation of environmental and development policy (cf. UN 1992). In Germany this led to the formulation of a national strategy for sustainable development (German Federal Government 2002).

Box 2.1 The normative content of the Brundtland report's definition of sustainability

The definition of sustainable development (WCED 1987: 43) is divided into three parts: first the concept is defined in general terms and then two explanatory extensions are added. The main definition focuses attention on the issue of meeting needs and, indirectly, of the distribution of goods between the generations, thereby opening up a long-term perspective. The text states that the opportunities of current and of future generations to meet their needs must be distributed fairly. The so-called problem of intergenerational justice entails finding ways of meeting this demand.

The first extension of the opening definition notes that, in addition to the problem of intergenerational justice, there is also the problem of fair shares within the generations currently alive, that is, the problem of intragenerational justice: within a generation as well each individual must receive an adequate supply of goods for meeting their basic needs at least.

The second extension draws attention to the link between environmental problems and the problem of intergenerational justice. Environmental problems often arise during the manufacture and consumption of goods. These problems limit future generations' opportunities to produce and consume. Thus the need to protect the natural environment is not explained by reference to an intrinsic value of nature but merely by reference to its instrumental significance. Nature thus appears as nothing more than a means by which humans meet their needs. The Brundtland definition of sustainability is thus based on an anthropocentric view.

2.3 The philosophical debate about sustainability

The formulation found in the Brundtland report is not so much a precise scholarly definition of sustainability but can rather be understood as a political demand to attend to the link between different problems such as the North–South conflict and environmental destruction and to develop correspondingly comprehensive solutions (SRU 1994: 46)[5]. Politicians' main difficulty in getting sustainable development off the ground in any comprehensive sense seems to be not simply a matter of conflicting interests alone but one of the term's indeterminacy as well – which, in turn, is a result of unresolved conflicts of interest. Successful sustainability policy therefore requires that the meaning of the term be clarified, as has occurred in the context of academic philosophical debate. Certainly the idea of sustainability has been received very positively in academia generally and in philosophy in particular, where a number of conceptions of sustainability have been developed[6]. In the following we briefly mention a few key aspects of the academic debate.

2.3.1 Sustainability and justice

Sustainability is essentially about preserving the natural environment on which all life depends, but it also has to do with the way people co-exist in the world and thus becomes a question of justice. It addresses not only intergenerational justice but also intragenerational justice between rich and poor countries and between the different social strata within individual societies. Extending the justice perspective to future generations would remain an abstract exercise if it were to ignore the many different existential needs and environmental problems facing poor people currently living on the planet. The term sustainability refers to the concrete intersection of inter- *and* intragenerational justice with regard to natural resources, goods and suchlike. When the Brundtland report demands that the current generation must not constrain future generations' opportunities to meet their own needs, it is referring to sustainability as something that demands a particular kind of distribution, namely, not primarily of goods but of opportunities to meet needs in terms of food, water, energy, health care etc.

Philosophers have put forward various theories of justice, each of which introduces a formal framework consisting of basic concepts, categories, patterns, instances and spheres of justice (Ott and Döring 2008: Chapter 2). A theory of intergenerational justice must additionally be able to solve certain specific problems caused by the fact that future individuals (unlike children and young people) do not yet exist (on this point, see Unnerstall 1999; Schröder et al. 2002: 153–170; Ott 2004). It must also – given the inherent uncertainty about the future – clarify which long-term risks are acceptable.

At the general level there are a number of competing theories of justice, including those of John Rawls (1973) and Michael Walzer (1983), the so-called capabilities approach developed by Martha Nussbaum and Amartya Sen (Nussbaum 2006; Sen 2009) and the more strongly Marxist-oriented approach of Gerald Cohen (2001). It is not possible to provide here an ethically differentiated discussion of these 'classical' approaches and more recent ones based upon them. Since each new theory of justice must of necessity address John Rawls' *Theory of Justice* (1973), we limit ourselves here to the question of whether or not a Rawlsian theory of justice can be rendered fruitful for conceptions of sustainability.

For Rawls, the theory of justice is an instance of practical philosophy. The core idea of his theory is a thought experiment. In order to arrive at his principles, he assumes that the members of a society vote on these principles in an artificial situation. In this situation all individuals are hidden behind a 'veil of ignorance' that conceals their individuality and social situatedness. Rawls argues that in this situation they would choose a liberty principle, an equality principle and a solidarity ('fraternity') principle:

- the principle of freedom equates with a largest possible system of liberties;
- the principle of equality equates with a principle of fair equality of opportunity to achieve desired offices and positions; and
- the principle of solidarity is manifested in the so-called difference principle: because nobody knows their own social position behind the veil of ignorance, everyone would choose a principle according to which even those occupying the worst position are provided for as well as possible[7].

For Rawls, the difference principle in every case assumes the existence of a principle of satisfaction of basic needs and thus fits well with the definition of sustainability contained in the Brundtland report[8]. However, the difference principle can also be interpreted to mean that the worst-placed individuals should be able to develop and exercise their capabilities[9].

Rawls devotes a special paragraph of his theory (§ 44) to the issue of justice between the generations (1973: 319), because he assumes that the difference principle is not applicable to this issue[10]. Justice between the generations should, for Rawls, be guaranteed by each generation observing a 'just savings principle' (ibid.: 291). To ascertain this just savings principle, current generations behind the famous 'veil of ignorance' need to ask how much they would be prepared to save if all other generations have saved and will save according to the same principle (ibid.: 292). This savings principle is the fourth principle of Rawlsian theory, so that freedom, equality and solidarity are complemented by a principle of responsibility toward the future. Interestingly, this principle is imposed as a restriction upon the difference principle; in other words, the best minimum possible may be raised only insofar as it remains compatible with the fair savings principle.

The concept of just savings, however, is clearly based on the model of saving monetary assets. This model is too limited for a theory of sustainability – or rather it would constitute a prejudgement in favour of the notion of 'weak' sustainability. However, as we shall show in Section 2.3.3, this has rightly been heavily criticised. For this reason one should extend the proper principle of just savings and speak conceptually of a fair intergenerational bequest of goods, or a 'fair bequest package'. Since current generations are not able to directly influence the happiness of individual members of future generations, their responsibility extends to leaving behind (bequeathing, endowing) various goods[11].

Given prognoses for a decline in natural resources and goods and the transformation of ecological systems, the focus of sustainability comes to rest on those things that might be more scarce in the future than in the past and the present, namely, natural goods (resources). One key question in the debate therefore concerns 'how many and which natural goods this bequest should contain' (Ott 2009: 69). According to Rawls, in every justly ordered society there ought to be a political institution which adjudicates and keeps a watchful eye on the collective goods of a society. For Rawls, though, the amount of collective goods depends only on the preferences of those currently alive. He does not establish a direct link between the fair savings principle and the safeguarding of collective goods. Thus it is important to link the issue of a fair bequest more strongly with the institutionalised protection of collective goods in a globalised perspective. However, even this brief sketch shows that a theory of sustainability certainly can be based on Rawls' theory, but must take it further.

2.3.2 Absolute versus comparative standard

As far as the distribution of opportunities for meeting needs between the generations is concerned, the alternatives to be addressed are whether to determine the claim of future generations relative to the level of prosperity of those currently living or whether to set a certain standard that applies to every generation regardless of what other generations have. The first option is known as a *comparative standard* and the second as an *absolute standard.*

The comparative standard is also an *egalitarian* standard, as there is no reason not to grant future generations the same claim as the present one. A comparative standard requires that an average member of a future generation must not be any worse off overall with regard to their quality of life as a member of a comparable collective[12]. The absolute standard is less demanding. It says that we owe future generations only the conditions of a good life worthy of human dignity but that we are not permitted to leave them less than we ourselves have inherited on average[13].

When working with the absolute standard, it bears asking quite generally: what are the (minimum) conditions for a good life worthy of human dignity? With regard to this issue, Amartya Sen and Martha Nussbaum have put forward an approach that is widely debated all over the world. This so-called capability approach sees humans as active, practical beings endowed with a rich array of capabilities. Whereas needs can also be met in prisons, the development and above all the exercise of these capabilities requires a large degree of human freedom (and is thus compatible with Rawls). Unlike Sen, Nussbaum has developed a list of human capabilities to which a universalistic claim is attached. The list relates primarily to political principles and goals of governmental action. Every person has an elemental right to enact all these capabilities above a defined threshold. The list does not in itself imply where that threshold lies. This threshold must be more than a purely formal right to exercise these capabilities. In Box 2.2 we present the list in paraphrased form.

Box 2.2 The capabilities approach

An interesting proposal that does not take the meeting of needs as a starting point is the capability approach put forward by Amartya Sen and Martha Nussbaum (Nussbaum 1988, 2000, 2006; Sen 1979, 1985, 1987; Sen and Nussbaum 1993). Martha Nussbaum (2006: 76–78) formulates on this basis the following list of capabilities that have to be realised in order to be able to lead a life worthy of human dignity:

1 *Life.* Being able to live to the end of a human life of normal length; not dying prematurely, or before one's life is so reduced as to be not worth living.
2 *Bodily Health.* Being able to have good health, including reproductive health; to be adequately nourished; to have adequate shelter.
3 *Bodily Integrity.* Being able to move freely from place to place; to be secure against violent assault, including sexual assault and domestic violence; having opportunities for sexual satisfaction and for choice in matters of reproduction.
4 *Senses, Imagination, and Thought.* Being able to use the senses, to imagine, think, and reason […] Being able to have pleasurable experiences and to avoid nonbeneficial pain.

(*continued*)

5 *Emotions.* Being able to have attachments to things and people outside ourselves; to love those who love and care for us, to grieve at their absence; in general, to love, to grieve, to experience longing, gratitude, and justified anger. Not having one's emotional development blighted by fear and anxiety. [...]

6 *Practical Reason.* Being able to form a conception of the good and to engage in critical reflection about the planning of one's life. (This entails protection for the liberty of conscience and religious observance.)

7 *Affiliation.*

A Being able to live with and toward others, to recognize and show concern for other human beings, to engage in various forms of social interaction; to be able to imagine the situation of another. [...]

B Having the social bases of self-respect and nonhumiliation; being able to be treated as a dignified being whose worth is equal to that of others. This entails provisions of nondiscrimination on the basis of race, sex, sexual orientation, ethnicity, caste, religion, national origin.

8 *Other Species.* Being able to live with concern for and in relation to animals, plants, and the world of nature.

9 *Play.* Being able to laugh, to play, to enjoy recreational activities.

10 *Control Over One's Environment.*

A *Political.* Being able to participate effectively in political choices that govern one's life; having the right of political participation, protections of free speech and association.

B *Material.* Being able to hold property (both land and movable goods), and having property rights on an equal basis worth others; having the right to seek employment on an equal basis with others; having the freedom from unwarranted search and seizure. In work, being able to work as a human being, exercising practical reason and entering into meaningful relationships of mutual recognition with other workers.

In the context of the capability approach, sustainability could mean that a state should be sought or preserved in which every person is able to enact this capability. This gives rise to a range of demands in relation to politics, economics, society and culture.

2.3.3 Strong versus weak sustainability

Central to many – though not all – scholarly conceptions of sustainability are demands relating to the ability of future generations to produce goods and meet needs. Solow (1992), for example, writes:

> If 'sustainability' is anything more than a slogan or expression of emotion, it must amount to an injunction to preserve production capacity for the indefinite future. That is compatible with the use of non-renewable resources only if society as a whole replaces used-up resources with something else.

However, even conceptions geared towards the meeting of needs offer diverse answers to the question of what exactly a *just* intra- and intergenerational distribution of opportunities to meet needs means in practice. One major controversy in the current sustainability debate revolves around the question of whether we are obligated to preserve nature in its species richness and with all its resources for the benefit of our descendants or whether we can exploit resources until they are used up and allow species – in a worst-case scenario – to die out, as long as we can provide a replacement for them.

The proponents of so-called *weak sustainability*[14] consider it perfectly permissible to use up resources completely or to drive species to extinction – provided an appropriate substitute can be created. Renewable and non-renewable resources are regarded as *natural capital* in this debate. According to 'Hartwick's rule' (Hartwick 1977), the criterion of weak sustainability is met when 'the yields from the consumption of natural capital are fully re-invested in produced capital' (SRU 2002: 63). The 'artificial' capital made by humans then takes on all the functions of the natural capital that has been destroyed or used up. The loss of natural capital can be borne because it can be substituted. The welfare standard of a society can be increased largely independently of nature. A highly artificial world can also meet a comparable standard ('non-declining utility over time'), provided a high degree of substitution elasticity can generally be assumed between the various natural and artificial capital goods.

The adherents of so-called strong sustainability[15] doubt the extent to which natural capital is substitutable with artificial capital. For this reason they call for natural capital (including cultivated forms of natural capital such as forests, vineyards and greened land) as well as for the preservation of a large amount of biodiversity not using up renewable resources beyond the point at which they reproduce themselves. The position of strong sustainability has by and large gained the upper hand in the academic debate (Klauer 1998: Chapter 3; Ott and Döring 2008: Chapter 3). The justification for this position is based predominantly on empirically verifiable arguments and on principles regarding how to deal with uncertainties[16].

The proponents of strong sustainability accuse the proponents of the counter position of putting too high an estimate on the substitution elasticity between natural and artificial capital (cf. also SRU 2002: 60) and therefore of being too hasty in their willingness to replace natural capital with manufactured capital. Another argument brought to bear against weak sustainability is that the multi-functionality of many ecological systems limits their substitutability, as a substitute would have to be provided for each ecological function (Harte 1995). The irreversible eradication of natural capital is also rejected because of the loss of options it entails. The critics of weak sustainability emphasise not only the instrumental value of nature but especially also 'the many different eudaimonistic and biophilic values that people associated with experiencing nature and landscapes' and the 'uncertainty surrounding our possible reliance upon certain forms of natural capital' (Ott and Döring 2006: 112). A rather more fundamental argument for strong sustainability arises from debates about the economic 'framing' of weak sustainability and the tendency of this position to disregard from current considerations the necessarily *future* utility that future generations draw from natural capital (cf. SRU 2002: 61).

The strong sustainability position also encounters objections, however. Klepper (1999: 313) rightly argues that even a thrifty use of non-renewable resources must sooner or later lead to their being exhausted. In consequence non-renewable resources ought not to be used at all – though this would serve neither present nor future humans. The rigid requirement to 'preserve nature in all its present forms', particularly in relation to material resources, is 'too general' (SRU 2002: 66). Some intermediate approaches such as that of Lerch and Nutzinger (1998) argue that opportunities for substitution should be tested empirically case by case, while others analyse the problem of the criticality of forms of natural capital (Brand 2009).

2.4 Operationalising sustainability

The philosophical debate about sustainability usually remains at a rather abstract level. The norms are so general that in specific situations it is often not clear what implications are to be drawn from them. The principles need to be specified. It would be helpful to know more precisely: which environmental policy measures need to be implemented today in order to ensure sustainable development? What constraints emerge from this for citizens? Can the measures that are required be enforced in society? Who should bear the costs? What legal problems arise? In short, how can sustainability be operationalised? 'Operationalise' here means (Klauer 2000)

- translating abstract norms of sustainability into tangible, empirically verifiable objectives;
- where possible, making the degree of achievement of these objectives measurable using indicators and, where appropriate, indicator systems; and
- formulating management rules that act as normative rules of thumb and give an idea of how the demand for sustainability can be met in a specific situation.

There is a range of practical approaches to operationalising sustainability, some of which have been developed by academics working in applied contexts and some by policy makers and administrators, and they differ accordingly. Certain policy sectors additionally require special policy strategies (such as for differentiated land use). In order to give an idea of the broad range of these approaches we present a number of examples, though we make no claim to having compiled a representative selection.

One approach is to define *environmental standards*. These are legal, administrative or civil law regulations in which certain legal terms such as 'harmful impact', 'precaution' or 'recognised rules of technology' are first translated into measurable entities and then into specific prohibitions, injunctions or permissions (*Akademie der Wissenschaften* 1992: 33, including reference to Jarass 1987; cf. also SRU 1996a: 254, 1996b). The idea behind these operational measures is that while the continued existence of natural systems and their capacity to develop is threatened by anthropogenic influences, the risks can be contained by limiting the influences (SRU 1994: 181–183; Redford and Robinson 1995: 404). Environmental standards acquire considerable influence by virtue of being anchored in law.

The first environmental standards in Germany emerged at the end of the 19th century in the form of health and safety regulations in the chemicals industry (SRU 1996a: 251). Over the course of time environmental standards came to be applied not only to health and safety at work but also to health and safety in general and eventually to nature conservation and environmental protection per se. 'Safe minimum standards' for the stability of natural systems were first called for in the early 1950s by Siegfried von Ciriacy-Wandrup (1952). The European Water Framework Directive (EC 2000) is a prominent example of powerful environmental standards. It formulates standards for bodies of water that are explicitly geared towards the objective of sustainable development. Article 4 contains the requirement that in principle all European ground waters, surface waters and coastal waters should achieve what is called 'good status' by 2015. As part of the implementation of the Directive, EU Member States have been required to develop and implement monitoring systems in order to test the status of waters at regular intervals.

A different approach towards operationalising sustainability that is not limited to any specific field of environmental policy but pursues a comprehensive set of aims was developed between 1998 and 2003 by the Hermann von Helmholtz Association of German Research Centres (HGF) under the leadership of the Karlsruhe Research Centre (Kopfmüller et al. 2001; Grundwald and Kopfmüller 2012). The starting point of this so-called *HGF concept* is an integrative approach which views the four dimensions of 'ecology', 'economy', 'society' and 'institutions/policy' not as areas that exist in isolation from one another but rather as an overarching whole (Kopfmüller et al. 2001). The following 'fundamental principles of justice' are named as key sustainability objectives (Coenen and Paschen 2000):

- to safeguard human existence;
- to maintain society's productive capacity; and
- to preserve options for development and action.

These general sustainability objectives are first rendered specific in terms of minimum requirements for sustainability within a 'hierarchy' of objectives and are underpinned where possible using indicators.

The HGF concept adopts an anthropocentric perspective and seeks to achieve an absolute sustainability standard. Intra- and intergenerational issues of justice are regarded as being of equal import. This anthropocentric stance is 'enlightened' to the extent that the protection of non-human life and of nature in general – with its origin in 'subtle human needs' – is incorporated and that a 'possible intrinsic value of non-human existence' is not disregarded from the start. Any inherent values of nature are regarded as lying 'outside the sustainability concept', however (Renn et al. 2007: 35).

Finally we wish to mention the *German sustainability strategy*, which can also be understood as a means of operationalising sustainability. It was published in 2002 by the then Social Democrat–Green coalition government and bore the title 'Perspectives for Germany – Our Strategy for Sustainable Development' (German Federal Government 2002). In addition to some basic information about the idea of sustainable development, the first part of the strategy contains 10 specific management rules for sustainability and some 30 prime objectives, most of which are quantified. These prime objectives are simultaneously understood as indicators for sustainable development: the degree to which the objectives have been achieved is intended to provide information about the areas in which Germany is on its way to becoming a sustainable society. One such objective is the so-called 30 ha goal aimed at restricting land use: 'The daily use of land for human settlements and transport infrastructure has risen overall in Germany to 129 hectares per day. This trend should be reversed and directed towards reaching a level of 30 hectares per day in the year 2020' (German Federal Government 2002: 288).

The objectives set by the German government in its sustainability strategy are ambitious and the arguments in favour of them largely convincing. However, they are not being pursued strenuously by the political decision makers. We will offer an example of this in Chapter 10, where we look at land-use policy in Germany, especially the goal of drastically reducing the amount of undeveloped land made available for development, from the stocks perspective. We will also see in Chapter 12 – in which we apply the stocks heuristic to German inland waterways policy – that the goal of a 42 per cent growth in the transport capacity of inland shipping by 2015, as stated in the German sustainability strategy (German Federal Government 2002: 178), was not only completely unrealistic but not conducive to sustainability either.

2.5 Sustainability policy and the concept of stocks: shortcomings and ways to ameliorate them

We can define sustainability policy as that which seeks to ensure that a community can continue to survive over the long term in social, economic and ecological terms. Within this, special emphasis is placed on protecting the natural environment on which all life depends. Essentially, then, sustainability policy is always also environmental policy – environmental policy with an *integrative* and *long-term* perspective.

Differences in detail notwithstanding, the various approaches to conceptualising sustainability and operationalising it agree on a number of key points:

- *Intra- and intergenerational justice*: The term sustainability addresses the fact that the way people (above all in the prosperous countries) currently live and work – the consumption of non-renewable resources, inequitable opportunities for development, the harm done to the environment – leads to serious problems in the long term. Many of the adverse consequences of our way of life are even now distributed unequally, but future generations in particular will also have to bear them.

- *Long-term perspective*: Sustainability implies that the long-term effects of today's actions are a key criterion for assessing policy options. This follows from the demand for intergenerational justice.
- *Comprehensive and integrated approach*: This refers to the need to judge and assess problems relating to sustainability not from a sector-based perspective alone but rather using a comprehensive and integrated approach.
- *Preservation of nature*: Finally, what most concepts of sustainability (perhaps with the exception of concepts of weak sustainability) have in common is that the quality of what is bequeathed to succeeding generations should not be arbitrary but rather must satisfy certain requirements. In particular, it can be assumed that a specific quality (standard) of nature needs to be preserved[17]. Occasionally there are also calls to attribute to nature or certain parts of nature an inherent value, that is, a moral value that is independent of its usefulness or value to human beings[18].

All four of these issues are essential to sustainability as a normative model for political and individual action.

Our analysis has shown that the normative content of the sustainability concept is already well thought through. There is a range of operational approaches for rendering specific the abstract norms of intra- and intergenerational justice and the preservation of nature in concrete situations and problems such that a general direction for solutions can emerge. Considerable shortcomings remain nonetheless, however, both in conceptual and operational terms. They relate especially to dealing with a long-term perspective and to the need for a comprehensive approach.

In the sustainability debate, just as in practical sustainability policy, too little attention is given to issues of time. The phenomenon of *time* is always presupposed and implied but is hardly ever analysed. And yet it is surely impossible to explain the idea of sustainability without referring to the aspect of time. To this extent, time is a transcendental category for any conception of sustainability. But this is by no means the only sense in which time is crucial, as we shall show in greater detail below. The task of taking a comprehensive look at complex problems is either undertaken in a reductionist and one-sided way or else it sets the viewpoints from different sectors and disciplines alongside one another in an additive way, without integrating them[19]. These are the two shortcomings we address in the following chapters, along with suggestions for ameliorating them.

The stocks perspective makes it possible to generate an approximate picture of the temporal dynamics of objects and of conditions for action, making them available to the person who needs to act. In this perspective one looks at things in terms of their permanence (persistence through time) and their temporal dynamic and can at the same time compare these different dynamics with one another in a synopsis. When framing a problem, the stocks perspective prevents us from sticking to a one-sided disciplinary approach and instead enables us to retain a certain degree of openness so that different aspects can be integrated into an overall picture. The stocks perspective as such is not based on any particular conception of sustainability, any particular body of ethics or any particular theory of justice. It is therefore 'unfettered' theoretically. Therein lies one of its strengths. However, it does not exempt its users from the necessity of reflecting on the genuinely ethical and conceptual issues involved. If offers no substitute in this respect.

It is to the concept of stocks that we now turn in Part II.

Notes

1 For this reason the Advisory Council prefers to speak of 'permanently environmentally sound development' (*dauerhaft-umweltgerechte Entwicklung*) rather than of 'sustainable development' (SRU 2002: 57).

2 Grober (2012) provides a highly readable cultural/historical account of the term 'sustainability'.

3 On the definition of sustainability and how it is operationalised, see Klauer (1999a, 1999b).

4 Interests that cannot really be represented by the interested parties are very much open to interpretation and indeed require interpretation – not least because it is not clear whether the current use of natural resources actually touches on these interests. One could argue on the one hand that strict environmental protection is required to protect the interests of future generations; however, one can argue equally that it is eminently conceivable in certain circumstances for further environmental harm to be compatible with their interests.

5 How best to define the term 'sustainability' is the subject of considerable debate in both the academic literature and in policy circles, but so far no agreement has been reached (cf. e.g. Repetto 1986; WCED 1987; Costanza 1991; Pezzey 1992; Munasinghe and Shearer 1995; Chichilnisky 1996, 1997; Klauer 1998, 1999a, 1999b; Ott and Döring 2008).

6 Cf. e.g. Ott and Döring (2008: Chapter 2), Kopfmüller et al. (2001), Ekardt (2011).

7 For Rawls, the difference principle applies only in the context of societies constituted through a nation state, rather than to all societies globally. This is why Rawls' later work on international law (*The Law of Peoples*, 1999) expressly does not contain a global difference principle. Thomas Pogge (2001) and Wilfried Hinsch (2001) have argued in favour of extending the difference principle globally, which would effectively lead to a policy of combating absolute poverty.

8 The difference principle does not, however, limit material inequality between individuals. Provided it can be assumed that inequalities are to everybody's advantage, there is no reason to limit inequalities. Rawls rejects a so-called inherent value of equality, i.e. equality for equality's sake, for the dimension of distributive justice.

9 In this interpretation the difference principle corresponds to a sophisticated absolute standard in the sense of the capabilities approach (cf. next section). This interpretation is rather similar to the intuition that every person should be able to lead a decent life, or, as Nussbaum puts it, 'a life worthy of human dignity'.

10 A number of meta-ethical problems in § 44 are addressed and resolved by Ott and Döring (2008: 100–102).

11 For the term 'fair bequest package', see Norton and Toman (1997: 559 ff.).

12 Determining the comparable collective and the concept of average quality of life naturally raise certain issues. We decline to judge whether these difficulties are so serious

that it is necessary to relinquish the intuition that future humans should not be any worse off than 'us'. For example, it might be counter-intuitive if an absolute standard were to allow 'us' to 'blow' the majority of current communal assets as long as enough resources remained to meet future basic needs. This would not even be compatible with Rawls' just savings principle.

13 Some proponents of so-called anti-egalitarianism (e.g. Frankfurt 2000; Anderson 2000) have spoken in favour of such an absolute standard. Rawls (1973) is also among them: he argues that the meeting of basic needs should always be guaranteed (cf. Ott and Döring 2008: 81–82).

14 Hartwick (1977, 1978a, 1978b) and Solow (1974a, 1974b, 1986), for example, have developed theoretical growth models in which the substitutability of resources by human-made capital goods is implied. Even if it is not clear whether or not this assumption is empirically justified, the implications of the models – namely, that growth in prosperity is possible even given declining resource availability – are relatively frequently used implicitly or explicitly as arguments in economic policy debates.

15 Cf. e.g. Pearce et al. (1990), Pearce and Turner (1990: Chapter 3), Klaasen and Opschoor (1991), Goodland and Daly (1995), Daly (1994, 1996) and Ott and Döring (2008).

16 A detailed justification of the mechanism of strong sustainability can be found in Ott and Döring (2008: Chapter 3).

17 To put it in the language of 'strong sustainability', it is said that certain elements of non-substitutable natural capital are to be preserved.

18 This issue of inherent value is one of the basic moral problems of environmental ethics (Ott 2010: Chapter 5), whereas sustainability theory concentrates on issues of 'interpersonal' justice.

19 The problem of insufficient policy integration comes clearly to the fore, for example, in the context of implementing the EC Water Framework Directive (Petersen and Klauer 2012).

Part II

The conceptual framework of stocks

3 The perspective of stocks

The idea of sustainability has to do with people's concern for the continued existence of society and humanity as a whole over the *long term*. Before we can solve the problems linked to sustainability we need to understand what they are, and this requires looking at things over very long timescales in order to attend to long-term temporal dynamics. Since the study of sustainability problems usually requires input from a variety of disciplines (sociology, economics, the natural sciences), it is extremely useful to be able to represent the temporal aspects of these problems within a shared conceptual framework capable of being used in every discipline involved as well as by practitioners. The following chapters elaborate the set of ideas grouped around the German word for 'stock', *Bestand*, as a basis for achieving this.

3.1 Origins of the concept of stock and its German translation *Bestand*

The German term *Bestand* together with its derivative forms conveys various meanings. To describe something as having *Bestand* or being *beständig* means that it has, as it were, 'staying power', that it is 'constant' in the sense of persistent, lasting or enduring. The term is used attributively. However, we can also use the term as a substantive, saying that there is a *Bestand* – that is, a stock, an amount – of something. Since both uses of the term are important in our analytical approach to sustainability problems, we wish to explain them briefly.

When *Bestand* is used attributively, it means that something is persistent, enduring or long lasting, that it continues to exist through time. The potential end point of this continued existence is often not part of the idea conveyed by the word: instead it is implicitly assumed that the object or thing will continue for a long, indeterminate (period of) time. In relation to the founding of an organisation, the adoption of a constitution or a scientific discovery, for example, we might say: 'This is something that's going to last'; it is something that has *Bestand*. Saying this conveys the sense that it is essentially robust at its core and is not so easily threatened by countervailing currents[1]. *Beständig* in this sense generally – if not always – has positive connotations. The opposite of something that has *Bestand* is *das Unbeständige*: that which is non-enduring, unstable or impermanent.

In many instances the latter refers to something on which we cannot rely. This use of *Bestand* is associated with a human characteristic known in German as *Beständigkeit* (Latin: *constantia*, English: constancy) and is considered in the tradition of moral philosophy to be a virtue.

When using the term in a substantive sense, we can refer to objects or things in terms of being a 'stock' (*Bestand*) of something. In the context of warehousing (stock keeping), a stock is an amount of things which look the same and are itemised according to their shared designation. Their number is registered at certain intervals, the main point of interest here being any change, that is, any increase or decrease in number of the stock. An entrepreneur will want information about the stock of ready-to-sell products in her warehouses and sales locations and about the stock of accounts receivable and assets in her books; a mayor will want information about the 'stock' of inhabitants in her town, the commander of a troop about the 'stock' of soldiers and equipment in his unit, and the hunter about the stocks of wild boar, deer or stags in his hunting ground. This substantial use of *Bestand* (as 'stock') typically refers to something with which one has a practical concern. Depending on how the stock changes, either we need to act or else we can let things continue as they are. *Bestand* in this sense can have a positive, neutral or negative connotation, depending on the concerns of those dealing with it[2].

Linked to *Bestand* in the sense of stock is the term *Bestandsaufnahme*, or stocktaking. Stocktaking is done when we want to be certain about the quantity and quality of a stock. The expression refers in the first instance to things that can be registered, but it is also often used in a figurative sense to refer to the attempt to gain full awareness of the most important facts of a given situation. Wherever there is a perceived crisis (in a company, a government or a society), it may prompt an impulse to 'take stock', which may then be described as being done with 'unflinching honesty'.

The term 'stock' was introduced to the ecological economics debate by Georgescu-Roegen (1971), his purpose being to steer the debate among economists regarding the concept of capital in a new direction. His concern was to place greater emphasis on the real or material aspect of what was known as capital, which seemed to him at the time to be largely hidden by a value-based, technical concept of financial capital. Georgescu-Roegen contrasts 'stock' with 'flow' – a change in stock. The conceptual pairing of stock and flow was intended to address the structures of change over time independently of market value or exchange value.

During the 1980s and 1990s both the concept of capital and – less conspicuously – the conceptual pairing of stock and flow, used as a means to study intertemporal decisions in economic systems[3], were introduced into the debate around sustainability[4]. At certain points in this process these concepts were interpreted in new ways. Material flows were a significant element in this, particularly in the debate about the closed substance cycle economy and life cycle assessments[5]. At the same time efforts were underway in ecology to understand ecosystems as networks of material and energy flows[6], a subject taken up by ecological economists to generate information about their sustainability[7]. The concept of stock developed in this book takes its point of departure from this revised understanding of Georgescu-Roegen's term. Unlike him, however, we are less concerned with distinguishing between stocks and flows than with observing long-term dynamics by directing attention towards the long-term persistence and constancy (*Beständigkeit*) of things.

3.2 Aim of the conceptual framework of stocks

Concern over the long-term survival of humanity – a basic motif in the idea of sustainability – has certain aspects in common with the concern of an entrepreneur who is keen to ensure the continued existence of her company and therefore registers all the relevant stocks and any changes to them. For a policy of sustainability, of course, the entire Earth can be seen as the warehouse where stocks are studied in terms of their dynamics, their increases and decreases, their emergence and their disappearance. Here we name a few examples of such stocks.

In the economy there are, first of all, natural phenomena that can be regarded as stocks, including resources such as water, air and soil, deposits of ore, oil and coal as well as timber, cereals, cattle, etc. In addition, though, the consumer and capital goods created from these are also stocks – things such as food and medicines, tools, machines, houses, and so forth. Waste and pollutants can also accumulate to become stocks. Indeed even the workers in a company or the inhabitants of a town or city can be represented as a stock. Both the natural objects and the human-made objects are material stocks.

Typically, however, the stocks that are important for sustainability policy are not just material in nature. For food or medicines to be produced and distributed to their users, a network of producers, logistics firms and traders is required. This includes (aside from the material objects themselves) contracts, agreements, legal regulations, conventions and suchlike. Although they are of an 'intellectual nature', these things too have *Bestand* in the sense that they endure over a period of time: they establish constancy and reliability in human relationships. We call such enduring non-material objects *immaterial stocks*.

Immaterial stocks include such things as formal rules like laws, regulations, injunctions and prohibitions. They determine what people have to do and not to do. Alongside such formal rules, informal rules such as conventions, traditions and habits also determine interactions between people in a variety of situations. They too have the character of *Bestand* in the sense of endurance. Other examples of immaterial stocks are behavioural patterns, knowledge, technologies, values, norms and preferences.

In contrast to material stocks, immaterial stocks cannot be dealt with using the language of a registry or inventory – or at least not as easily – and their changes cannot be described as readily in terms of increase or decrease. What both kinds of stocks have in common, however, is that they are characterised by a certain persistence, permanence or endurance, and that they constitute a setting for human action during the period of their existence. In this respect it is essential to any policy of sustainability that they are taken into consideration. Stocks can further sustainable development but they can also pose an obstacle to desirable societal changes and positive changes in our natural environment. If we wish to identify options for political action that are effective in the long term in relation to sustainability, then studying the relevant material and immaterial stocks can help us greatly in doing so.

The aim of the conceptual framework of stocks, then, is to achieve a better understanding of the dynamic interplay between nature, economics and society than we have done to date. The way we want to do this is by developing, on the basis of this framework, a common language and a shared conceptual scheme that encompasses ecology and the natural sciences on the one hand and economics and other social sciences on the other. The framework serves as a means to describe and analyse the dynamics of nature and society in parallel – their changeability and their inertia – in order to generate useful information about opportunities for and hindrances to action for sustainable developments. One key element in all this is the focus on practical action. The conceptual framework of stocks is not some kind of dynamic 'supertheory' but rather a heuristic (Chapter 11) for ascertaining and representing the temporal structures of the problem at hand (in the manner of an overview) and doing so using a transdisciplinary approach that does justice to the complexities involved.

For the discussion contained in this book we distinguish between

- the concept of stock;
- the conceptual framework of stocks (also referred to as the stocks framework); and
- the perspective of stocks (also referred to as the stocks perspective).

The concept of stock (*Bestand*) makes it possible to represent objects in terms of their temporality, changeability and inertia – this forms the subject of Chapters 4–6. This concept is embedded in an overall conceptual framework of stocks characterised by the three key aspects of time, stock and judgement. It is designed to provide information that enables action guided by judgement and oriented towards sustainability (Chapters 7 and 8). When actors use the method and key terms of the stocks framework to get an overarching view of specific sustainability problems, we say that they adopt a stocks perspective – this is illustrated in the case studies presented in Chapters 9 and 10. The concept, conceptual framework and perspective of stocks then feed into the heuristic for sustainability policies introduced in Chapter 11 and applied in Chapter 12.

3.3 Framing the problem, using a systemic approach and adopting a stocks perspective

In both scholarly study and practical contexts the way a given problem is defined and framed – i.e. which aspects of it are looked at, in how much detail, in what way, and how they are incorporated into the problem – proves to be a key to dealing with it successfully[8]. In this respect the conceptual framework of stocks makes a major contribution when it comes to looking at sustainability problems (cf. Chapter 11). To show how this occurs, we look first at the question of how such problems tend to be framed. The normal procedure for unravelling a problem consists in analysing it using systematic methods and models prescribed by the relevant scientific disciplines (Section 3.3.1). As a rule this involves trying to explain or predict the phenomena observed on the basis of causal relations. In contrast to this kind of 'systemic approach', we then sketch the perspective of stocks (Section 3.3.2), a perspective that shifts stocks to the centre of our attention. It should be noted that these two perspectives are not mutually exclusive – on the contrary, both are useful and indeed necessary to solve practical sustainability problems.

Why is the issue of problem framing important? Many scientific and technical approaches to solving problems in highly varied areas are wedded to a standardised and often narrow view of the problem, meaning that too little consideration is given to innovative and integrative solutions. Particularly in the case of serious, complex problems – as sustainability problems generally are – working out the proper way to frame them is already an important step towards finding a solution. This includes delineating the problem in an appropriate way and establishing a realistic representation of the actual situation with regard to particular values, norms and goals[9]. If this step is implemented and thought through carefully, a situation in which the policy makers or their advisers end up deciding too hastily in favour of a pre-given problem solving strategy can be avoided.

Any model-like representation of an actual situation will inevitably involve some degree of simplification. In consideration of their practical interests policy makers and their advisers need to reduce complexity in such a way that all the essential factors required to act are included without information overload setting in[10]. The question is how that is best done. The set of ideas around the concept of stock helps conceptually in simplifying the interconnections relevant to sustainability policy in a way appropriate to the problem at hand. This involves first and foremost describing the *temporal developments and structures* of both natural and societal factors for those concerned with sustainability policy[11] in a simplified and comprehensible way. In the following we compare and contrast the systemic approach with the stocks perspective.

3.3.1 The systemic approach of the hard sciences

The objects studied in the classical natural sciences as well as in mathematical economics are grouped into systems for a purpose, the term 'system' being interpreted in a specific way: systems consist of elements whose interrelationships are based on regularities or laws that are universal and are ideally expressed in mathematical form. Such systems are conceptual structures that are elaborated within each discipline and can be described as models augmented by empirical data. Adam Smith described this as follows in his essay "History of Astronomy": 'A system is an imaginary machine invented to connect together in the fancy those different movements and effects which are already in reality performed' (Smith 2004: 235). The purpose of systems in this sense is initially a theoretical one: they serve to generate knowledge within the paradigm of the academic discipline concerned by making it possible to link data 'systematically' in a causal arrangement[12].

When a discipline seeks to capture reality using its own specific systematic methods (whether to generate theoretical knowledge or to facilitate action) various steps are necessary to do so:

1 Empirical information about the reality is selected and processed in such a way that it can be represented and utilised within the system of the discipline concerned[13]. If, for example, we are working within the system of neoclassical economics, information about scientific laws or human behaviours can only be utilised to a limited extent or else in highly stylised form. Drawing on the influential definition provided by Lionel Robbins (1932: 15), the neoclassical economic system refers to those human behaviours that involve actions based on choice to deploy scarce means which have alternative uses. Other human behaviours, such as responsible action using the human faculty of judgement, cannot be usefully analysed within this system. The material, life-world object of economics, consisting of volumes and prices, is expressed in the form of quantity of goods, prices, costs and benefits. Scientific laws or regularities are integrated only in heavily stylised form[14].
2 A system of axioms that helps generate a simplified picture of reality – in other words, a model – is then devised in order to explore the laws or regularities that describe the changes in the data concerned. In neoclassical economics, for example, these include certain assumptions about economically active individuals that are conceptualised axiomatically as egoistic rational maximisers of utility (*homines oeconomici*) with given preferences.
3 Finally, the law-based relationships within the system are analysed. Interrelationships are often formulated in mathematical terms[15]. The aim is generally to establish causal relationships: relations of cause-and-effect are sought and their significance examined in relation to both the individual elements and the system as a whole[16].

Systems of this kind exist in the classical sciences as well as in economics. They are, in the first instance, constructs that are underpinned by the theoretical cognitive interests relating to a particular sphere of human knowledge.

However, these systems can also be used to solve practical problems. In this case, reality is viewed in a perspective we describe as a 'systemic approach'. A systemic approach such as the one common in academic disciplines requires – apart from the necessary empirical data – that the problem in question can be allocated to a specific scientific discipline (physics, biology, economics etc.)

and can be appropriately represented within its conceptual, axiomatic and methodical schemes.

The greatest strength of the scientific disciplinary systemic approach is that it generates – within the terms of the paradigm in question – information about actual situations that is logically comprehensible, verifiable and reliable. Equally, however, the systemic approach also entails a set of difficulties, two of which are as follows:

- The ideal of establishing a complete representation of a given reality (even if this refers to only the diffuse part that needs to be taken into account in relation to a given sustainability problem) cannot, in principle, be achieved – especially when we are dealing with complex problems. Given that this is the case, a decision needs to be made as to how precisely a given representation should reflect the reality it addresses. This involves a conflict between the divergent aims of comprehensiveness and precision on the one hand and clarity and practicability on the other: the more accurate and complete a picture of reality one seems to have, the less clear and manageable the representation becomes. The converse is also true, however: the simpler the representation, the greater is the risk of neglecting important aspects.
- A special problem with many scientific systemic representations is how to represent temporal issues in dynamic theories. Causal associations are represented as universally valid in the form 'whenever x …, then y …'[17]. This means that phenomena which differ from one instance to the next or those that occur only once cannot be adequately represented or explained. Contingencies that arise from (highly) complex situations or novelties cannot be adequately depicted in systems based on causal connections. In such cases historical developments appear at best as an illustration of abstract information and laws (cf. Schiller 2002: Section 3.1).

3.3.2 The systemic approach and the stocks perspective

The stocks perspective is not in opposition to the systemic approach outlined above but rather differs in terms of its particular emphasis. It addresses the dynamics of objects, in particular their persistence or changeability. As with warehouse stocks, the elements that make up a stock are viewed as being homogeneous in a certain way; as such, no attention is paid to their unique character or internal structure[18]. However, special attention is paid to the increase and decrease in the number of elements and to the overall lifetime of the stock, which is over when all the elements have disappeared. The relationships between the elements are deliberately (and in certain cases temporarily) ignored. Instead, the unique characteristics of a stock in terms of its temporal development are given special emphasis.

The critical difference between a systemic approach and a stocks perspective lies in the way temporal developments are addressed. The systemic approach tends to analyse its object in a general and therefore basically timeless – and above all ahistorical – way. The attempt is then made to use the general information thus acquired to arrive at specific, temporal dynamics which (in the form of predictions, for example) are regarded as a specific application of the general information. The movement of a pendulum, for instance, can be described and predicted by means of mechanical laws that are always valid, provided the initial conditions are known.

The stocks perspective, by contrast, places emphasis on the actually existing persistence (*Beständigkeit*) and inertia (*Trägheit*) of the objects in question and on the changes that occur phenomenologically, without necessarily explaining why they occur. If we wish to identify persistence in the past, it is sufficient to observe the history of the stock. But if we wish to recognise persistence in the future – something that is especially relevant when it comes to sustainability issues – then we need to make predictions about future trends. Scientific knowledge (and thus systemic knowledge) as well as empirical knowledge (observations, statistics and experiences) can be used to do this. The stocks perspective makes it possible to work with knowledge about degrees of persistence (*Beständigkeiten*) and instabilities (*Unbeständigkeiten*) as well as about things that are predictable or surprising. It has a historical perspective on developments over time[19].

Whether a given practical context is conceived of as a system or whether structural relationships are ignored and a stocks perspective adopted is not an objective property of the phenomena concerned but rather depends on the point of view of the observer or the person involved. Thus the development of a human being, for example, can be described not only in terms of the causal dynamics of a highly complex system, established either in biological or social scientific terms, but also as a set of changes that occur in the stock of cells or of certain behaviours. Similarly, the employees of a firm comprise not only a structure in the business management sense but can also be conceived of as a stock of human resources.

The systemic approach and the stocks perspective can complement one another if a system is understood as being comprised of various stocks. The stocks become elements of the system. If a company is regarded as a system, for example, the raw materials stored there, along with its machines and its workers and so on can all be represented as stocks. If we then go further to consider immaterial stocks, then the interests of those involved in the company, internal company arrangements, organisational structures, routines, production technologies, and so on are also elements of the company system.

The difference between a systemic approach and the stocks perspective is shown in Table 3.1. In the following chapters we will look in detail at two fundamental aspects of the concept of stocks, namely, material stocks (Chapter 4) and immaterial stocks (Chapters 5 and 6).

Table 3.1 Schematic representation of the differences between the systemic approach and the stocks perspective

Systemic approach	*Stocks perspective*
Cause-effect relations are the main focus of the study	Temporal processes are the main focus of the study
How does x impact on y?	How does the stock containing the element x develop or change? How does the stock containing the element y develop or change?
Models (formulated mathematically) on the basis of laws that reflect temporal processes in the ahistorical form 'whenever x …, then y …'	Evaluation of statistics, especially time series, recording of typical lifetimes and rhythms, phenomenological observation of processes in order to obtain information about *typical* processes
Scientific methods	Faculty of judgement guided by principles

Notes

1 Something that 'has' *Bestand* (i.e. is persistent or enduring) is not necessarily regarded as something that 'is' a *Bestand* (a stock of something). A state may endure over time but that does not make it a stock in the ordinary everyday sense.
2 A potentially positive or negative connotation may depend either on the type of *Bestand*/stock – a stock of foxes with rabies is a bad thing for a hunter – or on the quantity of its elements – a stock of rabbits may be desirable for the hunter within certain boundaries whereas it will be seen as an infestation if there are large quantities of them.
3 These issues were studied prominently in the context of neo-Austrian capital theory (Faber 1986: Chapter 3; Faber and Proops 1998; Faber et al. 1999; Winkler 2003).
4 Cf. e.g. Wodopia 1986: 188–191; Faber et al. 1996; Schiller 2002; Faber and Manstetten 2003, 2007; Faber et al. 2005a and b; Ott and Döring 2008.
5 Cf. e.g. BUND and Misereor 1996; Schmidt-Bleek and Klüting 1994; Schmitz and Paulini 1999.
6 Cf. e.g. Odum 1975: Chapter 4; Remmert 1980: 192–198.
7 Cf. e.g. Hannon 1973, 1995; Amir 1975, 1987, 1989; Klauer 1998: Chapters 6 and 8; Klauer 2000.
8 This is elaborated in Schiller et al. (2006) in relation to problem-oriented integrative environmental research.
9 Issues concerning making the right choice of systemic representation are discussed in Baumgärtner and Schiller (2001: 377–379) and Schiller (2002: Chapter 2).
10 In this respect, simplifications are a matter of subjective perception, as they are dependent upon the observer's or policy maker's reasons for seeking knowledge and taking action (cf. Baumgärtner and Schiller, 2001: 374–375).
11 Those concerned with sustainability policy are principally decision makers (e.g. politicians or the employees of the relevant public administration) as well as their advisers (academics, engineers, consultants etc.). They also include the representatives of specific interest groups (e.g. business federations or environmental organisations, lobbyists etc.). Ultimately, of course, any citizen who takes a stance in some way or another in relation to a given sustainability problem can also be regarded belonging to this group.

12 A clear analysis of the various functions of models in sustainability research can be found in Baumgärtner et al. (2008).

13 This procedure is especially far-reaching in the scientific *experiment*. Here, an idealised situation is created – an artificial reality which allows for the empirical study of a previously posed question or hypothesis in the context of the disciplinary system concerned.

14 For example, technical constraints on production are depicted in the context of productive functions. Elements of these constraints that are crucial in relation to environmental and sustainability problems, such as the ubiquitous occurrence of co-production (i.e. the generation of unwanted additional products such as waste products), are systematically ignored, however (Baumgärtner et al. 2006: Chapter 7).

15 This is not necessarily the case. The interconnections may also be conveyed linguistically, for example (as in systems whose elements are human beings).

16 It is frequently assumed that elements in a system may disappear or new elements may appear over time but that the functions performed by a disappearing element remain intact for the system as a whole and are taken over either by other elements or by new ones (substitution).

17 This also includes stochastic regularities such as Schrödinger equations.

18 The homogeneity of the elements of a stock is expressed in the formal definition by the property of appertainment (cf. Section 4.3.1, Definition 4.1): with regard to this characteristic a stock is homogeneous, i.e. it displays no internal structure.

19 By analogy with the conceptual scheme of structural linguistics based on the work of Ferdinand de Saussure, we might say that a systemic approach is a synchronous way of looking at phenomena whereas the stocks perspective approximates more to a diachronic way of looking at them.

4 Material stocks

4.1 Definitional approach

As already mentioned in the previous chapter, both material and immaterial objects can be persistent. In this chapter we shall look at material stocks[1]. Matter is an object of inquiry addressed by science and technology. The temporal development of material stocks can be studies scientifically and statistics can be collated regarding the way they change. In this chapter, then, we seek to formulate a definition of material stocks that accords with a mathematical and scientific approach.

In preparation for this definition we first set about defining the terms 'time horizon' and 'timescale under consideration' (Section 4.2), as these serve to define the temporal context in which the study takes place, which is determined by the observer. Having defined the notion of 'material stock' in Section 4.3 we turn in Section 4.4 to an analytical discussion of what can be described as a (material) stock and what cannot. The remaining sections of this chapter are devoted to a number of examples of material stocks (Section 4.5), to elucidating the general reasons for their persistence (Section 4.6) and, finally, to discussing what kinds of empirical propositions can be made regarding material stocks (Section 4.7).

4.2 Time horizon and timescale under consideration

One of the key preconditions for describing material stocks is that the observer (or policy maker) needs to be clear about the timescales and periods of observation on which they want to base their study. In the context of our formal definition, we use the terms 'time horizon' and 'timescale under consideration' to refer to these aspects. The *time horizon* T is the period of time over which the practical context concerned is to be described and the way it develops studied. Since in most cases a temporal description cannot occur at any random point along the time axis, we need to have an idea about a 'segment of time' during which the observations is to be carried out. We refer to this *segment* as the *timescale under consideration* τ.

This need not be a precise interval of time; rather, the timescale under consideration may be set according to a specified length of time. For example, the development of meteorological events can be described on a timescale of hours or days, which would be a study of the 'weather'. Looking at the way it develops over a timescale of years or decades, however, would be to study the development of the 'climate'. Each is a different issue that requires a different approach, even though it is fundamentally the same environmental system that is being studied.

In principle the choice of time horizon and timescale under consideration is limited by only one condition, namely, that the timescale needs to be much shorter than the time horizon. In all other respects the two are independent of one another. Both the time horizon and the timescale under consideration are not fixed objectively but rather emerge from the interests, or point of view, of the observer (cognitive interest) or the policy maker (motivation to act). Thus they are *subjective factors* which are initially located at the level of the observer or the policy maker.

Nonetheless the choice is not arbitrary. If policy makers are committed to achieving a certain objective, such as sustainability, it means not only that the goals and objects of their actions need to meet particular requirements but also that the time horizon and timescale need to be selected in accordance with these goals and objects.

4.3 Definitions

4.3.1 Material sets and stocks

Our definition of the term *material stock* is grounded in set theory and as such is universally applicable. It can be used, for example, in ecological, physical and technical as well as in economic and societal contexts. Before the actual definition of a material stock can be provided a number of auxiliary terms need to be clarified first.

> **Definition 4.1: Material set, property of appertainment** – A *set* is a combination of those elements that display a certain common property. This property, which defines the set, is what we call its property of appertainment. A *material set* is a set whose property of appertainment includes the proposition that its elements consist of matter. A set is *empty* if it contains no element.

The property of appertainment of a set is therefore the property which, by definition, has to be given in every element of the set[2]. This property, then, is one which describes the individual elements of the set in question and thus is located at a microscopic level of observation[3]. At the same time the property of appertainment describes the set as a whole and delimits it from its environment – that is, it can also be conceived of as a property at the macroscopic level.

The elements of a set can be characterised by more than a single property of appertainment. In the following, however, we shall discuss *one* property of appertainment that generally encompasses several sub-properties. Thus, a property of appertainment usually includes a spatial component and characterises the elements in a factual way – for example, the set of 'red cars registered in the city of Leipzig'.

We understand the property of appertainment of a stock to be an *objectifiable* property of elements in the sense that it is possible to come up with intersubjective criteria for whether or not the property of appertainment is given or not. Thus, for example, the place where an object is to be found can serve as part of the property of appertainment; it can be determined objectively. If the colour of the object is to determine appertainment, then a convention must be established beforehand concerning the wavelength range of visible light to be allocated to a specific colour[4].

Although the property of appertainment is objective or objectifiable, it can nonetheless be chosen freely by the observer when delimiting a specific set. This choice will depend on the theoretical or practical interests of the observer or policy maker. Consider as an example some machines in a factory building. If we wanted to find out how much electricity is used up during the production process, a useful property of appertainment of the set of machines in the factory will be the fact that (i) the machines are located in the building and (ii) they require electricity for their operation. A solely hand-operated machine would not be included here. If, however, the intention is to look at which of the machines belong to the factory owner, then logically the property of appertainment consists in the machines which belong to her (i.e. have not been leased, for example) and are located inside the factory building.

This example shows that the purpose of the study is crucial in selecting a meaningful property of appertainment and thus in delimiting the sets under observation. Accordingly the following applies to any sustainability problem: the properties of appertainment need to be selected in such a way that the policy-relevant issues come into view.

At this point we are now in a position to define the term 'material stock'. It is the aspect of time that constitutes the heart of our conceptual framework of stocks. This is why the key characteristic of a material stock (in our view) lies in its property of *persistence*. A material set of elements should only be described as a material stock when it exists over a certain length of time. This line of thinking leads us to the following definition:

> **Definition 4.2: Persistence, material stock** – A material set is persistent at point in time t_0 when it is not empty for a length of time beginning at t_0 that is different from zero on the timescale under consideration τ given by the cognitive interest or practical concerns of the observer or the policy maker. A persistent material set is called *material stock*.

Thus the key property of persistence pertaining to material stocks can only be stated relative to the given timescale under consideration τ. This timescale represents the measure by which persistence is quantified. With regard to the exact period of time in which the set in question may not be empty, Definition 4.2 can be further specified (this we do at the end of this section in Proposition 4.1).

The timescale under consideration that underpins Definition 4.2 is prescribed by the observer's cognitive interests or the policy maker's motivation to act. These are also the interests on which the time horizon T for the overall observation depends. As discussed in Section 4.2 above, the time horizon T and the timescale under consideration τ are factors that are prescribed by the observer, but they are not objectively given characteristics of the material stock in question. A third length of time is crucial when describing stocks, namely, the duration of the stock or the *remaining duration* at point in time t_0.

> **Definition 4.3: Duration of a material stock, remaining duration** – The duration of a material stock is the entire time span of its existence. The *remaining duration* of a material stock at the point in time of observation t_0 – that is, T^{t0} – is the remaining time span of its existence at point in time t_0.

The duration of a material stock is its remaining duration at the point in time when the stock begins to exist. Unlike the timescale under consideration, the duration of a material stock is a given objective characteristic of the stock, that is, it is independent from the observer; this characteristic constitutes a property of the object in question[5].

4.3.2 Dimensions and dynamics of stocks

So far we have characterised material stocks in relation to two aspects,. namely, the way they are set apart by means of a property of appertainment that has to be fulfilled by all their elements, and their temporal duration. A third aspect consists of other properties of a stock, which we describe formally as quantitative attributes. Studying specific problems with the help of the stocks concept often involves taking an interest in other properties of the stock at the macroscopic level. These may initially be properties which can be defined by means of a quantitative measure, but they may also be those for which no meaningful quantitative measure exists. To distinguish between these we use the term *quantitative attribute.*

> **Definition 4.4: Quantitative attribute, stock variable** – A quantitative attribute of a set is one which can be identified on a cardinal scale at any point in time within the time horizon T. A quantitative attribute K can be measured by a real function f_K: $[t_0, T] \rightarrow \mathbf{R}$ within the interval $[t_0, T]$. The function f_K is called the stock variable.

If we look, for example, at a pile of sand as a material stock, then its temperature, its volume and its weight on the earth's surface constitute some of its quantitative attributes. In the case of a fish population both the number of individuals and their overall biomass constitute different stock variables. Generally, then, it is possible to specify any number of attributes of a given material stock. Thus when looking at a specific problem it is necessary to select those attributes that are relevant to the issue out of the many possible ones available, thus enabling a description of the material stock in question.

Returning to the example of the inventory of machines in a factory building, the overall electricity consumption of the machines as well as their overall monetary value as an investment represent different stock variables. If we wanted to make a business management study of the profitability of production, then investment value would be an important stock variable. If, by contrast, it is the climate-related impacts of production in the building that we want to assess, then overall electricity consumption would be a relevant stock variable rather than investment value.

Before going on to discuss a number of other features of our definition of material stocks in the following sections, let us first introduce the concept of the dynamics of a stock. Dynamics are related to the stock variables of a material stock.

> **Definition 4.5: Dynamics of a stock** – The *dynamics of a material stock* refer to the temporal development of the stock variables observed on the timescale τ.

With regard to this definition[6] it should be noted that we still refer to the dynamics of a material stock even if the latter does not change within the period under consideration, i.e. even if the stock variables remain constant over time[7]. Furthermore, our notion of dynamics is relative to the timescale under consideration τ and the time horizon T (cf. Section 4.2). Both 'demarcate a window' in the temporal development of the stock variables – which generally occur on different timescales – for consideration. Temporal development which is more rapid than the timescale under consideration is ignored, as is temporal development which is so slow that it is not recorded within the time horizon. For any given issue, though, the way this 'window' is selected is by no means arbitrary: to the extent that stocks themselves change, everything depends on selecting the timescale and the time horizon in such a way that this inherent dynamic is adequately recorded (cf. also Chapter 8).

4.4 An equivalent definition of persistence

For the purposes of the concept of material stock presented here, it is initially helpful to work with an understanding of time that is characteristic of classical Newtonian physics – in Section 8.3.1 we refer to this concept of time as *chronos*[8]. Time is conceived of as an empty, countable and measurable entity that proceeds in a certain direction. Phenomena are imagined as being embedded in this time and they are assigned a date within it which is expressed in numbers.

Three aspects of time that can be measured using *chronos* are important for the concept of stocks, as follows:

- A material stock relates to a certain point in time t_0 at which it is observed; in relation to this point in time we can specify whether a set is persistent or not.
- In order to define the nature of its persistence, the timescale under consideration τ on which persistence (in the sense of continuity) must be given is important.

- The third aspect of time relating to our conceptual framework of stocks is the remaining duration T^{t0} of a material stock at point in time t_0, which is an objective characteristic of the stock[9].

By comparing these three aspects of time, our concept of material stocks can now be formulated somewhat differently and with greater analytical precision.

> **Proposition 4.1: Equivalent definition of persistence** – A material set is persistent at time t_0 if and only if its remaining duration T^{t0} is considerably greater than the timescale under consideration τ given by the context, i.e. $T^{t0} \geq A\tau$, with $A >> 1$.

Since the timescale τ constitutes the 'resolution' used by the observer to record the dynamics of the material stock, the condition in Proposition 4.1 means that the remaining duration of the stock extends across several consecutive observations[10]. This approach to expressing persistence is at the heart of our definition of material stocks. A comparison between the two periods of time can serve as a 'test' for whether or not a set of elements constitutes a stock. Proposition 4.1 can thus serve to establish empirically the persistence of specific observed sets.

4.5 Examples of material stocks

There are very many things which can be considered as material stocks in line with Definition 4.2. Some examples in relation to typical economic issues include existing quantities of coal, oil, mineral deposits, timber, cotton, grain, coffee, pearls, diamonds, gold coins, machines, computers, tools, buildings, roads, ports, ships, refrigerators, cameras and the railway network. All the things named here are reserves or capital goods as they are used, whether directly or indirectly, to provide a service to people. There are also human-made material stocks that do not count as reserves or capital goods, such as quantities of household waste, mud from harbour installations, scrapped cars, disused machines, ruined buildings, heavy metals in rivers, and so on. Whether or not a stock constitutes capital depends, among other things, on how it is used. Uranium, for example, was not a capital good before people began to use it. Once nuclear technology came into use, it became a capital good in the form of fuel rods.

There are also many examples of natural stocks: lakes, rivers, forests, desert regions, habitats and biotopes and animal and plant populations. Many human-made stocks and natural stocks are both at the same time: mud from harbour installations, ruined buildings, CO_2 stocks in the atmosphere and heavy metals in rivers can be regarded as both human-made and natural stocks. Ultimately, as already indicated, even people themselves can be described as a material stock in the sense of our set theory based definition. Examples include the population of a country, the members of a club and the employees of a company.

4.6 Reasons for the persistence of material stocks

With regard to most of the material stocks mentioned so far, their persistence is based on the durability or permanence of their constituent elements. For example, stocks of pebbles and gold coins are durable because their constituent elements – each specific stone or coin – are long lasting. However, in many cases the persistence of the overall stock surpasses that of its elements. The individual elements disappear but new elements come into being. Either they come from outside or else they are created anew. The population of Leipzig is a stock because new children are born and new residents move to the city. This means that, alongside the durability of the individual element, the reproduction and importation[11] of elements are the 'mechanisms' of persistence.

Figure 4.1 shows the four foundational mechanisms of stock dynamics – import (Element 1), export (Element 2), emergence (Element 3) and disappearance (Element 4). The circles represent the spatial boundary of a stock at two different points in time. The squares symbolise (for simplicity's sake identifiably different) elements of the stock. Element 3 becomes doubled between points in time τ_1 and τ_2 to become Elements 3a and 3b, while Element 4 ceases to exist as such.

The mechanisms of persistence of material stocks presented here play a variety of roles in relation to each specific stock under consideration. When we look at the volume of water in a certain stretch of a river in terms of its properties *qua* stock, it is dominated by import and export, as a stretch of river constantly has water flowing through it. What remain constants in this case, then, are the flow of water from upstream and the riverbed. In the case of stocks of populations, reproduction

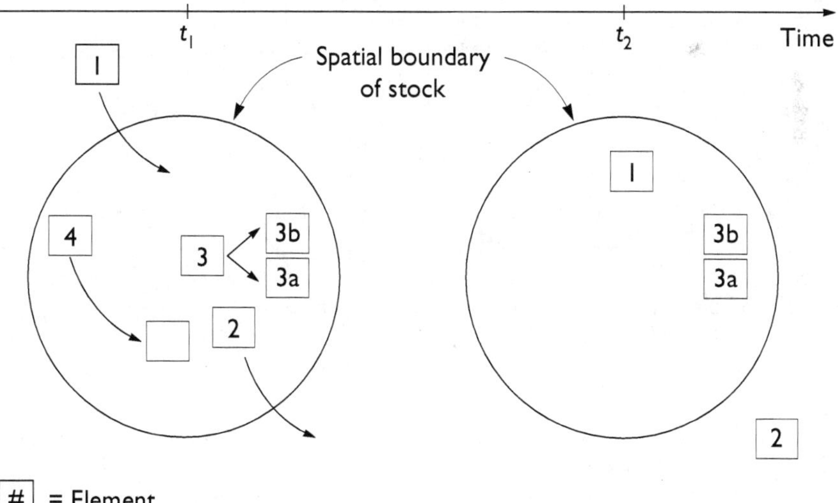

Figure 4.1 Mechanisms of stock dynamics in the depiction of a spatial property of appertainment

plays a key role in long-term persistence, as the lifetime of individuals is limited. Whether or not a given set of things is considered to be a stock is always a matter of empirical observation.

4.7 Empirical information about stocks

In the preceding sections of this chapter we have introduced the term 'stock' as a theoretical concept in relation to which it is initially irrelevant whether or not the conditions are given for generating reliable information regarding the persistence of a specific material set of things. This changes as soon as the aim is to discover by empirical means whether or not a specific object of study is a stock.

If we want to establish the persistence of a set of things in the past, this can be done on the basis of observing its uninterrupted existence. If, however, we take the point of time of observation t_0 to be the present, then it is necessary to know something about the *future* development of a set of things when judging its persistence according to Definition 4.2 or Proposition 4.1. This will necessarily involve a degree of uncertainty or lack of knowledge. In order to obtain, despite this, useful information *ex ante* about the persistence of specific objects of study, further information about stock dynamics is needed.

One potential source of such information about a stock's dynamics is, in many cases, *experiential knowledge* from the past. Even if knowledge of the history of a material stock is not enough in itself to illuminate the issue of its persistence in the present, it usually provides some clues nonetheless[12].

However, even if the persistence of a set of things in the past has been proven empirically, this does not always make it possible to predict whether or not it will continue to exist (i.e. its character *qua* stock) in the present or the future. Generally speaking, it is the dynamics of the set in question and its underlying mechanisms that need to be considered in order to ascertain this. In other words, it is necessary to draw on *scientific knowledge* (Section 3.3.2) to judge persistence. Due to the uncertainties that arise *ex ante*, stochastic concepts are often helpful here (Faber et al. 2005a and b).

If we look at living populations, for example, the number of individuals in an ecosystem must not drop below a certain threshold if the population's ongoing capacity to reproduce – and thus its continued existence over the long term – is to be safeguarded. Thus merely knowing that a population has existed over a period of time in the past is not sufficient to yield conclusions regarding its persistence in the present. In order to predict a population's dynamics in the future – and therefore its present and future persistence – further information is needed[13].

If we describe something that exists in the present as a stock, this means that it will continue to exist into the future and will therefore influence the future. Similarly, if we shift the point in time of observation t_0 back into the past, it follows from this that the stocks we now find in the present and which influence it are those which originated in the past. The persistence of a stock links the past to the future via the present. Stocks thus serve to convey influences from the past into the present and can therefore be considered historical factors (Schiller 2002: Chapters 3 and 4).

Notes

1 This chapter is based extensively on Faber et al. (2005a and b) and has been modified by the authors in line with the requirements of this book's overall argument.

2 A set is homogeneous in the sense that all its elements fulfil the property of appertainment. The elements may well differ, however, in relation to other properties, i.e. they may be heterogeneous.

3 Every object can be observed at various stages of aggregation. Here, the microscopic level means that the description is sufficiently detailed for the properties of the individual elements to come into view. By analogy, a macroscopic level is conceivable at which it is no longer the individual elements that are observed but the set itself, e.g. as part of a larger system. The stocks perspective (cf. Section 3.3) generally uses a macroscopic level of observation.

4 Properties of potential elements that are initially felt at a purely subjective level, such as the 'beauty' of works of art, would have to be rendered objectifiable as far as possible in order be used as a property of appertainment. It is here that one limitation to the term material stock becomes apparent: it is almost impossible to agree objectively upon the 'stock of beautiful pictures in Leipzig', for example; it is also virtually impossible to describe the essential character of this stock by quantifying it.

5 Being able to define the duration of a stock presupposes that the stock has been set apart, i.e. that a property of appertainment has been defined. As discussed above, a meaningful mode of setting apart the stock in question depends on the way it is to be examined – that is, it depends on the cognitive interests of the observer and the practical interests of the policy maker. The property of duration of a stock clearly depends on how that stock is defined, and so its 'objectivity' is not absolute.

6 Our concept of the dynamics of a stock does not include the reasons for the temporal development of stock variables at the level of its elements. The concept is thus phenomenological in nature. Given a corresponding cognitive interest the reasons for the dynamics of a stock can be looked at in a complementary study at the 'micro-level'.

7 Dynamics, then, means nothing other than what changes and what stays the same over time. This kind of concept of dynamics is perhaps unfamiliar in everyday language because the latter associates dynamics in general with changes in at least one dimension. However, both change and constancy in a stock or in its variables are important when studying the temporal development of a material stock as part of a larger system.

8 Alongside the notion of time common to Newtonian physics (*chronos*), other conceptions of time are also important for the conceptual framework of stocks and the stocks perspective (cf. Section 3.2 above); this is the subject of Chapter 8.

9 We explicate the link between this property of a stock and the concept of inherent time in Chapter 8.

10 It is not especially important to define the exact dimension of constant A in this context, as it will generally depend on the problem in question.

11 For it to make sense to speak of 'importation', a material stock must be characterised by a spatial boundary. In Definition 4.2 the concept of material stock was formulated only in terms of the dimension of time, with no explicit mention being made of the dimension of space. As mentioned previously in relation to the property of appertainment, however, a material stock generally possesses a spatial dimension. This is obvious in the case of ecological stocks and most economic stocks. A population always has a certain area of distribution – in some cases this may be the entire Earth. Similarly, any description of the vast majority of economic goods will include a reference to their location.

Consider, for example, a stock of capital goods, a company's CAD machines: in relation to almost every issue relating to these machines, it is the places where they are available that is key – e.g. 'all the CAD machines in Leipzig'. In formal terms a spatial dimension of material stocks is included in our conceptualisation as a component of the property of appertainment and as such is not initially highlighted in comparison to other properties.

12 A stock with no history whatsoever – i.e. a stock that starts to exist at the precise point in time of observation t_0 – can be regarded formally as a stock according to Definition 3.2, but it is a marginal case and thus does not accord with the substance of what we wish to express through the stocks concept.

13 Faber et al. (2005a and b) offer a formal example of how, in theoretical ecology, predictions can be made regarding the dynamics of stocks based on knowledge of structural conditions.

5 Immaterial stocks and institutions

with Mi-Yong Lee

5.1 What are immaterial stocks?

So far we have defined the concept of stock in relation to material objects. What we now consider in this (and the following) chapter are *immaterial* stocks. It will soon become clear that the mathematical-scientific approach taken in Chapter 4 to define a stock cannot be applied straightforwardly to objects such as values, norms, technologies, consumption behaviours, decision-making structures, organisations or laws. What these objects have in common is that, by their very nature, they are non-material and therefore do not exist independently of human actions and thoughts. Due to their durability and enduringness, however, they are obviously also persistent. They are also highly relevant to sustainability policy as they influence – whether directly or indirectly – human behaviour and actions.

It is not easy, however, to get an adequate conceptual grasp of immaterial stocks in terms of their character as a stock, that is, in terms of their inertia, stability and resistance. After clarifying some terms we elaborate how, in the context of our main concern (how best to design and implement sustainability policy), it is helpful to concentrate on analysing *institutions*, even if there are many other immaterial stocks besides these. The issue of the persistence and changeability of institutions is very important when it comes to designing policies aimed at achieving sustainability. The reasons why institutions remain stable and persistent or not will be dealt with at length in Chapter 6.

In the following discussion we look at the preconditions and foundations required to grasp conceptually the stability, persistence and dynamics of immaterial objects, especially those that influence human behaviour and actions. In doing so, our concern is continually to bear in mind the basic purpose of the conceptualisation of stocks, namely, to establish a means of making visible the dynamics of durable objects and their significance for long-term policy, especially sustainability policy.

Our discussion of immaterial stocks is aimed at

- simplifying complex issues in such a way that the spotlight falls on their dynamics and their inertia;
- ensuring the description of these issues is based for the most part on observation alone; and
- rendering transparent the subjective perspective of the observer or practitioner.

While these three aims also apply to the concept of material stock, they are joined by a fourth aim in the present context: since immaterial stocks are related to human thoughts and actions, it is barely possible to discuss them meaningfully without including people and their activities in our conception of them. So a further aim of our discussion of immaterial stocks is to

- contribute towards describing adequately a number of essential characteristics of human behaviour.

In comparison to mechanical processes and instinctive responses, human behaviour appears far less predictable. Furthermore, people who act consider themselves free agents who can act this way or another way. Given that this is so, any attempt at subjecting human behaviour and action to systematic analysis – as is attempted in mathematics-based economic theory, for instance – will only ever be partially successful.

Studying the essential characteristics of humans is the task of cultural theory, the social sciences and the humanities. They ask what is specifically human about human beings and how this humanness can be addressed conceptually, captured empirically and, where appropriate, influenced. From the point of view of sustainability policy, everything that can be considered as part of human behaviour and action plays a special role here. These issues fall within the purview of *anthropology*, the study of human beings. This being the case, our attempt to explain immaterial stocks and the manner of their persistence and stability leads us to enter this field of inquiry at several points, including discussion of relevant terms and theoretical approaches.

In Section 5.2 we present some of the difficulties associated with empirical observation of immaterial stocks by referring to a few specific examples. We then explain why we choose to concentrate on institutions in our subsequent closer study of immaterial stocks. Sections 5.3 to 5.6 focus on explaining where the term 'institution' comes from and what it encompasses. In Section 5.7 we show how other kinds of immaterial stocks can either be represented as institutions or placed in relation to institutions in terms of their sustainability-related aspects.

5.2 The observability of immaterial stocks

If we are interested in finding out about the long-term stability and dynamics of human societies, then clearly it is important to consider not only material factors but a variety of immaterial factors as well:

- the values that guide the behaviours of members of a society;
- the ideas they have about the world and through which they interpret their environment and their own existence, e.g. religious and secular world views and ideologies, including prejudices, conventions of thinking and taboos;
- the norms, laws and rules they follow;
- the interests and preferences that guide their actions;

- the knowledge they have about natural and social processes;
- the technologies they use to accomplish certain tasks and activities;
- the habits that lend their life uniformity and stability; and
- many more besides.

All these dimensions of human and social existence are of significance to successful sustainability policy. In addition, they are often persistent as well. If habits of consumption and modes of production play a role in the ecological aspects of sustainability, then clearly all the factors mentioned above need to be examined insofar as they exert an influence on them. A change in cultural values or the introduction of new technologies can mean that the overall situation in a society with regard to the sustainability of a given development must be judged completely differently than it has been previously.

When factors of this kind change, far-reaching changes may likewise occur in the quantitative attributes and dynamics of material stocks. We need only think of climate change as an example: new technologies such as energy-efficient homes and low-fuel vehicles; new laws such as a CO_2 tax; or a variation in other modes of consumption such as fewer car journeys, fewer flights and eating much less beef could achieve a marked reduction in greenhouse gas emissions.

Thus sustainability policy must take immaterial stocks into consideration as a priority. In doing so it is confronted with the problem that many immaterial things are not *observable* per se. Their occurrence, their durability, their dynamic and their disappearance can only be discovered from the things people actually do. Whether or not solidarity, for example, is a value and, if so, how it works can be observed indirectly by noting whether people talk about it and the way they talk about it as well as how people support or do not support one another. Similarly, the technologies that exist within a society take on significance only when they are actually put to use or at least when plans for them exist. Knowledge and world views can be observed if they are available in written form, but they are not relevant to sustainability policy if they are merely kept in archives. Of much greater interest are the knowledge and world views that actually have an impact on people's lives. As far as preferences are concerned, economists have long recognised that they can only be taken into account when they are observed as *revealed* preferences in the behaviours of market participants (Houthakker 1950).

Alongside the fact that many immaterial stocks cannot be observed directly, a further difficulty lies in the fact that they do not always exert any impact at all – they may remain dormant, as it were, in certain circumstances in the present, while different circumstances may cause them to emerge visibly and have an impact. Thus they constitute potential impacts. It may be, then, that in principle we know theoretically about a certain technology but that we cannot say whether it will ever be put to use. This depends not only on the technology itself but on the cultural, economic and political setting in which it exists, such as the availability of resources, the prevailing pricing system, the relevant legal regulations, the preferences of consumers and so on. Once all this is known, it may become apparent how likely or not it is that a certain technology will be used in a practical application.

In this way the immaterial stocks of values, knowledge, preferences and interests turn our attention back initially towards observable human behaviour. Values, norms, world views, knowledge, technologies, interests and preferences are *behavioural possibilities* whose importance and persistence need to be assumed in principle but which can only be captured empirically when they become visible in the form of actual human behaviours (cf. Section 5.4)[1].

Generally speaking, then, sustainability policy should take account of immaterial stocks whenever they actually influence people's behaviour or when there is a real possibility that they may do so. Thus if we look at the immaterial stocks mentioned above we need to recognise that we can only establish their relevance and persistence empirically in those cases where a correspondence is apparent between them and human behaviour or human interactions. In other words, the cultural, social, political, economic and ecological relevance – and thus the policy relevance – of values, norms, world views, knowledge, technologies, preferences and interests can only be opened up to scrutiny by observing and describing behaviour.

From the point of view of persistence and stability, however, it is less the behaviour of isolated individuals than the repeated, *regular* behaviour of many people that is of interest here. Regular behaviour is in many cases not only repetitive but can also be understood in relation to an explicit rule. Such rules, whose impact is recognisable in people's behaviour, are known as *institutions*. We will therefore focus the rest of our study of immaterial stocks on institutions. At the end of this chapter, in Section 5.7, we shall show that an analysis of institutions is also helpful in analysing the relevance and dynamics of other immaterial stocks.

5.3 Behaviour and behavioural patterns

In principle, there is an 'external' and an 'internal' aspect to human behaviour. The external aspect is observable: it can be recorded by an observer or by a camera. The internal aspect, by contrast, consists of motivations, interests and purposes which are only accessible to us indirectly – through introspection, if they are our own; the motivations, interests and purposes of other people, however, can be ascertained only by communicating with them or by interpreting what we can perceive them doing. Let us look first at the external aspect, observable behaviour, and ask what characteristics are relevant from the point of view of sustainability.

Sustainability problems are characterised by the following typical feature: it is not the one-off car journey undertaken by an individual from A to B but rather this individual's habit of travelling repeatedly from A to B by car that may lead to a sustainability problem. Similarly, for a change to occur to the stock of CO_2 in the atmosphere, it is not significant that a single individual has this habit but that many millions of people habitually use a car. The practical conclusion we draw from this is that observable human activities that occur regularly beyond a certain period of time ought to be recorded in terms of stocks. We use the term *behavioural pattern* to refer to activities which display these features. In other words:

- We see *behaviour* as an observable human activity that is engaged in by one or more people and can be distinguished from other activities.

- A behaviour is always part of a *behavioural pattern* whenever these activities occur repeatedly, i.e. they can be registered at different points in time or by different people in similar situations. This repetition often has the character of *regularity*.
- The *perspective of the observer* is important when it comes to identifying a pattern of behaviour.

Wherever the consequences of behavioural patterns, and especially the regularity with which they occur, are relevant to issues of sustainability, it is possible to study them more closely.

5.4 Behavioural patterns and understanding actions

5.4.1 Behaviour and actions

The very act of identifying a behavioural pattern often goes beyond straightforward observation and into the realm of *interpretation*. This is because the identification of a specific behaviour presupposes knowledge whose sources lie beyond the observation itself. If, for example, we observe that a person is greeting another person, reaching the conclusion that this behaviour means 'greeting' entails – alongside the observation of certain movements or verbal utterances – prior knowledge of what 'greeting' is. Indeed it is more generally the case that when a human observer sees other people behaving in a certain way, there will normally be additional assumptions feeding into these observations. For example, we assume that people behave this way for certain reasons – unlike the movements of a machine or the mechanised chatter of a talking doll.

The reasons for a specific behaviour can only be ascertained directly from a personal *internal perspective*. However, people can communicate the reasons they perceive in their internal perspective. This is how they explain their behaviour. These explanations may include such information as their motivations, intentions, purposes and values as well as their perceptions of appropriate means-ends relations. Explanations can be discussed and, where necessary, criticised as well. An observer who is aware of this also knows that in principle people are capable of changing their behaviour. In most cases a person who behaves in such and such a way could equally behave differently.

Reasons that cause a specific behaviour to occur are described as *motivations*. Motivations cannot be observed as such but can be communicated verbally as explanations for behaviour. Each type of behaviour for which explanations can be communicated and which can thus be related to motivations is described as *action* (Figure 5.1). The explanation need not necessarily be communicated by the people doing the action themselves. Habitualised behaviour or routines in work processes are often more or less mechanical in character. Those engaged in them will often not be able to say why or for what purpose they are doing so. Nonetheless, though, it is generally possible to deduce from the context of a work routine a (more or less) logical motivation[2]. If behaviour is the external aspect, then action, to simplify somewhat, is the internal aspect of human activity. This is why behaviour can only be understood as action, while action can only be observed in behaviour.

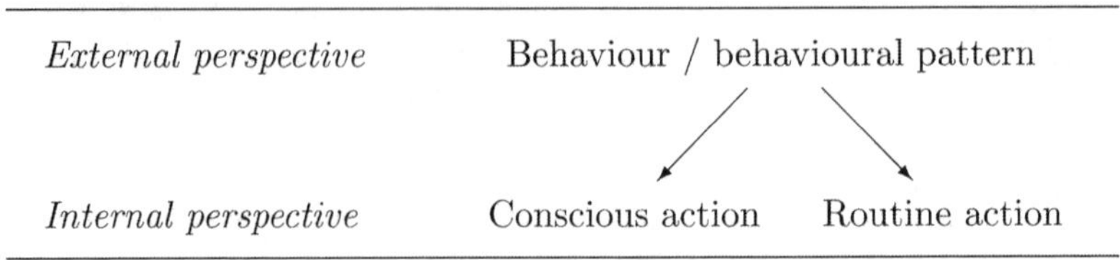

Figure 5.1 External and internal perspective: action and behaviour

From a stocks perspective, the foregoing account delivers in the following insights: the persistence and changeability of behavioural patterns can be adequately assessed only by studying the internal aspect of the modes of behaviour that comprise these patterns, that is, by studying the action in question. For this reason we proceed in the next section to elaborate the essential characteristics of action.

5.4.2 Essential characteristics of action

The boundary between the external and internal perspective, that is, the difference between action and simple behaviour, cannot be drawn sharply because when it comes to observing human behaviour we can rarely separate it out from all our prior knowledge about the action. We inevitably create a link between people's actions and our own internal perspective: when we observe another person's behaviour, we try to understand it as action by imagining what might have motivated it.

In the following we seek to formulate a number of attributes which can be applied meaningfully to action only and not to perceived isolated behaviour[3].

1 Action entails the possibility of articulating *goals* or *purposes* as the cause and motivation for it. The purpose may be an outcome which is achieved only once the action is completed (e.g. a certificate as the conclusion to the act of 'sitting an examination'), but the action may also be an end in itself (e.g. dancing, making music).
2 Action – especially conscious action – entails *freedom* in a particular sense: those who act have chosen this specific action from a range of alternative options, and those who see a person as the originator of certain acts will assume that that person had the option of acting differently if they had wanted to.
3 Action is designed to be *understood*. This follows from the fact that action happens for certain reasons. Normally people act in the context of a communication community whose members are able in principle to comprehend the reasons for their actions.
4 Action – one's own as well as that of others – is subject to *expectations*. In certain situations we expect of other people (and of ourselves) a particular kind of behaviour; equally, a person who acts knows that their action will be perceived within the context of other people's expectations.

5 Action is usually part of a *context of interaction* involving several people. Isolated actions, such as opening a door, may seem to be purely personal, but the chain of action (or higher-level action) to which this apparently isolated action belongs is generally related to the actions of other people.

6 The fact that an action can be understood and that it occurs in relation to a community imply that it is possible to ascribe a particular *meaning* to it. The expression 'meaning' refers to the notion that, from the point of view of those engaging in it, all action can be related to ultimate ideas or considerations which cannot be questioned and which are shared by all those who are either closely or loosely connected to the actors through sharing common values, attitudes, approaches, behavioural patterns and experiences. Meaning serves to embed actions in the lifeworld of a community or a society.

Understanding actions is a crucial prerequisite for describing phenomena of persistence in the realm of human activity that elude direct observation. At the same time the persistence of actions is closely related to observable behaviour; it is expressed in regularities – in patterns of behaviour.

5.5 Behavioural patterns, regularity and rule

5.5.1 'Laws of nature' governing behaviour: the economics approach

If we want to predict the persistence of material stocks in the future, we will often look for regularities in the stock dynamics and try to discover the *rule* that explains these dynamics. *Laws of nature* constitute one important category of such rules. It is assumed, in the classical natural sciences at least, that the objects they study are subject to such laws in the sense of being mechanically determined by them. The laws of nature themselves are not affected by the dynamics of change affecting the objects. They are regarded as timeless or eternal.

The dynamics of things pertaining to humans – such as behavioural patterns – can also potentially be studied and explained using this kind of approach. Parts of biology (such as socio-biology), behavioural psychology and influential strands of economics and political science have all attempted to establish laws for human behavioural patterns modelled on the laws of nature. The behavioural models based on *homo oeconomicus* that are used especially in economics and have found more general application in rational choice theory do not take account of the internal perspective of the agent. Instead they reduce all the agent's motivations to egoistic-rational maximisation of utility. This explanatory scheme implies that behavioural patterns and their dynamics can be described by analogy to the movements of particles, namely, as structural processes driven by external forces and subject to universal laws[4]. One example of such a law in economics is that of supply and demand. This law makes it possible to predict that a marked increase in price of a certain good will lower demand for it. This is not a law of nature, however, for in some cases it depends on the purpose and importance of the good in question in the context of a person's everyday life as to whether a change in demand will follow from a change in price.

Despite all critiques of rational choice theories, they are nonetheless useful in the context of a stocks perspective when it comes to structuring complex domains of action in a simple, clear way. For example, the trade in emissions certificates for greenhouse gas emissions and the waste water charge in Germany are sustainability policy measures that are based essentially on economic assumptions about human behaviour. Having said this, it is also apparent that such approaches are so reductionistic that they overlook key aspects of the dynamics of behavioural patterns. In order to address these aspects we need to turn from behaviour to action.

5.5.2 How action relates to rules

There is broad agreement in the social sciences and economics that human behaviour is *rule based* in a way that has no parallels in the non-human sphere. Unlike the objects of the natural sciences, people who act are doing so on the basis of rules of which they are aware and to which they knowingly adhere.

Thus the unique connection between human behaviour, behavioural patterns and rules and the way it differs from mechanical processes only becomes apparent when we switch to the internal aspect of human activity and discuss behaviour in terms of action. It then becomes possible to say the following: every action or set of actions relates internally (typically in a conscious and deliberate way) to rules. This does not mean that a given action occurs mechanically according to a given rule. Rather, we say that the person engaging in an action 'follows' a rule, 'obeys' it or 'behaves according to the rule'. With regard to a rule that inspires a certain action, though, we say that it is followed, it is *in effect*, it is recognised, or it is simply *valid*.

Rules which are followed by people are utterly different from laws of nature or constants of human nature. Whereas the latter are imagined as being timeless and unchanging, rules in effect are changeable in principle and can even be changed by intention. At the same time these rules of behaviour typically bring about stability, persistence, inertia and resistance (cf. Chapter 6). Given that this is so, it is not just observable behavioural patterns that are the object of study from a stocks perspective but also motivations, insofar as these can be formulated as rules in effect.

5.5.3 The relationship between rules and actions

The relation between rules and actions can vary greatly. There are very many ways in which an action may be related to a rule. These include a clear order or command that is carried out in precisely this and no other way, a general ordinance that can be adhered to in very different ways, or a prohibition whose impact becomes apparent only in the absence of a certain behaviour.

Rules that limit actions, for example, do so by means of prohibition. Within their boundaries, however, they leave room to act in any number of ways: they do not determine what each individual action should be. The fact that a prohibition is at work becomes apparent only when certain behavioural patterns are *not* observed or when they occur in such a way as to elude observation. At the same time it is necessary in the context of a stocks perspective to consider (where they are relevant to sustainability policy) the options for action that have been ruled out if they are ones that may become a reality. An action can occur despite a prohibition and, if it occurs repeatedly, can even become a pattern of behaviour.

Another kind of rule through which actions are determined or influenced is the precept. The existence of effective precepts can provide direct clues as to a certain action and, in many cases, to the occurrence of corresponding behavioural patterns as well. A precept also indicates the possibility of deviating behaviour: failing to act on a precept is an option that can be chosen in certain circumstances and with certain sets of motivations.

In addition to precepts and prohibitions there are many patterns of behaviour which, even though they occur regularly, are only indirectly linked to a valid rule. They emerge in the 'shadow of the rule', as it were. One example is certain permissible options for paying less tax, a behavioural pattern which is not immediately apparent in the rule itself but rather highlights a loophole in the system of rules governing tax legislation.

5.6 Rules and the study of rules: theories of institutions

5.6.1 Ways of using the term 'institution'

The link between behavioural patterns and actions on the one hand and rules on the other is referred to in the social sciences by the term 'institution'. This term is used in a number of different ways. Textbooks and dictionaries see in it a 'multi-layered social scientific term' (Prechtl and Burkhard 1999: 262), leading occasionally to warnings of 'undue exactness' (Richter and Furubotn 1998: 6) or else to the conclusion that 'No precise, generally recognised definition exists' (Gablers *Wirtschaftslexikon* 2001: entry on 'institution').

Given that the term 'institution' is defined in different ways, it tends to be used to refer to a wide variety of phenomena. The following are some examples:

- Certain fundamental arrangements in the life of a society are referred to as institutions, including marriage, the family and, where applicable, interpersonal connections such as the tribe or clan. In states subject to the rule of law, the constitution is considered an institution. Although these arrangements may find expression in a host of rules, they exist prior to these rules and can therefore survive far-reaching rule changes.
- The law as a whole is an institution, although its subsystems and even specific legal regulations can also be regarded as institutions. Thus the rules that govern road traffic can be seen as an institution, as can driving on the right-hand side in continental Europe or driving on the left in Britain. The rule about stopping at a red traffic light is also an institution.

- All the processes that occur in politics and administration are mediated via institutions. In a democratic state constituted by the rule of law this includes the separation of powers with their various institutions as well as decision-making procedures (elections and so forth) which regulate access to power as well as the legitimacy and use of power.
- Other rule-based structures and procedures that can be called institutions include research and education with their teaching and research institutions and their procedures for gaining knowledge, as well as corresponding processes in churches, voluntary associations, and so on.
- Events in the life of a society or a subsystem of society that are repeated at fixed intervals are also referred to as institutions: Christmas in a majority of Christian countries, the football World Cup, or the ceremonies conducted on national holidays.
- Any intentional behaviour that is enacted regularly can also be described as an institution. Immanuel Kant would take his daily walk at the same time via the same route each day: this walk can be understood as an institution (in relation to Kant himself). The same applies to a person who goes jogging or swimming on a certain day at a certain time or when a person engages in prayer at a certain time of the day. This kind of behaviour can become relevant in the life of a society if it 'catches on' and turns into a social movement (an example might be the demonstrative public Friday prayer sessions as a sign of protest as occurred, for example, in Iran after the presidential elections of 2009).
- Similarly, many consumption habits can be conceived of as institutions. Although they may seem to be an expression of personal preferences and dislikes, very many lifestyles along with their corresponding modes of behaviour are an expression of what is the 'done thing', what is currently en vogue, what is 'in'. A host of generally informal rules lies behind such phenomena. The institutional character of consumption habits has been described well by Veblen (1899).
- A certain lack of clarity exists with regard to the distinction between institution and organisation. From the point of view of institutional economics, the distinction is clear: institutions are the 'rules of the game without the players' (Richter and Furubotn 1998: 7), that is, rules without actual instances of putting them into practice. The entirety of such practical instantiations undertaken by the individuals responsible for doing so would be described as an organisation. In common linguistic usage, by contrast, the Catholic Church and the Supreme Court of a country are called institutions, by which we mean not just systems of rules but institutionalised instantiations of these rules, such as the Mass or the pronouncement of a judgement.
- Finally, every language is also an institution to the extent that it regulates the verbal expressive behaviour of its speakers. The rules of this institution include not only grammar but also many indeterminate instructions that determine which words, turns of phrase or formulas are to be expected or avoided under what circumstances.

While this list could be extended further to include more uses of the term institution, it serves here to illustrate the heterogeneity of the phenomena to which 'institution' refers.

5.6.2 On the definition of 'institution'

The literature reveals two basic ways of defining institutions: on the basis of valid rules or on the basis of regular patterns of behaviour.

5.6.2.1 Institutions as rules-in-effect

It is theories of institutions in economics especially that take the concept of rule as their point of departure:

> Institutions are viewed as durable rules which govern human interactions and which are also humanly devised (so, for example, technological constraints like the 'laws' of physics are not institutions). (North 1990: 3)

When rules are conceptualised as institutions it is the way they relate to actions that is key. They determine

> what actions are allowed or constrained, [...] what procedures must be followed, what information must or must not be provided. [...] [This applies to those rules] actually used, monitored, and enforced. (Ostrom 1990: 51)

Accordingly we can see institutions as *rules that are in effect*. In many cases, being 'in effect' implies that violations will be punished by some kind of sanction. The sanctioning authority may be a formal one, such as those of the legal system – courts of law, for example – or it may be an authority empowered to be such by legal regulations, such as a manager in an employment setting. However, societies also have social mechanisms for sanctioning individuals which are not usually formalised but may have far-reaching consequences nonetheless. Through the possibility of sanctions, rules acquire the character of an obligation[5].

Institutions are divided into *formal* and *informal* institutions. The former are rules that are formulated explicitly, usually in written form (e.g. laws), while the latter are implicit rules that are not written down and perhaps even remain unarticulated[6]. Examples of formal institutions include the legally binding rules of a society, precepts and prohibitions whose validity is backed up by authorities such as the court system and the police. Other formal institutions include means of payment, club statutes, house rules, standard contracts and suchlike. Examples of informal institutions include customs, conventions, rules of proper conduct and all instructions regarding behaviour which prescribe what 'is done' or what 'is not done'.

5.6.2.2 Institutions as behavioural patterns

The approaches outlined so far assume the existence of rules and consider their real impacts. In contrast to this, institutional theories in sociology take an empirical point of departure, namely, the observation of human behaviour. They begin by observing that behaviour evolves into habit or becomes 'habitualised' (Berger and Luckmann 1991: 70–71). Habitualised behaviour is described as an institution whenever this kind of habitualisation is associated with mutual expectations in social interaction. The decisive factor here is that partners in an interaction expect or demand a certain kind of behaviour from one another. This gives rise to a typical form of behaviour that matches these expectations[7]. When people encounter one another for the first time, for example, the way they greet one another and introduce themselves constitutes this kind of typical behaviour.

Thus institutions stabilise not only habitual and regular behaviour; they also stabilise mutual expectations of behaviour. The habitualised behaviour is often not only expected and demanded but is even coerced (Mackie 1990: 80) such that institutions acquire an obligatory character in this respect too. Even if institutions are understood in terms of behaviour, this does not mean that they are not part of an 'abstract system of rules'. What makes a rule an institution, though, is always a specific practice, i.e. a variety of everyday practical actions. The institution of greeting, for example, normally involves not only the obligation to utter certain set phrases but also certain movements, certain ways of looking at each another, and so on. Thus the requirements of an institution include not only the 'the normative content of the abstract rules and principles', but also 'various things actually

Box 5.1 Terminology: actions and behaviour, rules and institutions

Human activities have an 'external' and an 'internal' aspect. The external aspect is open to observation. The internal aspect is – in relation to ourselves – accessible through introspection. Where other people are concerned, we can gain access to this internal aspect (i.e. their motivations, interests and intentions) by communicating with them or by interpreting their actions. Behaviour is the external aspect and action the internal aspect of human activity. Behaviour can only be understood as action whereas action can only be observed in behaviour. Repeated behaviour is defined as a behavioural pattern and can be studied in terms of its regularities. By analogy, it becomes possible to understand action when there is an internal reference to rules. The term 'institution' can describe such rules that are followed by people and it can also be used to refer to behavioural patterns that occur repeatedly. Thus institutions can be conceived of both as 'rules-in-effect' and as behaviour which is repeated regularly. In many cases both modes of usage of the term 'institution' can exist side by side with no contradiction. It is possible to distinguish between formal and informal institutions. The former comprise explicitly formulated rules and the latter implicit rules that remain unarticulated. Rules can shape actions in a positive way – as with precepts or prescriptions – or limit them negatively – as with prohibitions.

being demanded, condemned, enforced or encouraged' (ibid.: 81). In order to understand institutions, it is often necessary to understand not only a certain rule or set of rules but also to look at the relevant context of everyday human actions.

5.7 On the connection between institutions and other immaterial stocks

As explained above, immaterial stocks such as knowledge, values, needs, wishes and personal interests have an internal aspect that eludes direct observation. This does not apply, however, to the external aspect. Our hypothesis is this: the external aspect of immaterial stocks is to be understood (largely) from the point of view of the institution. In order to illustrate this we consider in the following some important types of immaterial stocks:

- *Academic knowledge* is (largely) accessible through the institution of the academic community. Research organisations are a part of this, as are the numerous institutions that enable debate among academics: conferences, specialist journals, and so forth. The institutions of teaching are also a part of this, though. Ideally all these institutions adhere to the principle that academic knowledge should be publicly and universally accessible – a principle that was highly influential when universities were first founded in the West at the beginning of the twelfth century. Techno-scientific progress in the modern era can only be understood in connection with the institutions of scholarly research.
- *Technologies*, like scientific knowledge, can initially be found in texts (manuals, instructions). Technologies of concern to us – i.e. those which are used or can be used in production or consumption – are additionally to be found either in technological applications or, if they are new and are not applied, in patents. Just as patent law is an institution (one which plays an enormously significant role in technical progress), so too are applied technologies, which can only be understood within the systems of rules-in-effect of the entities that use them (e.g. a company's regulations) and within the national or transnational laws-in-effect which consistently set certain overall conditions and, in some instances, specific regulations for prospective technical applications.
- Being aspects of human consciousness, *values and internalised norms*, like the factors mentioned above, cannot be observed. And yet the shared values and ethical norms of a society are reflected for the most part in the rules-in-effect of social co-existence and in actually prevailing habits. This does not apply at times of transformation when old values are being replaced by new ones; at such times we can speak of a dynamic of change in the immaterial stock of values. The new values are by no means completely invisible, however: in a modern society it is barely conceivable for people to adopt new values without there having previously been some form of debate in various parts of society. Such debates are institutionalised in the discipline of moral philosophy on the one hand and in the public information channels used by the different

religions on the other. However, social, economic or ecological crises may also prompt these kinds of debates in other sites of public opinion formation.

- At first sight *preferences* appear to be even more an internal matter for private individuals than the immaterial stocks mentioned above. Nonetheless, preferences are evidently manifested in everyday habits, i.e. in regular patterns of behaviour shared by a large number of members of a society. Especially when these patterns of behaviour are stable they can be conceived of as informal institutions that can at times even become formalised (cf. Section 6.3.5). In many cases, indeed, it is institutions that decisively shape the preferences of a society's members. This is why institutional change often leads to changes in people's preferences. Both values and preferences acquire significance in social life – and therefore in sustainability policy – whenever they come together and become organised as *interests*. Organised interests in clubs, associations, political parties and other organisations are institutional structures that are directly relevant to behaviour.

Is it the case, then, that immaterial stocks can essentially be understood as institutions and that, in order to understand the dynamics of knowledge, technology, values, preferences, and so forth, we need to study the specific institutions associated with them? This question must be answered largely in the affirmative, albeit with one crucial caveat: the technologies, values and preferences of tomorrow entail an element of spontaneity when they come into being or when they are discovered or invented, and this element remains hidden before it is manifested in institutions. This element inherent to immaterial stocks was mentioned at the start of this chapter: 'behavioural possibilities'. In every society behavioural options exist that remain latent and unrealised. Although there are institutions capable of rendering some aspects of these possibilities recognisable – such as the patent of today being the potential technology of tomorrow – in a systematic sense some residual uncertainty and ignorance remains. The behaviour and behavioural options of tomorrow can only be guessed at vaguely today – with the possibility of misinterpretation ever present.

In the following discussion we place institutions at the centre of our study of immaterial stocks. There are two reasons for doing so. One is that the difficulties of looking at immaterial stocks – which are invisible as such – and of predicting their development are less pronounced in the case of institutions. This is because they are always accompanied by their visible external aspect, namely, behaviour. In many cases, in fact, it is even possible to access the internal aspect of institutions, namely, a (formal or informal) rule. Focusing on the institution thus enables us to gain knowledge about immaterial stocks. In the next chapter we will show how this simultaneously enables us to discover something of the dynamics of immaterial stocks.

A second reason for focusing on institutions lies in the fact that they are the main point of departure for steering individual behaviour by means of policy. Since people's values, needs, wishes and personal interests are hard to influence in ways compatible with sustainability policy, the classical mode of steering consists in introducing or changing formal institutions in the context of law making. Thus the ideas presented in the next chapter address a key issue of sustainability policy, namely, institutions' persistence and stability as well as their dynamics of change.

Notes

1 At this point we need to mention one difficulty entailed by distinguishing material from immaterial stocks. Some stocks, especially stocks of *value*, have both a material and an immaterial element. Let us consider a stock of capital as an example. A company's inventory of machines is part of its stock of capital. So this inventory of machines is certainly a material stock. But one can also define a company's stock of capital as the stock of means of production as valued in monetary terms. These are represented by shares in shareholder companies and are traded on the capital market. In this definition, capital is an immaterial stock. So as we can see, share values, monetary values and similar things generally have a material and an immaterial aspect. In such cases it is necessary to divide the stocks into the representative material aspect (material capital etc.) and the immaterial aspect (expectations, demands etc.).

2 Max Weber (1968: 24–25) distinguishes four types of action in this regard: instrumentally rational action, value-rational action, affectual action and traditional action. By the latter he means an action engaged in according to a customary habit, i.e. routines, whose meaning need not necessarily be immediately clear to the person engaged in the action but which in principle would be amenable to rational enquiry.

3 In doing so, we take Max Weber's definition of action (1968) as a given – cf. footnote 66.

4 Cf. Mirowski (1984: 365 ff.). For a critique of this view, see Manstetten (2000: 54 ff.).

5 In the German legal sciences tradition, by contrast, 'in effect' is understood in predominantly formal terms. Unlike our understanding, legal science contends that a law is in force if it has been passed and made public in accordance with the relevant juridical regulations. Whether or not it is actually applied or adhered to is initially irrelevant. In our case, however, the application of and regular adherence to a rule is constitutive of its being in effect. We regard rules that are broken in any more than a one-off way (i.e. as an exception) as being *not* in effect.

6 Kingston and Caballero (2009: 153–154) summarise this nicely, quoting North in doing so:

> The term 'formal' is often taken to mean that the rules are made explicit or written down, particularly if they are enforced by the state, whereas informal rules are implicit; another interpretation is that formal rules are enforced by actors with specialized roles (Milgrom, North and Weingast, 1990), whereas informal codes of behavior are enforced endogenously by the members of the relevant group. 'Informal constraints' [...] include 'codes of conduct, norms of behavior, and conventions' as well as 'extensions, elaborations and modifications of formal rules' and 'are part of the heritage that we call culture' ([North, 1990]: 36–40).

7 Berger and Luckmann speak in this context of 'reciprocal typification'. They write: 'Institutionalization occurs whenever there is a reciprocal typification of habitualized actions by types of actors. Put differently, any such typification is an institution' (Berger and Luckmann 1991: 72). Luhmann puts it in similar terms (1974: 13): 'Institutions are temporally, factually and socially generalised expectations of behaviour and as such form the structure of social systems.'

6 The persistence of institutions

with Frank Jöst and Beate Fischer

6.1 Two theoretical approaches to understanding the persistence and changeability of institutions

When attempting to examine policy processes in terms of their sustainability and with a view to actively shaping them, it is particularly important to consider institutions as a category of immaterial stocks. As detailed in the previous chapter, it is possible to gain considerable insight into the immaterial circumstances of human behaviour by analysing institutions as stocks. It is especially important here to understand the development of institutions over time, that is, their persistence through time, their stability, their inertia and their potential resistance to changes as well as their volatility. Understanding the temporality of institutions is a crucial precondition for being able to intervene actively in order to shape and to manage them – although it should be noted that interventions in any institutional structure often need to be planned over the very long term.

Economic, sociological and philosophical theories all offer ways of understanding the persistence of institutions. They start out from different points of departure and are based on differing hypotheses, so naturally they come to different (and sometimes contradictory) conclusions. In this chapter, we ask what contribution current theories can make towards understanding institutions from a stock perspective in relation to sustainability policy. We will look more closely at two theoretical approaches to analysing the persistence of institutions and will seek to mediate between the two. The first approach is one widely adopted in the field of institutional economics (Section 6.2). We then compare and contrast it with Arnold Gehlen's philosophical theory of institutions (Section 6.3). The reason we examine Gehlen's theory in such detail is due to the particular way it regards persistence not as a superficial, temporal property of institutions but rather as the very essence of institutions themselves. In the course of our account it is necessary to present some of the foundational assumptions of both institutional economics and of Gehlen's theory because what each has to say about the stability and changeability of institutions depends crucially on their assumptions about human beings, i.e. on their implicit or explicit anthropology.

In Section 6.4 we look at a further aspect of the persistence of institutions, namely, the problem of their legitimacy. In modern democratic societies political and legal institutions can only remain stable over the long term if their legitimacy is not constantly being called into question. In this connection we also ask whether it is possible to formulate a normative judgement of institutions, particularly with regard to sustainability policy. Section 6.5 contains a summary of the features that are typical of a stocks perspective on institutions and what significance such a perspective has for shaping sustainability policy – namely, it helps to avoid, as far as possible, elements of analytic reductionism, foreshortening and one-sidedness when looking at sustainability issues and developing appropriate policies; additionally, it can be deployed constructively to develop a realistic assessment of the possibilities for institutional change.

6.2 Institutional economics and the issue of persistence

6.2.1 Institutions as instruments for partially rational utility maximisers

Over the last 20 to 30 years – and in particular since the awarding of the Nobel Prize to Douglass North, Oliver Williamson and Elinor Ostrom – the importance of institutional economics has come to be more widely recognised. The so-called new institutional economics analyses first and foremost the formal and informal rules that regulate the exchange of goods and services. In contrast to early institutionalism (developed by Thorstein Bunde Veblen and others in the US during the early twentieth century but currently less prominent in current economic debate) the anthropological foundation of the new institutional economics is *homo oeconomicus* – the rational, utility maximising, self-interested individual (cf. Manstetten 2000). This individual is completely fixated on his or her own needs, formed in his or her own inalterable order of preference. This individual enters into social interactions with the sole purpose of achieving the greatest possible degree of satisfaction of his or her needs. It is the individual who (frequently only after many interim steps) builds or abolishes institutions according to his or her needs at the time. In this sense, institutional economics can be described as an individualistic approach.

From the perspective of institutional economics theory, the rationality of *homo oeconomicus* is regarded as a *bounded* rationality (cf. Simon 1959). If we assume that people have only incomplete information about the future behaviour of other people and perhaps even about their own motivations for acting in certain ways, then their rational self-interest demands that they seek ways of being able to predict others' behaviour wherever possible. This is what institutions are for, because when people allow themselves to be guided in their interactions by universally recognised (i.e. effective) rules, they can form rational expectations about other people's behaviour. This stabilisation of expectations provides certainty in an uncertain world with its many contingencies.

Thus 'the purpose of an institution is [...] to steer individual behavior in a particular direction' (Richter and Furubotn 1998: 6). Institutions perform this steering function by lowering the costs of desired behaviour or raising them for undesired behaviour. In institutional economics this steering function is performed according to the goal of managing cooperation and transactions efficiently. The (aggregated) preferences of egoistic, rational maximisers of utility serve as the ultimate standard for the efficiency of institutions.

Thus institutions are seen as being malleable and manageable by means of political will, a view largely regarded as belonging to the standard economics approach. As Karl Popper notes (1944: 123), institutions can be regarded 'as means to certain ends, or as convertible to the service of certain ends; as machines rather than as organisms'. In other words, institutions are instruments for influencing and regulating human behaviour. Their (continued) existence depends upon their capacity to function on behalf of individuals' pursuit of their own interests and purposes. If they fail to perform this function or do so inadequately – that is, if they become inefficient – they can be changed or adapted to new circumstances or new interests. To express this in formal terms: according to the paradigm of institutional economics a new institution will be established in the place of a previously existing one when the expected utility of this new institution is greater than the sum of the utility gained from the existing one plus the expected costs of reshaping it. This view of institutions, which can be described as an instrumental one, comes through in North (1990: 3, cf. Section 5.6.2 above) when he regards institutions as 'humanly devised'.

Nonetheless, as Kingston and Caballero (2009: 161) contend, standard economics has difficulty explaining 'why inefficient institutions often persist, or why less successful societies often fail to adopt the institutional structure of successful ones'. What these authors are pointing to here is the problem of the 'staying power' of institutions which frequently resist any and every effort at steering or influencing, so that they can be changed only over the very long term, if at all. In these cases the heuristic of *homo oeconomicus* fails to deliver.

6.2.2 Institutions and 'habits of thought'

Some proponents of the new institutional economics base their approach on older institutional theories[1] that emphasise non-instrumental aspects of institutions alongside the instrumental ones. Veblen (1899) sees the institutions that exist in a society as a manifestation of prevailing habits of thought connected to 'particular relations and particular functions of the individual and of the community' (ibid.: 190). This view is echoed in Aoki (2001), who defines institutions as stable, shared systems of convictions relating to the expected behaviour of the members of a society in various contingent situations. Without discarding the concept of rules entirely, these views address an aspect which exists, as it were, prior to or beyond the rule and the immediate purpose of its regulating function. Institutions are rules whose meaning and validity are rooted not in themselves but in the expectations, habits of thought and convictions that lie behind them. These include basic ideas about the world and internalised ethical norms and values. When looked at in and of themselves, rules may generally appear to be easy to change, provided one assumes they are the instruments of rational actors whose interests and rationality lie outside the rules themselves. If, however, the rules are inseparable from habits of thought and convictions, then they are no longer an object of the preferences of rational actors but instead become an integral part of their rationality and their preferences.

The fact that institutions are not simply an instrument for shaping exogenously given preferences has occasionally been addressed in institutional economics: 'By affecting habits, institutions can indirectly influence our purposes or preferences' (Hodgson 2004: 187). This occurs when

> people's individual preferences and habits are brought into alignment with the 'shared habits of thought' which constitute the institution. [...] In this view, institutions shape individuals at the same time as individuals shape institutions. (Kingston and Caballero 2009: 174)

The problems associated with this circular structure will occupy us in more detail further below.

When it comes to understanding behavioural patterns it is necessary, as Greif (2006: 30) points out, to find a way of gaining access to the norms, values and convictions that underpin a society's system of rules: 'An institution is a system of rules, beliefs, norms and organizations that together generate a regularity of (social) behaviour.' By conceptualising an institution as a system, Greif is highlighting the fact that it is often not enough to correlate individual rules to individual behaviours when seeking to understand the regularities in patterns of behaviour. Rather, it is necessary to take account of a structure of behavioural patterns and an entire system of rules together. Theorists such as Greif see an institution as the sum of all the factors that generate regularities in social behaviour.

Such a view is especially significant when it comes to intentionally changing patterns of behaviour. Frequently this involves taking account of not only those rules which are 'in effect' [effective] and are directly related to the behaviour in question but also other rules and habits of thinking and living that have an indirect influence: 'A new rule which fails to shift people's expectations in the desired way may have no effect at all' (Aoki 2001: 231). To avoid failure, the persistence of expectations needs to be taken explicitly into account when rules are to be changed.

If institutions are firmly rooted in people's ways of thinking and living, then they cannot – as standard economics would have it – be influenced straightforwardly by 'external' preferences. Instead, institutions develop in parallel to the general cultural, social and economic development of a society in ways which, rather like the evolution of life, lie outside the realm of human intervention. At the same time, the development of institutions takes place with a certain time lag in relation to other developments. At any rate this was the view adopted by Veblen (1899, quoted in Kingston and Caballero 2009: 162):

> Because these habits reside within individuals, institutional change involves the simultaneous co-evolution of both shared prevalent habits of thought (institutions) and the habits of individuals. At any time, therefore, the current habits of thought, both shared and individual, are 'received from the past',

> affected by the present, and together they jointly affect the future path of institutional change.

In this view, institutions are certainly capable of change, but this change does not occur through the deliberate actions of political actors or authorities based on their reason or their will. Rather, it is part of a broader process of social evolution which is not steered intentionally in a certain direction but occurs through a change in consciousness and ways of living that cannot be managed or controlled from the outside. If we go along with this notion, then institutions are not instruments aimed at adapting an uncertain social world as far as possible to the interests of the people who are active within them, but rather fixed forms in which interests and behavioural patterns have seeped into one another; these forms have been inherited from the past and, as such, are simply there in the present – regardless, initially, of whether those currently living like it or not.

This kind of view can lead to an extremely pessimistic take on the usefulness of institutions: rather than being instruments conducive to human interaction they may appear instead to be unyielding obstacles to human development. Ayres (1944, quoted in Kingston and Caballero 2009: 166) thus regarded 'institutions as impediments to progress, "ceremonial" outgrowths of prior technology and a negative, "past-preserving" influence'. This leads to the necessary conclusion (ibid.: 175) that '[i]nstitutions are resistant to change, in part due to people's emotional attachment to existing institutions, and in part because change threatens existing patterns of status, wealth, and power'.

6.2.3 Which institutions have how much 'staying power'?

In our discussion of theories so far we have simply referred to 'institutions' collectively. However, some proponents of institutional economics point out that it is necessary to identify more differentiated distinctions if we are to analyse the 'staying power' and malleability of institutions in greater detail. The distinction between formal and informal institutions is too rough and ready for this purpose. It may appear at first sight that formal institutions (such as laws or fully formulated contracts) are easier to reform than informal institutions (such as the traditions and customs of a culture). But appearances may be deceptive here. There are highly stable, formal institutions that have barely changed for centuries. Certain principles of Roman law such as 'Where there is doubt, decide in favour of the accused' or 'Ignorance is no defence' still apply even today. In Judaism, Christianity and Islam certain texts have been considered as holy scriptures for more than a thousand years and indeed for much longer periods; they have been handed down virtually unchanged and have been integrated into rites which in turn have persisted down the centuries with only minor changes, such as the Holy Mass in the Catholic Church[2]. By contrast, even informal institutions which appear to be doggedly persistent, such as certain taboos, can in isolated cases disappear very suddenly.

The fact that the persistence or malleability of institutions varies greatly depending on what kind of institution is at issue has been highlighted by

Williamson (2000: 596 ff.; quoted here in the summary provided by Kingston and Caballero 2009: 167; cf. also North 1990: 111). Williamson identifies four distinct levels of institutions according to the timescales on which change can be expected to occur:

> At the highest level are the 'institutions of embeddedness', including informal institutions, culture and norms, in which change occurs on the order of centuries or millennia. At the second level, constrained by the institutions of embeddedness, are the high-level formal rules: constitutions, laws, and property rights. At this level, change takes decades or centuries. The third level is that of the 'institutions of governance', at which the set of rules ('governance structures') which govern day-to-day interactions ('contractual relations') are assumed to adjust so as to minimize transaction costs. Adjustment at the third level typically takes years. Finally, at the lowest level, the prices and quantities specified in individual contracts adjust continuously. Williamson recognizes the possibility of long-run feedback from lower to higher levels, but he consciously ignores it.

The fundamental usefulness of these distinctions is not affected by the fact that the allocation of timescales to specific levels appears somewhat arbitrary and that counterexamples can be found as well. The first two levels have to do with the fundamental ordering of the informal and formal aspects of a society. Culture and the political, legal and economic constitution of a society are not a part of everyday politics. Of course, planned interventions are possible here too, but they need to be organised over much longer periods of time and require much greater effort than interventions at the third or fourth levels.

Williamson's distinctions can be used to illustrate something else, though: institutions at the third and fourth levels can generally be understood as instruments, that is, as means to achieve a limited and rationally reasonable purpose in the eyes of those who live with and within these institutions. These are the levels at which the standard theories of institutional economics usually operate. The fact that institutions are fixed forms that have been handed down from the past, that pervade the preferences of people who are living now, and are capable of influencing behaviours and practices regardless of their usefulness applies above all to Levels 1 and 2 – to the fundamental ordering and basic values of a society.

It needs to be borne in mind, nonetheless, that institutions at Levels 3 and 4 can also take on highly durable forms. One example of this is the so-called 'champagne tax' in the German system of taxation which, undoubtedly part of Level 3, was introduced before the First World War as a kind of 'wealthy people's tax' in order to make additional sources of revenue available for the upgrading of Germany's naval fleet. Despite being designed to serve this specific purpose, the champagne tax survived – more or less unchanged – not only the decline of this same fleet in 1918 but also every subsequent political change and reform, including the introduction of Germany's Basic Law (parts of which brought radical institutional changes at Level 2 and perhaps even Level 1).

Box 6.1 The institutional economics approach in brief

Institutional economics is an individualistic approach based on *homo oeconomicus*. Social interaction serves the exclusive purpose of maximising individuals' utility. Institutions are rules and systems of rules aimed at influencing and regulating human behaviour. Their purpose is to achieve efficiency in cooperation and transactions. Their existence depends on their capacity to satisfy individuals' preferences, which are given exogenously. Institutional change can be explained on the basis of cost-benefit considerations relating to the individuals involved. This view, which characterises the standard approaches of institutional economics, is unable to explain why ineffective and inefficient institutions remain in existence over long periods of time.

Alternative institutional economics approaches see institutions as deriving from habits of thinking and convictions. According to these approaches, preferences are formed endogenously within institutions. Thus institutions display a strong propensity to remain as they are in the face of attempts to change and shape them wilfully. Institutional changes that do occur tend to follow social and cultural processes of evolution.

Williamson's identification of four levels of institutions serves as a mediating link between the standard economics view and the alternative approaches:

- Level 1: Cultural institutions in which the life of a society is embedded: values, norms, culturally conditioned habits etc. Typical timescales for change: centuries or millennia.
- Level 2: Basic rules of a society: constitution, property rights, laws etc. Typical timescales for change: decades or centuries.
- Level 3: Governance institutions: contractual regulations, administrative ordinances. Typical timescales for change: several years.
- Level 4: Contractual regulations between individuals and organisations, relationships of economic exchange etc. Typical timescales for change: continuously.

Standard economics refers above all to Levels 3 and 4, whereas the alternative approaches focus especially on Levels 1 and 2. From a stocks perspective, Levels 1, 2 and 3 are of particular significance.

When we examine the theories of institutional economics in terms of their contribution towards framing and understanding issues dealing with the way institutions persist through time, how they change and how they are shaped and reshaped, a heterogeneous picture emerges. With standard economics at its core, institutional economics remains largely silent in relation to these issues. Standard economics patterns of thinking such as the concepts of efficiency and optimality or the assumption of exogeneity, i.e. the givenness of preferences, may even prove to be a hindrance in adopting a long-term perspective on institutions. However, provided individual theorists are capable of conceptualising institutions not only as necessary preconditions for economic activities but as influential factors in the life of individuals and societies per se, then they are certainly in a position to contribute relevant ideas to the temporality of institutions.

It is this temporality that constitutes the focus of the following discussion of Arnold Gehlen's institutional theory. His work elucidates the persistence of institutions in a rather helpful way.

6.3 Arnold Gehlen's philosophical theory of institutions and the question of persistence

Arnold Gehlen (1904–1976) was a German philosopher and sociologist whose main works were dedicated exclusively to formulating a philosophical anthropology – a theory of human beings. This philosophical anthropology also takes on board results from the empirical sciences, namely, biology and ethnology. At the heart of Gehlen's anthropology is a theory of institutions that seeks to discover the origins of the stability and persistence of institutions as well as the meaning of these temporal properties for people's lives.

6.3.1 Seeking the essence of human beings

In Gehlen's anthropology, humans are depicted as 'flawed beings'. Compared with animals, they lack the sure guidance of instinct. If humans are regarded as isolated individuals in their particular subjectivity, they appear to be naturally erratic in terms of their moods and their behaviour. Gehlen's basic thesis is therefore that, in their lack of security and orientation, humans need stability and persistence. This is the source of the elementary human interest in the constancy of the course of nature:

> This primary human interest in the regularity of the processes of nature deserves emphasis: It betrays a semi-instinctual *need for stability in the environment.* Since reality is unavoidably subject to time and to change, the most stability one can hope for consists in the same effects repeating themselves automatically and periodically, as indeed they tend to do in nature. (Gehlen 1980: 13)

Thus in nature as also in the history of human beings there are relations that are designed to remain the same. These, according to Gehlen, are institutions.

6.3.2 Motivation, action and habitualisation

Institutions develop because humans, unlike animals, have developed the capacity to act. By acting – that is, by behaving in one way rather than another in any given situation – the person acting commits him or herself, at least for the duration of the action. In doing so they move beyond their subjective fluctuating moods and engage in a specific performative act in which a certain stabilising effect is inherent. It is from this understanding of action that Gehlen's concept of institution emerges.

In institutional economics (as also in other theories of action) there is a general assumption that an action and the motivation for an action need to be clearly separated. The motivation is imagined to be a cause that exists outside the action itself and is located within the subject, as part of his preferences. In contrast to this, Gehlen feels it is not sensible to assume that a motivation arises separately from an action: 'After all, the need, the drive and the motivational idea, as performed (not merely thought) impulses or acts, already constitute initial stages of the action itself' (Gehlen 2004a: 29, our translation). According to Gehlen, motivations do not exist independently of concrete actions. Subjectively felt biological drives such as hunger or thirst would, in and of themselves, be no more than aimless, shapeless moods that have no practical relevance. They only become a motivation for action when they correspond to an action anticipated in a person's imagination. Hunger as a motivation for action appears in the form of a desire for something edible which the hungry person imagines as the goal of the action.

According to Gehlen there is a tendency toward repetition inherent in individual acts[3]. If acts were to occur solely in isolation they would remain largely incomprehensible. It is only through repetition that certain constant patterns become apparent and recognisable. This effect of re-cognition, as it were, is the precondition for actions to be 'unambiguous' (ibid.: 24). The more often a certain action occurs, the more natural it appears when this moment of recognition occurs: we have become used to this action and can locate it within an experiential context. In particular, that kind of action which already has something typical – we might say something 'habitual' – about it thus becomes meaningful and comprehensible for both actor and observer. Being understood is important to the person acting, though, because their action almost always occurs in relation to their fellow human beings and the community.

To sum up, then, there is a natural tendency toward *habitualisation* inherent in actions. This means nothing other than that actions occur on a regular basis and are expressed in repeated patterns of behaviour. Starting out from the notion of habitualisation, Gehlen introduces the concept of institution by delineating two key elements in particular: first, actions involving a tool and, second, the 'transcendence' of things and objects. Let us look more closely at each of these in turn.

6.3.3 Actions and habitualisation: the tool

Gehlen sees institutions as emerging from elementary aspects of everyday human conduct. An important interim stage in this is the concept of 'tool action' (*Werkzeughandeln*). In its simplest original form, human action involves dealing with resources, with tools, or instruments (*instrumentum*, Latin for 'instrument, tool'). However, tools acquire a life of their own beyond their instrumental character as such. This is illustrated by the following line of thinking.

A person who acts shapes and changes the conditions in the world around them in accordance with their intentions, or purposes. They pursue these purposes by changing their environment in specific ways using tools[4]. The tool can be used as a resource for certain purposes in a specific situation, and in a certain sense this is a general characteristic, meaning that it can be used in similar situations in similar ways to serve similar purposes[5].

At the same time, however, every tool itself implies a habitualised action. The act of cutting using a metal blade, for example, requires that it be used in a particular way appropriate to the tool itself, a way that offers certain options for dividing an object into separate segments while simultaneously excluding other options for doing so. Thus in a sense the person doing the action has the nature of their action prescribed to them by the tool – the 'tool action' needs to match the objective requirements. Thus tool action displays all the essential characteristics of a type of action known as a 'technique'. Every technique poses requirements for the proper use of the tools or machines associated with it. This use is already standardised in a specific way. Thus the action itself becomes habitual.

Gehlen's approach to actions involving tools illustrates an essential characteristic of all techniques. A technique that influences an act of production (*Produktionsvollzug*) – whether it occurs in a mediaeval workshop or in the electronically controlled assembly line of a modern manufacturing company – is much more than simply the application of a technology. By becoming routine, it is a way of life and a habit of living for all those who participate in it. Viewed in this way, every technique has the characteristics of an institution.

In the course of using a technique regularly, the motivations for doing so may change. The actual need for clean vegetables and chopped meat that one wishes to eat, for example – the original purpose of chopping something up – may be less important for someone whose work involves using a knife. Chopping up may become an end in itself. Thus a kitchen assistant chops up vegetables and meat because this needs to be done – no relation necessarily exists between any of his current needs and the act of chopping. For Gehlen, this means the following: 'Habitualised action' may sometimes have the 'effect of *suspending the question of meaning*' (Gehlen 2004a: 68). We do something because it has to be done, without having to consider or weigh up the whys and the wherefores or the meaning or purpose of the action itself. This *suspending of the question of meaning* is typical of many of our behavioural patterns. Every routine is based precisely on *not* pursuing the question of meaning, and human cooperation is made much easier when the actions it involves can be performed as a matter of course. Suspending the question of meaning relieves us of the need to reflect.

6.3.4 'Transcendences'

Just as action acquires a kind of autonomy in the face of changing moods and diffuse drives when habitualised, the tool and its associated 'tool action' depart from their original purpose and become autonomous. Performing an action with a tool confronts us with the 'inherent beingness' (*Eigensein*) of this thing. Handling the tool – learning how to use it, keep it safe and in good order – goes beyond the actual use itself that we make of it. It goes beyond our conscious use of it to fulfil the original purpose. Gehlen calls this characteristic of things their 'transcendence'. In the following we look more closely at what is meant by this.

Transcendence means 'going beyond' or 'surpassing' certain limits, or boundaries. The term transcendence is generally used in a religious sense: it refers to phenomena which transcend our world and surpass our experiential capacity, in other words, ones that lie *beyond* our world and our experience. Thus God has often been described as transcendent, meaning that it is not possible to encounter him in our world but only in the 'next world'. However, when Gehlen speaks of the 'transcendence of things' he is referring to a quite ordinary, everyday, personal experience. This is why he speaks of 'transcendence into this world' (*Transzendenz ins Diesseits*): the things we encounter and use have an aspect that surpasses or 'transcends' their use and their utility in the context of our purposes and ends. This can be described in two steps.

1 Things like tools have an independent existence apart from their use and the purposes they serve; in this sense they possess a certain degree of objectivity. Beyond the purposive use for which they constitute the means, they require proper handling and appropriate care. By looking after or perfecting a tool and by 'refining' (Gehlen 2004a: 32) one's mastery of it (prowess), something that had been a means to achieve something else becomes itself the object of a purpose. At first this purpose is still connected to the original purpose. The purpose of looking after a drill, for example, is to be able to use it to drill a hole in the wall whenever something needs to be hung up. 'As the counterparts to all manner of actual or potential needs, all manner of material and non-material things' (ibid.: 14) have an 'existence value' (*Daseinswert*). This value attaches to material and non-material things which can be regarded as 'fulfilments of needs that are chronically satisfied and are therefore no longer current'. Certain objects of use, such as a home, are simply there, even if we are not thinking about them and do not need them in the context of particular interests or purposes. As such they have the capacity to meet certain human needs in a continuous way, or rather to guarantee this meeting of needs over an extended period. They thus provide 'background fulfilment' which prevents the felt need from becoming acute. In this way they *relieve* us from the constant concern over satisfying certain needs or drives.
2 It can happen that the original purpose in using a thing fades into the background and that its use in a professional context becomes an *end in itself*. An example of this is someone who plays a musical instrument for its own sake, not to give pleasure to anybody else or to earn money or to meet some other need beyond the playing of the instrument. In such cases a thing acquires an 'intrinsic value by its pure existence' (*Selbstwert im Dasein*). We no longer merely act by using things (as means) but rather we act on the basis of things or with a view to things.

The way things become independent of their function for people, the way people relate to things in their non-functional form, and finally the influence on our own living of things that have become an end in themselves – these are experiences of transcendence in everyday life[6].

The transcendence of things can decouple itself entirely from needs and the necessities of life. In certain human circumstances the 'intrinsic value by simply existing' possessed by 'moments of transcendence into this world' (*Transzendenzen ins Diesseits*) grows to become an 'intrinsic value in the absolute sense' (ibid.: 17)[7]. One example of this is the God of the monotheistic world religions to whom humans dedicate their lives and whom they venerate or love for His own sake. Equally it is also possible for humans to engage in a particular behaviour for its own sake by adhering to certain rules (ritual commandments such as keeping the Sabbath holy in Judaism, for example, or ethical commandments such as the admonishment not to lie) for their own sake.

6.3.5 Habit, institutions and permanence

For Gehlen, institutions emerge from this 'intrinsic value in the absolute sense': 'Originally institutions were transcendences into this world in the fullest sense' (Gehlen 2004a: 18). This means that institutions become detached from their original purposes and 'transcend' into something permanent that is important for human life because it gives it a sense of security. They thus acquire an 'absolute intrinsic value', for permanence as such is 'itself a value' (ibid.: 47). Thus Gehlen highlights the permanence, persistence and stability of institutions as their key characteristic, as more prominent than their function, their utility or their social meaning.

Gehlen does not give a precise definition of 'institution', but it is possible nonetheless to describe some of the essential characteristics of his conception. Each institution is based on habitualised action, where the motivation for the action is itself shaped by the repeated individual acts. Viewed from the outside, institutions emerge when regularities in human behaviour are given, that is, recurring patterns of behaviour.

This 'habitual structure' of action is merely the 'substructure' of the institution. Habitualised action becomes an institution when it becomes an 'intrinsic value by simply existing' or acquires the same. When this occurs, it becomes an independent, permanent set of actions which are (also) performed for their own sake. The institution can only be this kind of self-purposeful doing when the action of which it consists possesses the characteristic of ritualised, presenting action – or, when it 'transcends into this world'.

An example may serve to illustrate this. A person may have the habit of eating a sandwich at midday while walking from A to B. For Gehlen, this would not amount to an institution. Only if a person regularly ate a meal at a particular time at a laid table and in a specific order would this be an institution for him. This kind of eating always has ritual and aesthetic – i.e. non-functional – elements. It is, however minimally, something special, something a little ceremonial, or at any rate something more than just aimless living.

For Gehlen the binding power of institutions depends precisely on their ritualised, non-functional elements. 'The great authority that judges and doctors still possess is based to a very large extent on their official attire' (ibid.: 28). Official attire says nothing about the specific qualities of the person wearing it and yet it prompts respect and thus influences others' behaviour towards the wearer.

The essential characteristic of the institution for Gehlen is its permanence, its persistence and its stability, which are based on their non-functionality. Institutions are forms of action in which this action is placed on a permanent, rule-defined basis. This *rendering permanent* is a kind of anthropological need for institutions beyond their specific steering tasks and their functions. It is the need for an at least partial relief from the incessant coercion to engage in personal reflection and to make personal choices. Institutions offer relief in several respects:

- They free the individual from the obligation to make isolated, individual decisions, to the extent that they help in 'tackling life's purposes together'.
- In institutions 'people are guided towards precise and commonly agreed feelings and actions, […] so that they do not have to become tied up in emotional knots at every turn or force themselves into decisions of principle' (ibid.: 93). In this way, institutions provide certainty with regard to expectations, in terms of both a person's own behaviour and the behaviour of others. Not only certain practical, permanently available objects of use (see above) but also institutions provide background fulfilment. Important examples of this are institutions such as marriage and the family (which make the need for social contact secondary) and the democratic state based on law and order (which makes the need for security and freedom disappear from people's immediate perception). One indicator of the fact that the democratic nation state performs background fulfilment is our tendency to identify security and freedom with the form in which they are guaranteed through the state and the law – thus, for example, we speak of legal certainty, freedom of movement, freedom of opinion and freedom of association.

6.3.6 The autonomy of institutions

Certain motivations may contribute to the emergence of institutions, and it may be that deliberate intentions underpin their coming into being. Nonetheless, institutions tend to become autonomous, independent entities. This *process of becoming autonomous* is manifested in the following ways:

1 The purposes of the institution become decoupled from the motivations of individuals.
2 Institutions themselves can change or even generate new motivations and needs. This indeed is how institutions come to be subject to their own internal laws or regularities, which is how they become stabilised[8].
3 Finally, however, according to Gehlen, institutions are even capable of making individuals comply with them (the institutions).

We will take a closer look at each of these three aspects in the following sections.

6.3.7 Separation of motivation from purpose, and the transformation of purposes

In terms of their origins, institutions usually derive from purposeful action and therefore have a purpose themselves. This purpose originally also constitutes the motivation out of which individuals act with respect to the institution in question. However, over the course of time and in addition to its original, actual purpose the institution may offer space for quite different motivations on the part of the acting individual. The original purpose may fade into the background or even disappear entirely and the new motivations may come to the fore. What then occurs is a '*separation of motivation from purpose*' (Gehlen 2004b: 33). Thus the individuals' motivations may on the one hand become decoupled from the original purpose of the institution while on the other a new purpose may develop within the institution which becomes autonomous in relation to the motivations for action.

We can illustrate the separation of motivation from purpose using the following example. The pursuit of profit that Gehlen calls the 'drive to acquire' (*Erwerbstrieb*) is a characteristic motivation for action within the institutional edifice of the economy. This drive, according to Gehlen, is by no means an 'independent psychical urge'. It should not be seen as an egotistical disposition rooted in humans' essential being, as *homo oeconomicus* models often suggest. The drive to acquire does not exist independently of the economy; rather it is 'an attitude imposed upon those in positions of responsibility when it is their job to ensure the survival of a firm in conditions of competition' (Gehlen 2004a: 38). Thus the ability of institutions in the economic system to mould and even generate their own motivations comes to the fore in the pursuit of profit manifested by economic actors[9]. According to Gehlen, the so-called 'drive for power' is also, like the drive to acquire, generated institutionally within the institutional edifice of politics, as the reflex of a necessary function of political and other institutions that exercise power. The institution thus 'determines for its part the attitudes and actions of those active within it' (ibid.: 39).

Institutions also display the internal laws and regularities that serve the institutions' own purposes in their capacity for *transforming their purposes*. They can 'adopt purposes' or discard them (ibid.: 39–40). 'The original purpose may have long since become a marginal condition and the system may have opened itself to completely new sets of motivations' (ibid.: 40). For example, 'a large industrial complex may [...] see itself forced to develop its own internal or even external political conceptions; profitability, once a key purpose, may in the course of this change to become a marginal condition for completely new objectives, while the motivations behind striving for profitability may shift' (ibid.: 39). By virtue of their autonomous existence institutions dominate human actions and their purposes: 'people act on the basis of them, in keeping with their inherent requirements and their laws' (ibid.: 18).

6.3.8 Objectification of drives, orientation towards needs

Given that institutions separate human actions from drives, they are able to reshape primordial, anthropologically based urges or, as Gehlen puts it, to 'objectify' them.

The 'institutions of law', for example, have 'largely stabilised legal behaviour and made it a habit' to the extent that people do not pursue any particular purpose but rather act lawfully simply out of habit (Gehlen 2004a: 75). In Gehlen's terms, needs are guided by institutions. These ideas draw attention to the fact that needs, motivations and drives as well as purposes are typically moulded and mediated by institutions.

This is precisely the issue which sustainability policy must take into account. Viewed in this way, non-sustainable dispositions such as oft-lamented 'greed', the tendency to consume items for their prestige value or to drive large cars, are not direct expressions of (possibly corrupted) human nature but rather a function of institutions or institutional arrangements. This is why there is no point in simply criticising the fact that people drive large cars. What sustainability policy needs to do, rather than seeking to change problematic consumer behaviour by promoting certain values, is instead to change institutions (Petersen and Schiller 2011). This is all the more true given that institutions are clearly capable of making people 'comply' with, or conform to, certain ways of acting and indeed particular affective dispositions.

6.3.9 How institutions secure people's compliance

Gehlen believes that institutions have an autonomous ethos which makes the people who act within them conform to a particular type of behaviour[10]. In other words, an institution shapes a kind of social convention regarding how people are to behave within it. The ethos of institutions imposes *responsibility* upon the individual. As 'the formal mechanism of duty' (Gehlen 2004a: 67) responsibility may appear as 'institutional liability' and, in some circumstances, as unlimited responsibility. This means that the person in a position of responsibility may have to be liable not only in terms of everything he or she possesses but with his or her very life for accomplishing an institutionally allotted task.

What Gehlen sees as the 'ethos of institutions' is manifested in various kinds of sanctions. These may range from holding individuals criminally responsible, making them liable under civil law or attributing political or social responsibility to them, through to diffuse, culturally specific forms of sanction that are applied when a certain type of behaviour deviates from the norm. Those who fail to do what 'is done' in certain circumstances – by wearing different clothes, moving differently or expressing themselves differently than expected – may experience *ex negativo* how (informal) institutions demand their compliance.

This feature of demanding compliance that is displayed by institutions contributes significantly to social stability. At the same time, however, in a process of mutual reinforcement it may contribute toward an institutional edifice and those who live within it becoming a kind of closed system that self-immunises against critique and requests for change: there seems to be no standpoint outside the institution from where it might be possible to question whether the duties demanded within the system are justified.

Gehlen's theory that institutions possess an ethos makes no contribution towards moral philosophy. Rather, its contribution lies in showing that institutions are able to generate moral affects – such as feelings of guilt or shame, or outrage toward others – among those individuals who do not act in accordance with the demands of the institution or do not wish to do so. For example, the hero in Mark Twain's novel *The Adventures of Huckleberry Finn*, set in the US of the 1840s, feels extreme guilt as a result of helping a runaway slave to escape instead of handing him over to the authorities to be punished. These are the kinds of feelings which generate the staying power of institutions such as slavery.

6.3.10 Mechanisms of persistence of immaterial stocks

Gehlen's conception of institutions, then, is based fundamentally on the permanence of his object. As such it provides an opportunity for better understanding the 'mechanisms' of persistence in immaterial stocks more generally. Rather like motivations for action, we often imagine values, preferences or knowledge to be objects that are stored in the consciousness of the actors concerned or contained in books and data storage media. Such objects generally only acquire significance and relevance, however, when they become tangible in institutional contexts and manifest in behavioural patterns and interpersonal systems of rules. Since these factors, which were described above (cf. Section 5.2) as behavioural possibilities, are relevant to sustainability policy, we want to examine the institutional aspect of their persistence more closely. To do this we shall look at the following immaterial stocks and their mechanisms of persistence: world views, knowledge, technologies, values, preferences and interests.

World views are institutionalised in, for example, religions and programmatic ideologies advocated by social movements and political parties. Outside such structures they rarely have an impact on people's behaviour. Within these structures, however, all the elements identified by Gehlen in his theory apply to an especially large extent: background fulfilment, needs orientation, transformation of purposes. The permanence of religious teachings, ways of life and organisations as well as that of certain anti-religious ideologies and movements is linked especially to processes of institutionalisation.

For example, a liberal world view that allows everybody a certain degree of freedom in how they conduct their personal life leads to people having to justify their actions or behaviour less often. Here, sustainability policy finds itself with nothing to say: it is almost impossible to address the issue of resource-intensive and environmentally harmful ways of life and modes of production outside the framework of legislation, as this is regarded as an illegitimate intervention in people's personal and entrepreneurial freedoms.

Knowledge. The institutionalised form of knowledge – the scientific community with its research and teaching, its publications, its funding mechanisms and its institutions (such as large research institutes and universities) – can readily be depicted in a stocks perspective. Whereas specific items of knowledge often become obsolete very quickly, the forms in which knowledge is generated, stored and disseminated are highly persistent and long-lasting, as are the typical behavioural patterns to which they correspond. The fact that sustainability problems are rarely presented in any comprehensive, practitioner-oriented way (as explained elsewhere in this book) has a lot to do with the inertia of research institutions.

Technologies are applied techniques and, as such, are a part of behavioural patterns. They are therefore incorporated into people's everyday actions, which are often infused with them to such an extent that it bears asking, along with Martin Heidegger (1950), whether it is appropriate to see technology as a means to external ends. The patterns and routines associated with a particular technology can often take on an autotelic quality (i.e. appear to be ends in themselves).

Values, preferences and interests. The values and preferences of people with important roles in politics and the economy can normally exert an impact only when they are manifested in *interests*: interests can be thought of as institutionalised values and preferences. The interests that have an impact in politics, the economy and society all display features that Gehlen attributes to institutions. An entrepreneur, a trade unionist, a party member or a politically active individual might only articulate their interests in public when they have re-fashioned them to the extent that they can be understood at least in relation to the interests of like-minded people or people whose thinking differs. In the process of this, the traces of personal preferences need to be progressively removed and universally valid values referred to instead, albeit to varying extents. Thus interests cannot be formed in a random way; they are shaped crucially by the existing institutional edifice in question. It is the persistence of organised interests in different social domains that often makes it possible to predict with reasonable accuracy what opinions will most likely be expressed by entrepreneurs, trade unionists, party representatives, members of automobile clubs and workers in environmental organisations. Even resistance to existing institutions can become a kind of institution. As a rule of thumb, one can say that preferences and values that are organised as interests in a manifesto (or similar) or in a public position turn into behavioural patterns and institutions. Thus all the problems associated with establishing, designing, changing or getting rid of institutions also apply to interests. Gehlen's ideas about institutions being subject to their own laws and regularities and about the transformation of purposes and orientation towards needs that are prompted by institutions can also be applied to interests.

6.3.11 Gehlen's diagnosis of the present-day situation: the weakness of institutions and their consequences for sustainability policy

In his books *Urmensch und Spätkultur* (Early Man and Late Culture, 2004a) and *Die Seele im technischen Zeitalter* (Man in the Age of Technology, 1980), Gehlen diagnoses and offers a critique of one of the weaknesses of present-day institutions. For Gehlen, the fact that institutional theories such as institutional economics take the isolated individual as the point of departure for their research is an indication of the fact that they are unconsciously following a trend found in modern societies, namely, that of making human subjectivity the normative standard of personal and societal development. This trend, which in Gehlen's view misunderstands the essence of institutions and, as such, the essence of human beings themselves, is the expression of a transformation in social consciousness in which it appears that the strength and impact of institutions is increasingly at risk. For Gehlen, 'the general characteristic of *subjectivity* [...] is the stigma of humans in a period when institutions are being dismantled' (Gehlen 2004a: 8). Modern subjectivism is not the cause but rather the consequence of the weakness of institutions.

By putting forward theories of this sort, Gehlen is moving beyond the framework of a universal, timeless institutional theory and is effectively presenting himself as a diagnostician of the present. A chief characteristic of contemporary 'late culture', according to Gehlen, is the dismantling of institutions. This does not mean that there are fewer institutions but that the systems of rules that exist in modern societies no longer have life-shaping force and are manifested in a bureaucratic organisation of life while everyday life lived outside these systems of rules becomes amorphous, insecure and lacking in orientation. What is characteristic of our times is, he says,

> the conditions of physical proximity, and the lack of structure and form, in which the people of our time are forced to vegetate; and [...] the elusiveness and abstractness of our institutions, which are mostly 'immaterial states of affairs'. (Gehlen 1980: 74)

What modern institutions are lacking, according to Gehlen's analysis, is the vivid, ritual aspect. This is why these institutions are deprived of one essential source of their stability.

In the conditions of the modern world individuals are thrown back upon themselves because they are lacking in *objectivity*. For this reason 'modern subjectivism is rooted in the wider cultural situation' (Gehlen 1980: 75, 2004a: 127). Ultimately it derives from the fact that

> this entails that our convictions, our obligations, even our opinions lack a solid point of reference. We do not possess an invariant reservoir of usages, habits, institutions, symbols, ideals – the 'cultural real estate' against which we may confidently measure our conduct. On the contrary, we can never afford to relax the tensed up, awake state of our consciousness; we must maintain a chronic state of alarm, continually monitor our circumstances, continually ethically reorient our conduct, continually articulate and revise our basic commitments. (Gehlen 1980: 67–68)

Modern subjectivism places too many demands on our moral sense of orientation because 'ultimately our senses set the boundaries within which we are capable of reliable moral responses, and thus limit their reach to proximate realities'. (ibid.: 70). These excessive demands lead to a

> moral confusion (not identified as such because widely taken for granted) that consists in feeling responsible for 'the West' but not for one's city of village; for 'culture' but not for one's bookshelf; or even for 'religion'. (ibid.: 79)

If we were to apply this argument to the debate about sustainability, we would probably come to the conclusion that attempting to take responsibility for the long-term development of human and biological life on Earth certainly is too much to expect.

Undoubtedly Gehlen's diagnoses reflect a conservative position. Starting from this basic conception it is difficult to even begin to define an approach that might enable institutions to be critiqued and shaped in any meaningful way. Nonetheless it does provide important food for thought in the context of the ideas presented in this book. Since sustainability policy, to our mind, needs to be capable of working within institutions that offer a long-term, stable setting for sustainable development in nature, the economy and society, such a policy needs to give consideration not only to reasonable institutions but also to the forces and powers that shape, stabilise and dissolve institutions in specific circumstances. A culture of subjectivity may (in times of general institutional weakness and if the right conditions exist) contribute towards the abolition of unreasonable institutions and their replacement with better ones, but the question is how the stability and effectiveness of reasonable institutions can be guaranteed. The danger is that institutions which serve the cause of sustainability but have emerged more or less through chance circumstances may disappear again as a result of equally random circumstances.

6.3.12 What follows from Gehlen's theory of institutions with regard to sustainability policy?

What Gehlen calls an institution initially seems not to fit particularly well with the definitions found in institutional economics. This is due to his different point of departure: Gehlen does not base his concept of institution on rules or systems of rules or habits of thinking. For Gehlen, an institution is a stable, persistent pattern of behaviour to which people ascribe intrinsic value. This intrinsic value will often force them to stipulate rules for these patterns of behaviour. However, in Gehlen's view no single, isolated rule should be regarded as an institution; rather, a system of rules as a whole can be described as an institution if there is a set of practices or a way of life that goes with it. The modes of definition used in institutional economics, by contrast, mean that many things are described as an institution which, for Gehlen, could at most be subsumed under this term through a process of deduction.

Despite the above comments, no clear line can be drawn between Gehlen's concept of institutions and that of institutional economics. The difference is one of perspective and not of the object itself. For example, the distinction made by

Williamson between the four levels of institutions (see Section 6.2.3) can be used to forge a connection between Gehlen and institutional economics. Gehlen's institutions refer to the formal and informal rules of a society including certain culturally shaped patterns of thought and behaviour which give people's lives a lasting order and form. They correspond to Williamson's 'institutions of embeddedness' (Levels 1 and 2). As intrinsic values and as purpose-transforming figures of authority, institutions in this sense of the term possess a pronounced non-instrumental facet. In contrast to this, rules and patterns of behaviour that are changed or might be changed over a period of years or decades – Williamson's Level 3 (governance) and Level 4 (relationships of exchange) – cannot be regarded as intrinsic values and thus not directly as institutions in Gehlen's terms; rather, their foremost function is an instrumental one.

Taking this distinction into account, we can summarise Gehlen's concept of institutions as follows. Wherever people live their daily lives, they are embedded within institutions that prescribe for them certain orientations and ties. Even if institutions are 'humanly devised' (North), an institution quickly becomes a form of 'stock' which itself, in its autonomous existence, shapes people along with their interests and motivations.

At the same time, Gehlen's theory is designed in such a way that it almost rules out the possibility – let alone the practical option – of redesigning, transforming or even just expressing critique of institutions. Gehlen quite rightly thinks it is 'impossible to change a society's behaviour by simply presenting or propagandising about "values"' (Gehlen 2004b: 68); similarly he also cautions, quite rightly, that alternative 'norms [...] [have to be] developed from direct experience of reality' (ibid.). However, when it comes to asking to what end we should preserve institutions, and what are the means and the standards by which we should modify or redesign them, Gehlen is silent. Indeed he cannot answer this question because in his conception it is the very institutions themselves which have always already determined how people will view the world and how they will interact with it. This being so, it is not possible to use Gehlen's theory as the basis for a sustainability policy aimed at achieving institutional changes. What his theory does do, however, is highlight the difficulties any such policy is bound to face. If any attempt is made to make practical changes, then – as Gehlen's theory warns us to – be prepared for resistance towards discussions of meaning and self-critical reflection.

Generally speaking, Gehlen's approach suggests that it is wise to tread carefully when changing institutions while at the same time being prepared for the 'long haul'. He draws our attention among other things to the following questions: what 'background fulfilment' does an institution have that stabilises it and that has to be replaced if change is to occur? Does it make sense to get rid of an institution if it is no longer fulfilling its original purpose? Or are we more likely to preserve it because the institution has since transformed this purpose into one that has its own justification? At any rate, it is likely that the impact of 'moral persuasion' and of technical interventions will be less than is perhaps hoped for.

One thing Gehlen overlooks, though, is that 'suspending the question of meaning' can also weaken institutions. In the next section we look more closely at how important it is to consider the meaning and purpose of institutions.

Box 6.2 Arnold Gehlen's theory of institutions at a glance

Gehlen's core point is the dominance of institutions over individuals. As changeable, unsteady beings that lack control via instinct, humans need the stability that institutions provide. Institutions are forms of action that render that action permanent and subject to rules. Their origins lie in repeated acts which (i) become habitual and (ii) acquire intrinsic value for human existence. Religious rites are a paradigmatic example of the institutions of ancient cultures, although the institutions of modern societies also contain elements of ritual.

Institutions cannot be controlled by those who act within them, but rather shape their motivations and everyday life practices. As such they serve to provide relief and ease: they prescribe how people should act and thus save them from having to make a choice; they suspend the search for meaning and reduce the need to engage in conscious reflection. Within institutions *motivation is separated from purpose*: an individual's motivations become detached from the original meaning of the institution while the purpose of the institution may be changed, expanded and even completely transformed.

Institutions are able to guarantee permanently the satisfaction of certain human needs. Since these needs are met and are barely noticeable any longer, institutions provide 'background fulfilment' – they only become noticeable by their absence. In addition to this there are needs, motivations and purposes which are typically shaped and mediated by institutions, such as the pursuit of profit in business or the desire for power in politics. Institutions impose an 'institutional liability' on individuals that can manifest in sanctions, be it in the form of criminal responsibility, political or social responsibility, or diffuse informal forms of sanctioning. The fact that institutions make individuals conform to certain behaviours contributes towards social stability but at the same time helps to immunise the institution itself against critique and calls for change. Gehlen's theory tends to regard the persistence of institutions as a value in itself. He does not say anything about the goals, the means or the standards according to which institutions should be preserved, modified or redesigned.

Gehlen's theory cannot be used to provide a basis for a policy of sustainability aimed at institutional change. In contrast to institutional economics, Gehlen offers an interpretation of institutions centred on persistence. Stability as such is a goal of human striving, and an institution's very persistence through time constitutes a value over and above its role in achieving particular purposes. Gehlen's theory focuses here on those institutions described by Williamson as 'institutions of embeddedness' – that is, institutions associated with the culture and constitutional structure of a society. A stocks perspective that is guided by practical interests such as those reflected in sustainability policy can take from Gehlen's theory the insight that institutions by their very existence often constitute a considerable element of power beyond their utility for particular purposes.

6.4 The legitimacy of institutions as a factor in their persistence

6.4.1 Legitimacy as an element of power

There is one essential aspect relating to the persistence of institutions which neither institutional economics nor Gehlen takes adequately into account. In modern democratic societies that operate under the rule of law, the political and legal institutional structure cannot be stable unless 'the needs of the individual's reflexive subjectivity are satisfied institutionally' (Schelsky 1970: 21). This means that individuals assert the right to reflect on anything and everything. They demand to be allowed to form an opinion about existing institutions, to judge them positively or negatively, and to give expression – where appropriate, public expression – to their consent or rejection. Unlike Gehlen, Schelsky believes that the articulation of subjectivity is part of the institutional stock of democratic states.

Schelsky's formulation 'the needs of the individual's reflexive subjectivity' refers to the fact that responsible citizens have certain expectations. Laws and rules as well as informal institutions should be deemed valid only if they are *legitimate* – or are recognised as legitimate in the citizens' judgement. Contrary to Gehlen's assumption, the question of meaning thus often plays an important role in the (ongoing) existence of institutions; it cannot be suspended indefinitely, as the following example shows. In the context of a discussion about the Polynesian word 'taboo', MacIntyre (2013: 129–130) writes that Captain Cook's sailors were surprised to observe the contrast between what 'they took to be the lax sexual habits of the Polynesians' and the 'rigorous prohibition placed on such conduct as that of men and women eating together'. Such behaviour, the sailors were told, was 'taboo'. Upon asking what this word meant, however, no information was forthcoming because, according to MacIntyre, 'the native informants themselves did not really understand the word they were using'. Clearly the question of meaning had successfully been suspended, although this gave only apparent stability to the institution of taboo. This was demonstrated by the 'ease with which Kamehameha II abolished the taboos in Hawaii 40 years later in 1819 and the lack of social consequences when he did' (MacIntyre 2013: 130). In this case, suspension of the question of meaning had merely concealed the fact that the 'spirit' of the institution had been lost, which is why it could be abolished so easily. Stable institutions do, then, presuppose that the question of meaning has been answered thoroughly and satisfactorily.

When institutions cannot be legitimated in line with public opinion because they no longer have any meaning they are not changed automatically – but they can be publicly criticised and called into question. In constitutional democracies, the test of institutional legitimacy is itself a construct consisting of both formal and informal institutions, ranging from the diffuse expression of public opinion, the media, non-governmental organisations and political parties through to the instances of the legal system.

To some authors' way of thinking, the institutionalisation of the debate about legitimacy leads to a situation in which critique of existing institutions has no practical impact. Instead of bringing about change, says Schelsky, the 'critical demands made by this reflexive subjectivity' are silenced in such institutions. This occurs because the aim of these demands, in his view, is 'not directly to change the material conditions or the world of the institution per se; instead they seek to have this critical reflexion and its expression rendered permanent, i.e. to have it institutionalised as well' (Schelsky 1970: 25).

Other thinkers, including the North American federalists of the eighteenth century and the philosopher Georg Wilhelm Friedrich Hegel, have elaborated in contrast to this the view that the requirements for legitimacy articulated in public opinion can become a determining force in the modern state. Although Hegel in particular adopted a highly critical stance towards public opinion, he nonetheless saw ways in which it can arrive at a critical and practically effective judgement of these institutions within the institutional construct of the state (Hegel 2001: 242f., 351–356; Petersen 1996: 258–264). In liberal democratic countries the attempt is made to accommodate citizens' ideas of legitimacy not only by supporting the formation of public opinion but also by providing procedures of democratic decision making. It is permissible (with a few exceptions) to change political and legal institutions. This being so, they need to be designed in such a way that such change can occur at least in principle, that is, that they can be redesigned, abolished and replaced by new ones by means of a procedure which itself is recognised as legitimate. Such procedures are themselves institutions whose particularity consists in enabling orderly institutional transformation to occur. This means, further, that these procedures of institutional change themselves need to possess a certain persistence and be relatively immune to calls for change[11].

Ideas about legitimacy that set the tone in a society constitute a powerful factor that helps to stabilise institutions – or to shake them to their core. Institutions such as the caste system in India up until Gandhi or slavery in the United States up until the war of secession were only able to persist because a large number of people in these societies believed these institutions to be legitimate. The same is true of the institutions of democratic states: they can only remain stable if they are generally believed to be legitimate. Conversely, problems arise in terms of the social order if institutions are felt to be illegitimate or meaningless, counterproductive or superfluous over a long period of time. This can lead to citizens refusing to participate in communal tasks[12] or it may lead to social unrest or revolution – consider, for example, the Peasants' War in Germany around 1525 and the French Revolution.

What follows from this discussion, then, is that the institutions of sustainability policy likewise need to be both effective and recognised as legitimate by public opinion over an extended period of time.

6.4.2 Legitimacy and sustainability

In both politics and public discourse, the legitimacy of institutions is considered to be a matter that goes well beyond those ideas of legitimacy that exist at any one time in a society and, as such, are highly contingent. In other words, criteria for the legitimacy of certain institutional arrangements which are more stable over the long term clearly exist. For example, even if the overwhelming majority of people in a society currently approve of discriminating against a certain minority and would declare this to be legitimate, it is nonetheless possible to argue that the majority decision is 'not right' and that discriminatory actions are therefore illegitimate. In a similar vein, when debating sustainability policy it is possible to ask whether – regardless of the current majority relations in a society – certain institutions that limit civil liberties for the benefit of sustainability goals (or, conversely, water down sustainability goals in favour of civil liberties) are legitimate. When weighing up the arguments between social justice for current generations and the benefits for future ones, or between economic growth and nature conservation concerns, here too we are bound to ask what is right and good rather than to content ourselves with the answer that what is right is what a current majority decides is right. In the case of sustainability problems, an additional aspect is that the solutions themselves need to aim to be permanent, that is, they need to be designed in such a way as to outlast changes in prevailing short-term notions of legitimacy.

Considerations of this kind are normative in nature because they are concerned with appropriate norms and how these can be justified regardless of the contingent opinions prevailing in a society. This concern is unavoidable if we want to assess the worth of institutions and to know whether a certain institution is good and whether its existence or establishment is justified. The principles we draw upon to deal with these kinds of questions (human rights, justice, political freedom, obligations toward future generations, the inherent value of species etc.) do not lend themselves to discussion within a descriptive theory such as economics or sociology. Neither is the stocks perspective suited to contribute anything in this respect. Nonetheless we wish to consider in broad-brush terms a number of normative issues to do with institutions, as they form an important part of the setting of sustainability policy.

To inquire into the normative basis of institutional legitimacy as opposed to the form of legitimacy that is rendered valid in actual reality by virtue of public opinion is to enter the field of moral philosophy. This field is dominated by conflicting theories. A variety of approaches can be used to establish the ethical foundations of an institutional design for sustainability policy. These include utilitarian approaches (Birnbacher 1988, 2006), contractarian approaches (Rawls 1973: 284ff.) and discourse theoretical approaches (Habermas 1984a, 1984b, 1987; Apel 1994) as well as rational theory approaches in the critical Kantian tradition (cf. Kersting 1997; Höffe 2001) and natural law approaches (Catholic ethics and social teachings, cf. Gabriel 2005)[13]. Despite their heterogeneous starting points and approaches to grounding such an ethics, these theories nonetheless share a number of fundamental conclusions when it comes to issues of sustainable development. For example, they all postulate certain human rights, principles of democracy and the rule of law as well as certain norms of distribution. They all assume the right of subjects to form their own views and to exercise self-determination. A further shared conclusion is that limitless consumption of natural resources and the uncontrolled destruction of natural habitats cannot be justified. Thus we can conclude that institutions of sustainability policy are legitimate when they contribute towards the pursuit of these principles.

However, what is striking is that many ethical approaches have no analytical concept of institution. This is because the premises for justifying norms are generally developed in a conceptual space in which no institutions as yet exist – one example of this is Rawls' 'original position'. If any practical consequences are to be drawn from these premises, it is at this point that institutions come into play, albeit usually in a reductionist form that is limited to merely functional aspects – all aspects relating to the institution's intrinsic and existential value, whose importance Gehlen had emphasised, are excluded from consideration. The institution appears as an instrument or as a technical means of setting (positive or negative) incentives to control human behaviour such that it appears desirable on the basis of the ethical theory in question. Viewed in this light, the institution is – to overexaggerate slightly – nothing other than a mechanism of coercion. This is the view already encountered in similar terms in institutional economics and is also the one adopted in the discourse theory of Habermas (1998).

It is possible to defuse the notion that institutions exert force and thus bring an element of heteronomy to people's lives by pointing out that the coercion they enact is a result of what the individuals themselves ultimately want. This is how constitutional economics justifies the coercion exercised by the constitutional state, namely, by arguing that at the constitutional level a representative *homo oeconomicus* should approve of this force on the grounds of egoistic utility (Buchanan and Tullock 1962, cf. Petersen 1996: 85–103). For Habermas, institutional coercion ideally brings about nothing other than the reasonable consensus of all participants at the level of discourse between free and equal citizens.

Two important normative issues are generally omitted in this technical view of institutions:

1 From Gehlen's perspective the question arises whether or not the stability of institutions constitutes a value in itself – considering the possibility that, rather than the existing ones, there might be no institutions at all. Seen in this way, cannot every institution that exists be seen to have earned itself a certain basic merit?
2 Taking this further, we can ask: is it not problematic to conceptualise ethical reasoning as existing only outside institutions? Should ethical reasoning not be thought of rather as potentially also being present within the institution itself? This approach gives rise to a particular view of ethical reasoning: rather than pitting *what-ought-to-be* against reality, ethical reasoning would seek to formulate *what-ought-to-be* in terms of *what-can-be*, that is, in terms of the likely prospects for putting *what-ought-to-be* into practice within the current institutional structures. This would entail trusting that existing institutions are more or less reasonable despite all their failings. Without this trust, all attempts at putting into practice what is ethically required would merely amount to empty demands[14].

To the extent that normative theories deriving from practical philosophy attempt to give institutions that are deemed to be good and right some kind of form in reality, they come into the purview of the stocks perspective. The reason for this is that such an attempt cannot be undertaken, not even in purely theoretical terms, without making (implicitly) descriptive assumptions about reality and its temporal development. This is especially true of normative theories pertaining to sustainability.

6.5 The stocks perspective in relation to institutions

Let us turn now to the question of how the stocks perspective can help to clarify the significance of institutions for sustainability policy. In doing so, we assume that the prior normative question regarding which sustainability goals should be pursued has already been answered. The next step is to examine, from the stocks perspective, whether existing institutions support the process of achieving those goals and, where necessary, to work out how they need to be changed. For this reason, the stocks perspective has both a *critical* and *constructive* role to play.

6.5.1 The critical role of the stocks perspective in relation to institutions

Many philosophers, institutional economists as well as organisations at various levels and politically active citizens tend, on the one hand, to underestimate the inertia and persistence of institutions and to overestimate the possibility of introducing new institutions. On the other hand, they fall prey to resignation when their 'positive intentions' founder on the rocks of a 'negative reality'. Being sure that we are pursuing the right goal causes us to gloss over the difficulties encountered along the way, but it also causes us to overlook the opportunities that might present themselves.

Scientists and philosophers sometimes encourage these mistaken notions systematically by adopting their respective narrow disciplinary view – at least in those instances where the limits to this view are not considered carefully. The segment of reality illuminated in each case leaves a number of important factors in the shadows. The result of this unconsidered bias is that necessary changes are implemented either in an overhasty manner – and therefore fail to be effective over the long term – or not at all.

The critical contribution made by the stocks perspective consists first of all in rejecting all elements of reductionism that spring from such an attitude. Taking shortcuts when representing reality may, for methodological reasons, be unavoidable if we wish to make theoretical progress in a specific discipline, but it can lead us astray when it comes to practical issues[15]. The behavioural patterns and rules that are at issue need to be studied as impartially and comprehensively as possible, independently of disciplinary presuppositions and limitations. This demand for impartiality and comprehensiveness does not in itself elicit knowledge, but it does help in recognising what is only apparent knowledge which, if applied in practice, would lead to poor results. By enacting this critical role, the stocks perspective reminds us that organising human affairs is a *holistic* exercise. It draws attention to elements of reductionism, abridgement and bias. In its critical turn the stocks perspective cautions us to proceed carefully and to persevere; it can also show us what happens when these cautions are not heeded. Williamson (2000: 610) illustrates what this means in relation to shaping institutions by describing the institutional shaping of societal relations in post-Soviet Russia[16]. We should not allow the fact that such prominent errors tend to be the exception in sustainability policy[17] to deceive us. As sustainability goals become more widely and more firmly embedded in the consciousness of a society, the risk of poorly thought through measures manifesting in inappropriate institutional arrangements grows.

6.5.2 The constructive role of the stocks perspective in relation to institutions

Assuming that the normative requirements of sustainability policy are generally agreed in a given domain, a stocks perspective can be used *constructively* both to evaluate the existing institutions and to assess the opportunities for establishing new ones.

1 First of all, existing institutions will be looked at in terms of which requirements they have already met, either fully or partially, and what kind of innovations they are capable of facilitating – or, alternatively, what new forms of institutionalisation are needed. The idea put forward by some authors during the 1980s (e.g. Hannon 1985) that the rule of law and democracy would have to be abolished in favour of a dictatorial state based on environmental legislation if the key sustainability goals were to be achieved, will be rejected: it appears that it is precisely democratic states based on the rule of law whose persistence enables institutional reforms relating to sustainability to occur.
2 In political debates the ingrained nature of disadvantageous (vis-à-vis sustainability) patterns of behaviour is often put down to a lack of political will or to the disproportionate power of particularistic interests. This view (usually directed especially at individuals involved in political processes) is justified to an extent. However, a stocks perspective will additionally seek to identify the persistent behavioural patterns or formal (and often informal) rules that are concealed behind such imprecise concepts as 'political will' or 'disproportionate particularistic interests'. It will do so because what is described in sustainability discourses as a lack of political will, for example, almost always has to do with existing formal institutional arrangements or else with (informal) combinations of activities on the part of individuals, interest groups or organisations; these are more or less persistent and can certainly be addressed as institutions in Gehlen's sense of the term. This serves to shift attention from the level of individuals to that of institutions. Here, though, the meaning of institutions is to be conceived of in terms of their non-functional, non-instrumental elements in particular.

3 The task arising out of Gehlen's theory is to examine each institution – prior to any envisaged plan to preserve, change or abolish it – in terms of what it does and what impacts it has beyond its official purposes and controlling functions. While the conceptual tools of law and institutional economics are well-suited to analyse the 'official aspects' of institutions, what these disciplines lack is a language for studying those elements of institutions mentioned above that are associated with the transformation of purposes, needs orientation and background fulfilment etc. Going beyond Gehlen, it is also necessary to take account of views of legitimacy in relation to existing institutions or those that are to be established.

4 The persistence of existing institutions – particularly those at Levels 1 and 2 but often also at Level 3 in Williamson's scheme – cannot be understood without looking at their *history* and at the history of their context. A stocks perspective that emphasises the element of time will always constitute a historical perspective when it comes to human relations and conditions. The empirical methods that belong to an adequate theory of institutions consist not only in data and time series from economics, sociology and cultural theory but also in the narratives presented by historians. These narratives are not subject to the strict (and simultaneously reductionist) methods deployed by disciplines such as economics and are therefore especially suited to address the temporal aspect that is central to a stocks perspective as well as to include comprehensively those factors which elude disciplinary perspectives.

5 The history of institutions associated with sustainability policy is comparatively short. But it too can and must be present when the question of institutional change comes up. Moreover, the narrative of this history is always linked to narratives related to other institutions, ones that exist independently of the problem of sustainable development. Persistence and change in sustainability policy must always be seen in the context of all other institutions and behavioural patterns. What this means in practice will be illustrated in the case studies presented in Chapters 9, 10 and 12 of this book.

What follows from this discussion is that dealing appropriately with persistence in human relations requires a form of knowledge and a faculty that extends beyond scholarly knowledge and technical prowess. It is the particular character of this knowledge and this faculty that we turn to in the following chapter, which deals with judgement.

Notes

1 Many of the quotations give in the following can also be found in the article by Kingston and Caballero (2009).

2 Liturgical reforms intended to make detailed changes to the way the Holy Mass is conducted yet without affecting the institution as a whole have occurred, but only at intervals spanning centuries. The next reform to follow the Tridentine reform of 1570 was that of the Second Vatican Council in 1968.

3 It might justifiably be argued against Gehlen that expressions of spontaneity, creativity and surprise are just as much part of human behaviour as the expressions of standardisation he emphasises, such as habit, repetition and convention. The surprising traits are the more striking ones, whereas the 'taken-for-granted' ones – the instances of convention and habit – are often overlooked. But apart from the fact that spontaneous actions are the exception in the everyday flow of human behaviour (this is why we notice it), they can only have an impact if they are in some way comprehensible to others. This comprehensibility, though, is only given to the extent that the spontaneity relates to contexts generally characterised by repetition and habit. In support of Gehlen, we might even say that successful spontaneous actions are possible, if anywhere, within a stable framework of standardised actions (institutions).

4 Instruments or tools 'join people's needs and thoughts to existing conditions' (Gehlen 2004a: 11).

5 The comments made here about tools also apply, *mutatis mutandis*, to linguistic concepts. Thus Gehlen is also able to refer to the tools of the Stone Age as 'stone concepts': if linguistic concepts are theoretical resources aimed at ordering and describing reality then 'stone concepts' are their practical equivalent, namely, resources for (re-)working and shaping reality.

6 On this basis Gehlen attempts to fashion an explanation for the origin of experiences of transcendence in the religious realm. This explanation is important in our context because it leads into Gehlen's understanding of institutions. In primitive societies people's lives depend not only on having access to tools but also on invisible powers that play an important role in their lives. These powers – the gods – and the influence they wield are connected on the one hand (like the tools) to the ends pursued by humans. Humans are dependent upon the benevolence of the gods, for otherwise their efforts are in vain. On the other hand, though, the gods are – according to Gehlen – acknowledged as possessing 'intrinsic beingness' (*Selbstsein*). The cult of the gods is not primarily an instrumental one. Instead, the invisible powers are considered to be gods because they are believed to possess intrinsic existence - to the extent that 'their relationship to their own needs is secondary' '[die] Beziehung auf die eigenen Bedürfnisse zurückgestellt [ist]' (Gehlen 2004a: 15). In the religious ritual of veneration of the gods, ritualistic acts are repeated in the same way over and over again. It is precisely by changing nothing that these acts recall the *permanence* of things and invisible powers to which intrinsic value is attributed. Consciously recalling permanence as such transcends the overwhelming experience of fleetingness and impermanence in human existence.

7 This absolute intrinsic value is a property of 'those things, beings, institutions etc. to which a behaviour is related that applies to their independent existence itself and their reality as such – virtually up until the relinquishment of any existential value (for one's own needs)' (Gehlen 2004a: 17).

8 This aspect is also recognised in the discipline of economics, though less in institutional economics than in the economic theory of bureaucracy (Downs 1967) and in constitutional political economy (Buchanan 1975).

9 Karl Marx recognised this too, even if he expressed it in different terms: in his pursuit of profit the capitalists are merely 'characters who appear on the economic stage' who 'are but the personifications of the economic relations that exist between them' (Marx 1959, beginning of Chapter 2); the capitalist is 'capital personified and endowed with consciousness and will' (Marx 1959: 152).

10 This theory is roundly rejected by, among others, Habermas (1985: 122) in his critique of Gehlen. This rejection relates not to the theory as such, though, but to the fact that Gehlen blurs factual and normative issues. Rehberg too (1990: 130) points to inconsistencies and contradictions in Gehlen's institutional theory. It is hard to disagree with the observation that there is, factually speaking, an ethos of institutions, but Gehlen's attribution of a normative aspect to this fact is inappropriate from a philosophical perspective.

Only institutions which have something good about them from the point of view of a reasonable ethic can – to the extent that they are good – provide grounds for ethical commitments.

11 In line with Williamson's scheme regarding different levels of institutions (2000, cf. also Section 6.2.3 above), this means that as a rule these procedures need to be embedded at Level 2, the level of the constitution (cf. Buchanan and Tullock 1962).

12 This occurred, for example, during the decline of the Roman Empire from the early years of the third century A.D. onwards.

13 On this, cf. also Section 2.3 above.

14 The idea that reason – in and of itself autonomous – is present not only in the reflexive capacity of the moral subject but also in the actual (real) forms of the subject's actions, namely, institutions, was developed by Hegel (2001) in his philosophy of right. What exactly this 'presence' of reason means in any specific instance is not always easy to say. The fundamental aim of this view, though, is to reconcile subjectivity with institutions.

15 The fundamentally different modes of procedure and types of knowledge entailed by scholarly inquiry on the one hand and practical action on the other are the subject of Chapter 7 on judgement.

16 The failed attempt to establish orderly arrangements based on the rule of law in Russia during the 1990s is regarded by Williamson to be the result of a misplaced euphoria on the part of politicians and their advisers, who allowed themselves to be guided by an 'undue reliance on ex ante property rights'. These were abstract normative requirements that were to be implemented by instrumental means. Williamson rightly acknowledges that not a few *ex post* experiences ought to have been anticipated, particularly in view of the 'shortfalls of the institutional environment in Russia' (Williamson 2000: 610). If the existing conditions could have been perceived without ideological bias, 'the effort to reform Russia would have proceeded in a more modest, molecular, deliberative way'. A similar argument could be made in relation to the adverse experiences encountered in the course of reorganising societal conditions in Afghanistan after 2001 and in Iraq after 2003. A policy of sustainability whose institutional arrangements are similarly poorly adapted to the given circumstances as in these cases would probably quickly lose all credibility and end in failure.

17 These exceptions include the Clean Water Act of 1972 in the US, cf. Chapter 8.

7 Judgement

As we pointed out in the introduction to this book, using the concept of stocks requires the faculty of *judgement*. Having elucidated the concept of stocks in some detail, we now turn in this chapter to the concept of judgement and then show in Chapter 8 that the concept of stocks can be understood as a principle of judgement. What, though, does 'judgement' actually mean?

7.1 What is judgement?

The term 'judgement' is often used in everyday speech and yet it appears to be inextricably linked with a certain vagueness that is apparently hard to reconcile with scientific or philosophical concepts and principles. We say that a person demonstrates judgement when he or she accurately judges the character of another person or is able to 'size up' a situation – but not if she or he develops a complicated mathematical proof. People typically show judgement in cases where it is possible to 'have a different opinion'. Such a difference of opinion is not possible with regard to a mathematical proof but often is in relation to judging people and situations. Nonetheless, correctly anticipating the behaviour of a person and mastering a situation is no proof of having made a correct judgement, as it would still be possible to object that the person making the judgement had simply 'got lucky'.

So there appear to be some instances where it is possible to have a different opinion and others where it is not. Judgement seems to relate only to the former, whereas – according to a widespread view – it is only with the latter that you can really 'know' something and where there is a right or a wrong. Is judgement, then, always a matter of opinion? The term 'judgement' has not presented itself to us arbitrarily: rather, when we use it we are indebted to the philosophy of Immanuel Kant, who dedicated a whole book to this mental faculty – the *Critique of the Power of Judgement*[1] (Kant 2001).

Kant had already concerned himself with the faculty of judgement in his *Critique of Pure Reason*, defining it there as follows: 'If understanding in general be defined as the faculty of laws or rules, the faculty of judgment may be termed the faculty of subsumption under these rules; that is, of distinguishing whether this or that does or does not stand under a given rule (casus datae legis)' (Kant 1855: 104).

However, what we might ask is this: 'subsumption under these rules' or under concepts – which for Kant are the same thing – is that not something we constantly do when we think? What is supposedly special about this 'ominous judgement'? (Ortmann 2006: 168). Elsewhere Kant offers us a further clue. We need judgement, he says, when we wish to make practical use of or follow a theory (i.e. a system of rules or concepts). This is because:

> (...) no matter how complete the theory may be, a middle term is required between theory and practice, providing a link and a transition from one to the other. For a concept of the understanding, which contains the general rule, must be supplemented by an act of judgement whereby the practitioner distinguishes instances where the rule applies from those where it does not. And since rules cannot in turn be provided on every occasion to direct the judgement in subsuming each instance under the previous rule (for this would involve an infinite regress), theoreticians will be found who can never in all their lives become practical, since they lack judgement. There are, for example, doctors or lawyers who did well during their schooling but who do not know how to act when asked to give advice. (Kant 1991: 61)

Thus judgement must 'subsume' specific or practical circumstances under rules and concepts. This is necessary when action needs to occur: the doctor's advice says how a specific individual who is sick should be treated. But exactly how judgement subsumes and comes to formulate such advice is something Kant does not divulge to us at first. All he tells us is that it is 'a special talent [...] that cannot be taught at all, only practised' and 'a peculiar talent, which does not, and cannot require tuition, but only exercise' (Kant 1855: 105). In other words, judging can be neither learnt nor indeed taught – and yet judgement is essential to us: 'Deficiency in judgment is properly that which is called stupidity; and for such a failing we know no remedy' (Kant 1855: 105).

Let us now look at an example from high-brow popular literature. In his novel *Durch die Wüste* (*In the Shadow of the Padishah: Through the Desert*) Karl May (1962[1892]) describes his hero Kara ben Nemsi, who has just thrown an impolite Ottoman officer out of his apartment, reflecting as follows:

> One has to understand how to treat an Oriental. A Westerner who regards himself as disrespected has only himself to blame. A modicum of personal courage and the largest possible dose of immodesty, supported by the dear virtue which we here would call coarseness, are the best possible means to success in certain situations. However, there are also circumstances in which one is forced to take a fair amount of impudence. In these cases, though, it is highly advisable to pretend one has not noticed a thing. Naturally it takes not just knowledge of the circumstances and consideration of the individual case but also plenty of practice in order to decide what is better and more prudent: coarseness or patience and self-control, one's hand on one's weapon or – in one's pocket. (May 1962: 319, our translation)

Although Karl May is not talking explicitly about judgement here, the elements that are important in Kant are present here as well. Karl May and Kara ben Nemsi are reflecting about a practical question, namely, about the right way 'to treat Orientals'. They too mention certain rules. But which rule is to be applied depends on 'knowledge of the circumstances and consideration of the individual case' and is ultimately a question of 'plenty of practice'. Yet this means that the advice we receive remains quite general and vague. It gives us a few pointers in the form of two general rules (for which, by the way, no reasons are given), but ultimately we do not find out how we are to do the right thing in dealing with 'the Oriental'.

Immanuel Kant and Karl May tell us, however, that judgement enables us to *know*. We know how 'to treat an Oriental' and we know how we are to behave as a doctor when 'giving advice'. But how do we know? This is what seems to remain hidden or 'ominous'.

In this chapter, we seek to show on the one hand that judgement is indispensable, both when acting and when acquiring knowledge – including scientific knowledge – and on the other that it certainly is possible to say something definite about it, that there are indications of how judgement can be practised or taught. We will approach the faculty of judgement via an indirect route in the following. We want to start out from a kind of knowledge which, unlike the knowledge entailed in judgement, is not ominous, hidden or opaque but, quite the contrary, is evident to everyone, namely, the knowledge of science (Section 7.2). Then we shall point out the limits of this knowledge (Section 7.3) and contrast it with another sort of knowledge, so-called practical knowledge (Section 7.4). Starting out from the observation that this practical knowledge is closely connected with judgement (Section 7.5), we shall then, in Section 7.6, explicate the meaning of judgement itself. Section 7.7 is more closely concerned with the relationship between science and judgement, before in the final section, 7.8, a number of conclusions are drawn in relation to sustainability politics.

7.2 Knowledge, science and politics

Our first question should be this: which faculty or which kind of knowledge differs from judgement and its associated knowledge? Let us stay with Kant for now. Kant distinguishes judgement above all from understanding[2]. Understanding is the faculty we use to form clear concepts, formulate judgements and draw conclusions. Understanding reaches insights into reality on the basis of controlled experiences, e.g. by experiments.

The Kantian differentiation of mental faculties is illuminating. In his *Critique of Pure Reason* (Kant 1855), Kant explains that the only knowledge we can have of reality initially is acquired by understanding on the basis of its principles, concepts, conclusions and the controlled experiences. This view seems nowadays to be widespread, if not predominant. This is due to the important role played by science today in nearly every sphere of our lives. Modern science – especially when it is guided by the paradigm of the modern natural sciences – is precisely the mode of knowledge of reality that corresponds in a special way to the structures of understanding described by Kant. After all, Kant understood his analysis of understanding as a philosophical reflection upon modern science (cf. e.g. Kant 1855: XXVI f.). Indeed, we can even say *cum grano salis* that the knowledge from which we can demarcate judgement is the knowledge of science. To be more precise, it is a knowledge which, according to its own self-conception, is guided to a greater or lesser extent by science. At this point we need to outline briefly the unique characteristics of this knowledge.

At first glance our knowledge consists of two different elements. On the one hand, we know of specific facts and concrete circumstances. We know, for example, that the Rhine flows into the North Sea, that Germany has a smaller surface area than France and that on September 11, 2001 the twin towers of the World Trade Center in New York collapsed after two airplanes flew into them. On the other hand, we also have knowledge not of individual facts but of general relationships, of regularities that govern the world. On the basis of such regularities we recognise and know that the individual facts exist in a necessary relation to one another. The collapse of the World Trade Center is connected in some way with fire, heat and gravity. It is by having knowledge of such laws that we can *explain* the facts. Explaining something means we can give a reason for why it is the way it is.

Knowledge of interconnected facts on the basis of laws is a kind of knowledge specific to science. Science gives us not only knowledge of laws but also certain knowledge of individual facts, because it is able to give us reasons why these facts exist. Using the law of gravity or the law of falling bodies, science can explain why a stone, when held in the air and then let go, falls to the ground. Science can also point out the errors we make precisely because of our naïve perceptions. For example, when we perceive the sun circling the Earth – an impression reinforced in language when we say the sun rises and sets – science teaches us that our senses are deceiving us and that it is the other way around.

Equally, science enables us to know facts of which we would otherwise have no knowledge. The fact that CFC emissions attack the ozone layer in the stratosphere and that CO_2 and other greenhouse gas emissions lead to a dangerous process of heating of the atmosphere is something we know not through direct perception but through scientific calculations based on assuming the validity of certain laws and on measurements, which in turn are based on the application of scientific procedures. Viewed in this way, it may appear as if all our knowledge is mediated by science. In relation to the facts that are known to us, science gives us knowledge about the reasons for them, thus rendering this knowledge certain. Science also teaches us about the regular interconnected circumstances that determine reality, and it enables us to recognise things that had previously not been known.

Science knows about circumstances and facts when it is able to *explain* them. Explaining means naming reasons or *causes*, so that each explanation of a set of circumstances is a *causal explanation*. In his *Logic of Scientific Discovery*, Karl Popper states: 'To give a *causal explanation* of an event means to deduce a statement which describes it, using as premises of the deduction one or more *universal laws*, together with certain singular statements, the *initial conditions*' (Popper 2005: 38). But how do we discover the laws themselves? What is important to note here is that initially science formulates laws in the form of a hypothesis, that is, as a supposition about a law. This supposition is then tested in experiments. An experiment consists in creating certain 'initial conditions' and testing whether or not the procedure or set of facts that has been predicted on the basis of the hypothesised law actually occurs. If this prediction is confirmed in a series of experiments, the hypothesis is taken as proven[3].

Let us summarise the characteristics of scientific knowledge. The knowledge of the sciences is – or should be – precise. It consists of individual facts on the one hand and of regularities based on individual facts on the other. Knowledge about both individual facts and regularities can be expressed fully in statements or so-called *propositions*. Such propositions constitute objective *information* that exists independently of the individuals giving or receiving it. This knowledge can thus be described as *propositional* knowledge (Wieland 1999: §13). In addition, scientific knowledge is reasoned and can always be explained by reference to known, generally recognised premises and initial conditions. Thus scientific insights can be *deduced* from these premises and initial conditions.

The characteristics of *precision*, *propositionality* and *amenability to rational explanation* make the knowledge provided by science such that it can be communicated universally. It can be taught, learned and applied in different situations; it is not tied to individuals. In principle, every individual is capable of understanding and accepting this knowledge and the rational explanations for it by using their faculty of reason – they do not need to have conducted the experiment themselves from which the knowledge originates[4].

What, though, are we to make of the claim that 'scientific knowledge' is the only kind of knowledge or the only paradigm for knowledge? Before we address this question, we would first like to discuss its role in the political sphere. We mentioned above that the dominance of the notion of knowledge outlined above has to do with the key role science plays in modern life. Science also plays this key role in politics, in particular in the area of sustainability politics. In nearly every sector, policy makers rely on the knowledge and advice provided by scientists; at the same time the considerable authority of science in the public sphere is manifested in the fact that politicians instrumentalise scientific expertise in order to justify the decisions they make.

Sustainability politics is dependent on science in a quite specific way because the ecological and resource-related economic consequences of our way of life and mode of production can only be estimated scientifically. This is why public discourse on sustainability is dominated by concepts and strategies which have been developed by academic organisations and often bear the authoritative seal of science. These strategies contain a range of management rules whose selection depends especially on whether the strategies in question favour a strong or a weak definition of sustainability or a mediating position (cf. Section 2.3.3). The distinctions between these strategies are based not so much in the mode of scientific argumentation but more in ethical-normative positions. For example, the Hartwick rule (Hartwick 1977, 1978a, 1978b) permits in principle the substitution of natural capital by man-made capital. Now whether one accepts this rule or not depends, among other things, on the importance one attaches to the right of future generations to make decisions freely – in other words, say, on whether one advocates a discourse-ethical or a utilitarian approach.

Sustainability policy strategies depend on both prior ethical-normative decisions and on scientific knowledge. In both respects, however, every strategy – as far as we can see – claims to be able to present cogent reasons for its recommendations. Viewed from this perspective, the conceptual framework of stocks would have its place in science.

Within the concept of knowledge outlined in this section (to use Kant's terminology, one based on understanding), each sustainability strategy – to put it in rather broad-brush terms – would lead to watertight, fully cogent recommendations and decisions. Doubts would exist only to the extent that we do not (yet) have sufficient knowledge about all the relevant circumstances of the situation in question. In principle, however, we could come up with solid and confident recommendations if only our capacities were sufficient to acquire all the necessary knowledge. Yet as we mentioned at the start of this chapter, difficulties arise if we approach political decisions using the concept of scientific knowledge alone.

7.3 Difficulties associated with 'scientific knowledge'

The conception of knowledge presented above is widespread. Knowledge should be able to be clearly formulated, well-founded and universally communicable. This is how it facilitates rational decision making. Yet we also know that real decision making in politics and elsewhere rarely matches this ideal image. The reason why recommendations made on the basis of sustainability policy strategies are rarely followed may not have to do solely with the resistance put up by powerful interests or with the shortsightedness of the decision makers. There seem to be reasons why scientific expertise plays a rather minor role in political decisions and why decision makers often follow their own *intuition* rather than scientific advice (Kieser 2006: 64).

Why is this so? Probably because when putting sustainability politics into practice, people – as in other areas of social life – often (possibly even typically) have to make decisions for which no watertight rationale can be provided, whose correctness cannot be proven, and which do not emerge straightforwardly from any norm for action or from scientific reports. The following difficulties arise, among others:

1 It is often not clear in *factual descriptive* terms how a specific instruction to act is to be interpreted or applied and to what a certain concept can be applied or not.

2 In *normative* terms conflicts can arise between objectives that are of equal importance, and it then becomes necessary to weigh up certain factors against others without any clear rules or recommendations for doing so.
3 What is also typical is that the person making the decision is confronted with *uncertainty* and/or *lack of knowledge*. It is not possible to acquire the necessary knowledge about the situation demanding action, either because there is not enough time or capacity to do so or perhaps because it is impossible per se to know certain things (Sigel et al. 2010).

As a result of these difficulties, it seems that there is always a gap between well-founded norms and knowledge on the one hand and the decision to be made on the other. This appears to lead straight to a dilemma: 'The need for reasonable, well-founded decisions arises at exactly the point where they are impossible' (Ortmann 2006: 170). Sometimes *decisionism* is regarded as being the only way out of this dilemma – that is, the theory according to which decisions are, in actuality, always without grounds (ibid.). Decisionism considers all decisions to be good simply by virtue of being decisions, given that they cannot be rationalised in any case.

Naturally there have always been doubts and criticisms concerning the exclusivity of the alternative between the reasonable and watertight rationale of decisions on the one hand and decisionism on the other. These doubts are generally directed at the idea of scientific knowledge, as clearly one can have cogently rationalised knowledge only of objects which themselves are necessary in some special way. For example, I can know for certain that the sum of the angles of a triangle (in Euclidean geometry) is 180° because that is the way it is, objectively speaking, in a triangle. Those things which cannot be any other way than they are, are necessary[5]. And certain knowledge about natural phenomena assumes that strict laws which determine these phenomena by necessity apply in nature.

The social world as well as the world of politics, however, is obviously not an object determined by necessity. There are many things here which are not as they are out of necessity; rather, they could be quite different. These situations are described as *contingent*. In particular, human actions do not follow such laws, and that is why one can predict neither one's own actions nor those of anyone else with certainty. However, contingency is no mere coincidence, and the social world is not merely unregulated chaos, even if there are no strict laws governing it. There are numerous regularities and routines, typical patterns of behaviour and habits and institutions; and action itself is not solely spontaneous and unpredictable. Thus, situations themselves and the characters of those involved may lead us to expect a certain course of interaction among the latter, but not with any degree of certainty.

So it certainly is possible to establish various things about the social world which have the status of general rules of thumb. We can say, for example, that things usually or generally happen in a certain way, such as: 'After three hours of discussion in committees it is usually possible to reach agreement'. Such generalisations bear a certain similarity to strict laws, but they are not as precise as these laws. This has to do with two things. First, when these kinds of generalisations are made about the social world, it is often not possible to define the matter at hand in any precise way. Second, these generalisations do not apply without exception. Here, though, the exception proves the rule rather than rendering it invalid, as would be the case with laws of nature. Due to their lack of precision and inexact quality, generalisations about the social world do not make it possible to produce precise predictions as laws of nature do.

Such generalisations or rules of thumb are not merely provisional statements which might become laws at some point in the future and from which it would be possible to draw necessary conclusions. Therefore, it is argued, the social world and its imprecise and inexact regularities are not the exclusive domain of deductive understanding – the faculty of scientific thinking – but of a particular mental faculty often described as 'practical knowledge'[6].

Yet the necessity of adding this dimension of practical knowledge to scientific knowledge is not limited solely to the social world. It is not enough to identify various areas of reality for which specific mental faculties are responsible. Practical knowledge is required not only in the social world but also in scientific research. A deductive procedure and a deductive explanation presuppose that the relevant scientific laws are known, as it is only through reference to known laws that individual facts can be explained. Finding these laws, though, requires more than just the faculty of reasoning. This is because laws of nature often cannot simply be derived from repeated observations; often they contradict naïve experience and are thus counterintuitive. The fact that gravity acts the same on all bodies is actually not what we observe in the world around us. This is why finding such laws is itself an art which mere reason alone cannot master and which we can understand as a *heuristic* (see Section 7.6) – likewise a domain of practical knowledge[7].

7.4 Practical knowledge

If this kind of practical knowledge exists, though, the question arises as to what else we can say about it. Practical knowledge has repeatedly turned up as a theme in the history of philosophy, and yet there has always evidently been a degree of difficulty when it comes to making it genuinely tangible. At first sight this type of knowledge seems somewhat deficient when contrasted with the knowledge of science; it is described variously as 'imprecise' (Aristotle 2014: I, 1; 1094b12 ff.), 'uncertain', and merely 'probable' (Oakeshott 1991: 24). Nobody disagrees with Aristotle's thesis that practical knowledge – in contrast to scientific knowledge – is *not* knowledge that can be proven, that is, knowledge underpinned by a water-tight rationale and backed up by axioms (e.g. Aristotle 2014: VI, 5; 1140a32 f.). Aristotle also finds that practical knowledge is related to all that is contingent – things that could be different than they are – whereas the knowledge of science can have as its object only that which is of necessity the way it is.

Descriptions of practical knowledge also illustrate, either implicitly or explicitly, that this kind of knowledge is about 'how to do things'; in other words, it is *know-how*, whereas scientific knowledge is '*know-that*' knowledge. Scientific knowledge

Table 7.1 Contrast between scientific and practical knowledge

Scientific knowledge	*Practical knowledge*
Certain, exact	Uncertain or inexact
Grounded on reasons, demonstrable, provable	Cannot be demonstrated and proven
Object: necessary facts	Object: contingent facts
Propositional	Not propositional
Knowing that	Knowing how
Can be taught and theoretically learned	Not teachable *in abstracto*, has to be exercised
Can be conveyed as information	Cannot be conveyed as information
Not tied to a specific person	Tied to a specific person

knows about facts and relations, so it can be expressed (as mentioned above) in statements or propositions. This is not the case with practical knowledge. 'I know how to ride a horse', 'I know how to conduct a negotiation' or 'I know how to give medical advice' is different from 'I know that petrol is lighter than water'. In terms of their grammatical form, 'how to ride a horse' or 'how to conduct a negotiation' are not propositions but indirect questions. This grammatical peculiarity signals that we cannot really say precisely what a person knows when they possess practical knowledge. Practical knowledge, then, is *non-propositional* knowledge. As such it cannot be taught or conveyed in the same way as the propositional knowledge of science. What is peculiar for practical knowledge is the fact that it is always and essentially specific to the person who possesses it.

Scientific knowledge and practical knowledge can be compared with one another schematically, as shown in Table 7.1.

7.5 Practical knowledge and judgement

The comparison presented in Table 7.1 makes it clear once again that what we mean by practical knowledge is not easy to grasp. Indeed some descriptions of practical knowledge in the literature are rather vague and imprecise; often, they only say what practical knowledge is *not* (cf. for example Burke 1803: 269). At the same time, however, thinkers such as Aristotle have shown that practical knowledge is always a matter of relating a specific, isolated case to a general concept and subsuming it within this concept[8].

With practical knowledge, then, we have exactly that which Kant calls judgement (*Urteilskraft*): the act of subsuming individual specific cases within general concepts and rules, above all in a practical context, as with a doctor's 'counsel'. Practical knowledge is also often associated conceptually with the faculty of judgement, and it is indeed difficult to mark out a clear separation between judgement and practical knowledge. With regard to a doctor who has to give medical advice, we might just as well say that he needs judgement as that he needs to have practical knowledge – both statements would mean roughly the same thing.

The terms 'judgement' and 'practical knowledge' often seem to differ only in a few nuances. The difference consists mainly in the fact that each emphasises a different aspect of the same thing: practical knowledge, for example, often highlights the aspect of experience required by this knowledge – experience is something that can be accumulated over time. Kant, by contrast, sees judgement as a mental faculty that is essential to human beings and part of their inherent make-up – and unlike understanding, this faculty requires continual, steady practice.

Aristotle believes that practical knowledge is needed only for right action; contemporary political philosopher Michael Oakeshott (1991), by contrast, views it as an indispensable element of every human activity – whether practical or theoretical. Thus we can say that practical knowledge, as Oakeshott understands it, differs only minimally from the concept of judgement in Kant. This is because judgement is a case of *knowing how*: judgement knows how to deal with concepts and how to apply them.

7.6 Characterising judgement

In his *Critique of the Power of Judgment*, Kant provided a similar definition of judgement to that contained in his *Critique of Pure Reason*: 'The power of judgment in general is the faculty for thinking of the particular as contained under the universal' (Kant 2001: 66). To think 'the particular as contained under the universal' seems fairly unspectacular initially. Identifying objects as a specific application of a concept does not seem to be anything special. 'This is a tree' or 'that is a dog' are, in Kant's usage, *judgements*, and yet making these judgements is a perfectly normal, everyday thing to do. Nonetheless, this everydayness should not allow us to gloss over the fact that indeed we cannot prove these kinds of judgements or provide a watertight rationale for them, and that actually they are in a certain way specific to a particular individual: each person has to make this type of judgement for him or herself rather than merely accepting it from someone else. If we wish to convince someone else that the object in front of a building is a tree, we can do so only if this other person sees the tree as a tree and makes the judgement, 'That is a tree'.

A look at more complex cases reveals that this subsuming of the particular as contained under the universal is by no means a trivial matter. Let us take an example from environmental politics. The precautionary principle is a general rule according to which 'damage or harm to the environment or to human health should – regardless of an incomplete knowledge base – be avoided or reduced to the greatest possible extent in advance'[9]. Yet what exactly 'reduced to the greatest possible extent' means cannot be determined in general terms: it always depends on a range of sometimes unique circumstances. Refraining from doing something would not be a genuinely *safe* application of the precautionary principle either because, in the case of natural disasters, for example, it is this very inaction that has adverse consequences for the environment and human health.

Similarly, we cannot present any universally valid way of applying the precautionary principle or some similar rule, as it really does depend on the circumstances in question. Indeed, a universally valid rule that could be applied mechanically would contradict the very concept of judgement itself. We do, however, want to bring out three characteristics or features of judgement which give rise to a particular set of methods for proceeding in such cases. These features give an indication of how judgement actually works. As such, then, they are rather like procedural principles that can serve as a guide for the practical use of judgement.

7.6.1 First feature: bottom-up rather than top-down

How do we fit a concrete individual case into a general rule? We can do it in two ways. First, we start out from what is general (a concept, a rule) and determine which cases fit into it. Kant calls this 'determinative judgement'; it proceeds from 'above', the general, to 'below', the specific (*top-down*). Alternatively, we start out from specific or special cases and reflect upon what might be the concept or rule into which they fit. This is what Kant calls reflective judgement, and it proceeds from below to above (*bottom-up*). Kant discovered that when we make a judgement (when we subsume the specific within the general) we *always* start out from the specific, that is, we always proceed *reflectively*. Even if, for example, we look for objects that fit into the concept of 'tree', we look at the objects in terms of whether this concept fits them[10]. This means that determinative judgement is only a derived function of judgement which at all times presupposes the activity of reflective judgement.

With regard to the precautionary principle, this means, for example, that even if we initially have to specify this principle, in the end, we will consider specific scenarios and ask how they conform or fail to conform to the precautionary principle. A good example of this is the way a judge proceeds at court: for each individual case, she or he must consider under which legal rule it is to be subsumed. This reflective activity of judgement comes to light especially in research conducted in the nomological sciences, i.e. those guided by laws. Here it is necessary to generate suppositions regarding what general law might be able to accommodate the individual observations made. It is not possible to deduce such a law from individual observations – as Karl Popper says in his *The Logic of Scientific Discovery*, you have to guess (Popper 2005: 278). When you are looking for something, you make a guess, and if you make a clever guess, you will find what you are looking for. This technique of finding has also been given the name *heuristics*.

7.6.2 Second feature: heuristics and bridging principles

Judgement, then, does not deduce; it seeks and finds. 'Find' in Greek is *heuriskein*, and this is where our word *heuristic* comes from. Heuristics is the art of finding something that cannot simply be concluded or deduced from our knowledge, such as a scientific law, a solution to a problem, or a good decision.

A heuristic always contains certain rules or principles – basic statements and rules of thumb – that can guide judgement on its search. Such rules form bridges between our knowledge of the general and the specific. So we might see these rules as *bridging principles*. Later on we shall see that even the concept of stocks can be conceived of as such a bridging principle. Those who seek knowledge must use their judgement; in doing so, says Kant, they always proceed heuristically, i.e. they apply such principles.

On this basis Kant formulated a *universal principle* of judgement. Each specific heuristic derives from this principle and renders it concrete for a particular situation or set of situations. The universal principle of judgement says, to put it simply: when using judgement, people assume – as a cognitive necessity – that the world is structured in a way that is accessible and comprehensible to them. This is the only reason it makes any sense to search for principles, rules or laws. The domain where individual specific cases exist is not total chaos to the faculty of judgement, then, but has some kind of order.

Tellingly, Kant explicates the role of this universal principle by reference to modern science, thus showing that the acquisition of scientific knowledge also requires judgement or practical knowledge (Kant 2001: 13–15, 67–68, 69–71). Science, which looks for laws in reality, must already possess the conviction and the notion that such laws exist (or may exist) in the first place. Kant names the domain of individual specific cases 'nature', and this is why he says that judgement assumes nature *a priori* to be a well-ordered whole. According to Kant the universal principle of judgement is expressed in certain 'rules whose necessity cannot be demonstrated from concepts' (ibid.: 69), namely, in rules that cannot be derived from anywhere and that certainly do not reside in the concept of nature itself. Naturally, however, we take these rules as a basis for every act of investigating nature: '"Nature takes the shortest way" (*lex parsimoniae*); "it makes no leaps, either in the sequence of its changes or in the juxtaposition of specifically different forms" (*lex continui in natura*); "the great multiplicity of its empirical laws is nevertheless unity under a few principles" (*principia praeter necessitatem non sunt multiplicanda*); and so on' (ibid., cf. 14–15). It is by all means plausible to interpret these rules as heuristics; 'unity under a few principles' is a maxim Newton used to unite the law of falling bodies with Kepler's laws of planetary motion into a 'universal law of gravitation'.

A number of points are important in relation to the bridging principles of a heuristic. They are not simply assertions about the world but rather guidelines by which judgement proceeds. Thus they are essentially procedural rules. It is characteristic of the principles and rules that exceptions to the rule are permitted. Whatever is correct in terms of the individual principles also applies to heuristics in general: in some situations a heuristic can be helpful, in others perhaps not.

We do not wish at this point to discuss in detail the heuristics that may be of use to the faculty of judgement in politics and sustainability politics (this will be the main topic addressed in Chapter 11). Instead, we wish to examine the characteristics of heuristics by taking the behavioural model of *homo oeconomicus* as an example.

The *homo oeconomicus* model describes human action in terms of maximising one's own utility under restricted conditions. Neoclassical economic theory is based on this model and uses it to find ways of explaining economic processes. This has sometimes meant that *homo oeconomicus* has been seen as an 'image of the human being per se', that is, as an ontological principle according to which people really are always utility maximising *homines oeconomici*. This then formed the basis for what has been called 'economic imperialism' (Radnitzky and Bernholz 1987), which examines all spheres of life on the basis of the *homo oeconomicus* model, as well as for the claim that this model alone permits meaningful analyses of human action and behaviour.

This claim has provoked intense debate in economics in which critics of neo-classical standard economics have proven in empirical studies that in many situations people do not behave as *homo oeconomicus*. As a result the school of business ethics founded by Karl Homann has proposed that *homo oeconomicus* should be understood 'as a heuristic' (Suchanek 1993). This is because, as a heuristic the *homo oeconomicus* model does not involve making any ontological assertions about the reality of economics and politics but rather serves merely to render visible typical traits and tendencies, to reveal structures and to inspire policy recommendations. 'The homo oeconomicus model serves to render comprehensible the behaviour of people confronted by certain incentives' (Suchanek 2001: 146). It can be used 'to solve important problems without necessarily believing that every person is (nothing but) a homo oeconomicus' (147). If we go along with this and regard the assumption of humans as rational maximisers of their own utility not as an assumed regularity but rather as a heuristic, it is but a short step to add another heuristic to that of *homo oeconomicus* – for example that of *homo politicus*[11].

Terms such as *homo oeconomicus* and *homo politicus* have more than just a heuristic function, however. They also play a constitutive role in scientific descriptions and explanations. In other words, they formulate propositional knowledge. The way a term functions solely as a heuristic principle – that is, without simultaneously playing a role in scientific explanations – can thus be seen by looking at a term that Kant himself sees as being linked inextricably to judgement, namely that of the organism, or the 'organized being' (Kant 2001: 244).

We regard an organism as a purposively organised whole in which the individual parts reciprocally maintain one another as well as the whole itself. Kant therefore calls the organism a 'natural end' (2001: 242). However, precisely because the concept of purpose plays a crucial role here, the concept of the organism cannot be an element of scientific knowledge of nature or of reality. This is because there is no such thing as 'causality based on purposes' in scientific explanations of natural phenomena. Thus no explanation of natural phenomena can make use of the concept of purpose. For example, the sentence 'This plant is an organism' does not reflect scientific insight. At the same time, though, we cannot do without the concept of organism when it is a matter of 'researching the particular laws of nature' (ibid.: 280), because it is only by looking at natural beings as organisms that we are led during our research of them to the correct questions[12]. The concept of organism or 'the principle of ends in the products of nature' is therefore not a descriptive concept but rather a 'heuristic principle' (ibid.). Thus to say 'This plant is an organism' simply means, when understood correctly: 'I only regard it or judge it as such an organism, that is, *as if* it were organised according to purposes'. When conducting research on this plant I allow myself to be guided by this way of looking[13].

7.6.3 Third feature: the role of feeling

When contrasted with understanding, judgement has a defect, namely, in terms of preciseness and certainty as well as in terms of providing a rational justification for its judgements. Something that does play an important role in judgement, however, is feeling (Wieland 2001). 'Feeling' is a term that is easily misunderstood. Its meaning here is not the same as 'emotion'[14], which is the opposite of cool, considered understanding; rather, what is meant is feeling in the sense that one might say 'I have the feeling something's not right here' or 'I have a feeling we ought to wait'. Feelings are not just sensations. They have an object: we feel a thing or a situation.

What are feelings like this telling us? In a Jewish joke, a Hasidic Jew – a pious East European Jew – sings the praises of his rabbi: 'Just imagine, our rabbi saw all the way from Posen that there was a fire in Bentschen'. – 'But there wasn't a fire in Bentschen'. – 'Hey, who cares! Think of the distance!' What is funny about this? The rabbi, so we are led to think, is obviously no visionary, he does not have the 'look' (prophetic abilities). But his disciple does not want to believe this and sticks rather ridiculously to his claim that the rabbi definitely did see something. He may have seen the wrong thing, but that seems to be a minor flaw. Perhaps the Hasidic Jew is right, though. After all, we might very well pose the question: if there is such a thing as visionary insight, then must there not also be false, incorrect visionary insight? And is not the existence of false visionary insight an indication that correct visionary insight also exists?

If we apply this to our problem, this means that feelings are also telling us something – usually when understanding is of no further help. In some situations feelings give us a false clue, but at least they point us in a direction where understanding cannot. Feelings may be unreliable and may, like the rabbi in the joke, see a fire where there is none; but they really do see the fire, whereas understanding is merely blind in such cases and sees nothing at all.

Thinkers such as Aristotle, Adam Smith and Immanuel Kant have emphasised the fact that feelings are indispensable in many decisions and judgements. Kant wished to show this is the case for judgements in general, Aristotle for right actions, and Adam Smith for ethics. Smith devised a *Theory of Moral Sentiments* (Smith 2002), in which he seeks to show that we can judge correctly in an ethical sense only when we develop the feeling appropriate to each specific situation, be it gratitude, goodwill or resentment. All three thinkers agree on the following points:

1 There are issues where we are dependent on the judgement of feelings and where understanding cannot help us any further.

2 Feelings are capable of both truth and error; they can show us what is right and they can also deceive us.
3 Usually, though, our immediate feelings in a particular matter are unreliable, deceptive and often wrong.

It follows from these three points that we reach correct judgements not by shutting out our feelings but by clarifying them. In this way an indeterminate feeling turns into considered intuition. We also say that a person develops a *sense* of a thing. In the next chapter we shall look at how it is important, when seeking solutions to sustainability problems, to develop a sense of time.

What makes our feelings deceptive, however, are our inclinations, our interests and our personal sentiments. Inclinations and interests cloud our feelings[15]. We reach correct judgements or have a good intuition or the right sense of a thing to the extent that we are able to distance ourselves from these inclinations. A variety of paths are suggested for this: Aristotle assumes that right decision making lies in action taken somewhere in the mean between two extremes – such as brave action as a mean between cowardice and foolhardiness. We will generally be inclined towards one of these extremes more than to its opposite. Aristotle recommends in this case that we act against our inclination and thus gradually come closer to the proper mean. According to him we should use the alleged wrongness of our feelings to reach the right decision by indirect means. If, for example, I am inclined to take no precautions at all, then I should increase my efforts to take precautions; in this way I am more likely to do justice to the precautionary principle. If, on the other hand, I am overcautious and try to insure myself against all kinds of things, I should become more spontaneous and waver less.

Kant and Smith propose a different path from that of Aristotle. They suggest that there is a 'normal feeling' for what is right. We can come to have this normal feeling by distancing ourselves from our own personal inclinations and interests. We are able to do this when we seek to judge a situation from the standpoint of another person. So we need to ask ourselves at all times: how would the others see this? In this way we can judge from the standpoint of the 'impartial spectator' (Smith) or, as Kant says, pursue a 'broad-minded way of thinking', whose 'maxim' is 'to think in the position of everyone else' (Kant 2001: 174). Kant also calls this 'broad-minded way of thinking' *Gemeinsinn* or *sensus communis*, which is roughly equivalent to the term 'common sense'.

'To think in the position of everyone else' means asking oneself how others would judge a matter and thereby seeing one's own inclinations, interests and idiosyncrasies in a new light. However, this cannot happen by simply going along with the judgements of others, as their judgements might likewise be clouded by 'private conditions' (ibid.: 173) or inclinations. Thus the key is to relativise both one's own and the others' judgement by reflecting on it, that is, by comparing it to the ideal of a judgement that is uninfluenced by personal inclinations and interests[16]. This 'broad-minded way of thinking' is, in this view, not something one simply has: rather, one must nurture it through constant practice; one must acquire it by constantly seeking to understand others' perspectives.

7.7 Judgement and science

In Section 7.2 we were concerned with the character of scientific knowledge and established a connection especially to the nomological sciences (i.e. those based on laws) (see Note 4); it is to this issue that we would like to return here. The nomological sciences are usually contrasted to the human sciences (humanities), which focus not on *explaining* facts and circumstances but on *understanding* meaning. The contrast between the two is formulated in particularly concise fashion in a text written by theologian Karl Rahner:

> In the natural sciences exactly proven results can be taken over from one specialty to another and from one researcher to another. They can be understood to some extent, and in any case they can be made use of without having to *evaluate* the method and how it was acquired and the certainty of its results. But in the human sciences the real understanding of an assertion and the evaluation of its validity depend upon one's *personal participation* in the discovery of what is asserted. (Rahner 1978: 7, our emphasis)

We can understand Rahner's differentiation in the following way. The results of (natural) scientific research are not only statements or propositions but also information, even for the outsider. The latter can make use of them without 'having to judge' the method and the scientific procedure involved – indeed, he or she need not even be aware of the method and procedure. The human sciences also generate statements, true enough, and yet they do not have the character of transferable information. In order to understand the statements of the human sciences and to find them useful in some way, we have to judge them and to re-enact the way the discipline concerned came up with them.

We wish to illustrate this with an example. Let us compare the sentence 'The acceleration of gravity is 9.8 metres per second squared, with the statement 'The ethical system of Immanuel Kant is a contemporary variant of the ancient ethics of the Stoics'. With no knowledge of gravitational theory, we can use the first sentence as a piece of information and thereby predict that a stone dropped from a height of 20 metres will hit the ground after about 2 seconds with a speed of approx. 70 kilometres per hour. By contrast, the statement about Immanuel Kant is of no use to us whatsoever if we understand nothing about ethics or the history of philosophy and cannot see how the person who posited the thesis came to formulate it. Another difference is this: statements emerging from the human sciences do not have to be definitive and unambiguous to count as 'scholarly' and 'well-founded'. Thus, alongside the statement 'The ethical system of Immanuel Kant is a contemporary variant of the ancient ethics of the Stoics' it is possible to have a thoroughly opposing one which, for example, traces Kant's ethics back to his pietistic roots – and which likewise counts as 'well-founded'.

Whereas understanding the results from the natural sciences does not require any special power of judgement, this is clearly not so for the results from the human sciences. Thus the nomological sciences and the human sciences seem to differ more in the *methods* they are using than in their objects. At the same time they represent extremes between which other sciences can be located. For example, the disciplines of history, political science and sociology often proceed on the basis of certain methods that demand less judgement (cf. Wieland 2001: 177–178), generating knowledge about both specific things and particular regularities of a general nature – e.g. the connection between environmental awareness and education or income. In other words, using observation (guaranteed by the methods used) and empirical data collection they are able to generate law-like generalisations. Finally, economics – insofar as it is guided by mathematics – has a particularly close affinity with the natural sciences, namely, to the extent that it too formulates laws (such as the fundamental theorems of welfare theory) which are widely considered to determine economies. Even political science and sociology reveal traits of the nomological sciences when they adopt methods and models from economics (e.g. *rational choice theory*).

However, statements of law emerging from the social sciences are usually seen as merely 'indicative of a tendency'. They have to be interpreted, and that too demands judgement. Even the assertions of history as a discipline are often not simply pieces of information. This is true both for assertions about historical developments (what exactly was it that led to the outbreak of World War I?), and for assertions about certain events; here, too, the credibility of sources has to be *judged.*

7.8 Judgement in politics and sustainability policy

To conclude this chapter, we wish to discuss a number of consequences that arise from our consideration of judgement in relation to politics in general and sustainability politics in particular. What function does judgement have in politics? It enables fires in Bentschen to be spotted from Posen – in other words, it makes it possible to anticipate things which cannot be predicted with certainty by understanding. What we can say with certainty is that in politics in general Kant's 'broad-minded way of thinking' plays the crucial role; those who are most successful in achieving their goals are those who are best able to comprehend and anticipate other people's interests and perspectives. We were able to demonstrate this, for example, in a study on the German environmental administration (Petersen and Faber 2000).

At the same time, sustainability policy makers in particular are confronted with a host of often disparate scientific and non-scientific insights on which they have to base their activities and decision making, indeed, even their problem definitions per se. Heuristic elements which bring these insights into a unified perspective regarding sustainable actions and *subsume* them within its goals are needed here. We would like to elucidate this in a little more detail.

Whether a political problem is a sustainability problem at all cannot be decided without scientific expertise; equally, it cannot simply be 'read off from' such expertise. Why, for example, is land use – new land dedicated to industrial areas, human settlements and transport infrastructure – of more than 100 hectares a day in Germany a problem of sustainability, and why should a reduction to 30 hectares a day be sustainable? This is a question we shall address in Chapter 10.

Targets such as the 30 hectare target contained in the German government's sustainability programme (German Federal Government 2008) are obviously intended to provide a 'ball-park figure'; at times they seems to be selected at random. Why do we not set the target at 60, 20, 10 or – as some sustainability researchers are demanding – 0 hectares? Science can tell us neither in simple terms why daily land use of more than 100 hectares is not sustainable nor why one of 30 hectares should be sustainable. Other considerations must come into play here.

When answering the question why land use is a problem of sustainability in the first place, the *experience* that the mere quantity of newly allocated land is an indicator for other sustainability-relevant developments – such as for an increase in traffic and pollutant emissions – is of crucial importance. Such experience is different from scientific knowledge or a law. At the same time, the 30 hectare target may be a reasonable interim target on the way towards sustainable land management. It may be based on the assessment that it is not possible to achieve more in a period of nearly 20 years. Setting a target that is too ambitious would have no impact. The 30 hectare target also offers an opportunity to try out new regulatory instruments for land use – such as the trade in land-use permits. Such instruments can – once they have proven their worth over time – facilitate further reductions in land use.

These kinds of considerations in turn presuppose, among other things, a feeling or an intuition for temporal dynamics. The following chapter will show how the concept of stocks can contribute towards developing a sense of time. Such a sense for processes, changes and windows of opportunity is important for sustainability policy, which necessarily has to take account of long periods of time. Later on, in Chapter 11, we will develop the concept of stocks into a heuristic that enhances this very sense of time.

Box 7.1 Summary: judgement and knowledge

Knowledge is a precondition of good policy decisions – especially when it comes to complex issues. Knowledge exists in the form of individual facts ('The Rhine flows into the North Sea') and of general laws. Science gives us certain, well-founded knowledge, and that is why politicians seem to be reliant upon the expertise of scientists.

However, objectives and knowledge about the world generally do not lead to any particular course of action: knowledge has to be applied or interpreted, and it rarely marks out a route towards any particular decision. So in any given instance there is a gap between our knowledge and its application, a gap that cannot be bridged by defining this knowledge in increasingly specific terms. The application and interpretation of scientific knowledge demands a kind of knowledge that we call *practical knowledge*.

Scientific knowledge is propositional; it can be formulated as propositions and conveyed in the form of information. It is a kind of knowledge that entails 'knowing that ...'. *Practical knowledge*, by contrast, is not propositional but is rather knowledge of 'how something is done' – 'knowing how'. Practical knowledge is a property

(*continued*)

Box 7.1 Summary: judgement and knowledge (*continued*)

of individuals and cannot be conveyed in the same way as a piece of information (cf. Table 7.1).

Practical knowledge is not a stock of knowledge but is more generally the capacity to relate knowledge of a general nature to concrete cases and situations demanding action. It is essentially what Immanuel Kant subjected to closer analysis as 'judgement' (*Urteilskraft*). Judgement is 'the capacity to think the particular as contained under the universal' and it possesses the following three features in particular:

1 Judgement never takes a general concept as its point of departure but rather the particular. It does not proceed in a *top-down* manner but works rather in a *bottom-up* fashion; it starts out from a specific case and looks for a suitable concept or rule that fits the case.
2 Judgement proceeds heuristically, that is, it is guided by general rules that take the form of universal statements about reality, such as 'Nature does not proceed by leaps and bounds' or 'To every thing there is a time'. However, these statements lay no claim to objective validity. They are procedural principles which judgement lays down for itself. We do not know whether or not nature does indeed proceed by leaps and bounds. But when searching for general laws of nature we start out from this assumption, otherwise we would find no such laws at all.
3 Heuristics demand that we be able to use them in a playful fashion. As Karl Popper says in his *Logic of Scientific Discovery*, hypotheses have to be guessed at. Doing so presupposes one has a feeling about the thing. A feeling gives us access to reality – even if it is accompanied by uncertainty. Feelings too are a source of knowledge, and they generally point us in a certain direction: 'I have a feeling that X isn't telling the truth'. We may not be able to provide a rationale for them, but unlike mere sensations, we can explain them. We rely on such feelings, but we do not have to trust them blindly. Feelings can be communicated. We can cleanse them of clouding by personal inclinations and sentiments and can clarify them by endeavouring to see the matter at hand from the perspective of others.

Notes

1 Despite the Cambridge edition title of Kant's work, his term 'Urteilskraft' will be translated in the following as either simply 'judgement' or as 'the faculty of judgement' according to the demands of readability.
2 He also distinguishes it from reason, but this distinction need not concern us here.
3 Albeit – as Popper (2005: 280) and Critical Rationalism (e.g. Albert 1985: 46) correctly note – we must always speak here of a provisional proof.
4 We must concede at this point that we have characterised 'scientific knowledge' in a somewhat one-sided manner. We have framed this knowledge completely in the sense of nomological, contemporary science, i.e. based on the concept of laws, as it is probably most purely represented by contemporary physics. We are aware that there are other sciences besides the nomological ones, such as the human sciences (humanities) and the historical and social sciences, which likewise generate propositional statements, including ones that are at least general in character – i.e. statements which to a specific

extent are derived by means of sound methods. Nonetheless we observe particularly in media and political discussions a tendency to regard the nomological sciences as an ideal and as a standard by which all other sciences should be measured – making it apparently easy to understand why severe doubt is cast upon the academic credibility of theology in Critical Rationalism (e.g. Albert 1985: 132–164) and why that of psychoanalysis is disputed outright (Popper 1974: 985). We shall return to the distinction between the nomological natural sciences, the humanities and the social sciences in Section 7.7, after providing a detailed explanation of the power of judgement.

5 This necessity is itself not absolute but rather relative in a certain way. The fact that there is such a thing as gravitational pull can be regarded as a random given fact. But when this pull comes into effect, planets and objects falling to the ground on Earth cannot behave in any other way than the way they do. Cf. Popper on this point, too (2005: 450): 'But the natural laws, though necessary as compared with singular facts, are contingent as compared with logical tautologies'.

6 In, for example, Hennis (1963); on the concept of practical knowledge, see Oakeshott (1991).

7 Kant (1855: xxxi) notes of Copernicus that, with regard to the planets, he 'ventured on the experiment – contrary to the senses, but still just – of looking for the observed movements not in the heavenly bodies, but in the spectator'.

8 'For if someone knows that light meats are digestible and healthy but is ignorant about which sorts of meat are light, he will not produce health; but someone who knows that bird meats are healthy will produce health more' (Aristotle 2014: VI, 8; 1141b17 ff.).

9 Translation of German Wikipedia definition, accessed 13.02.2014.

10 Without having Kant's theory of power of judgement in mind, philosopher Ernst Tugendhat (1992: 26) once remarked: when we ask ourselves whether lions exist (that is, whether we can subsume specific objects in the world within the concept of 'lion'), 'we don't study potential lions to see whether they possess the predicate of existence; instead, we look at objects in the world to see whether some of them are lions' (by asking ourselves whether they fit the concept of 'lion').

11 We have shown elsewhere that the heuristic of *homo politicus* is also valuable in spheres that are a special domain of economic political theory, namely, bureaucracy and administration (Petersen and Faber 2000).

12 The concept of purpose states the 'principle of unity under which causal processes have ordered themselves to become a natural purpose. It is only thus that we become aware of phenomena of the organic as particular ones' (Spaemann and Löw 1985: 136). We can grasp 'organic beings' 'given the constitution of the human understanding' only as purposively organised (Kant 2001: 282), and it is only this concept of a 'natural purpose' that enables a science to formulate fruitful questions about living things, in whose explanations the concept of purpose no longer appears and indeed must not appear. Purposes exist only in Aristotle's physics, which is no longer a science of nature in the contemporary, modern sense.

13 Karl Popper also addresses the role of heuristic principles in his *The Logic of Scientific Discovery* (2005: 39), when he sees the causal sentence or the conviction that Nature is determined by strict laws as a methodological rule: 'the simple rule that we are not to abandon the search for universal laws and for a coherent theoretical system, nor ever give up our attempts to explain causally any kind of event we can describe'. Likewise we can see rules as operational principles, which Aristotle posits and which help us to achieve virtue in action and to avoid vice.

14 Gigerenzer (2007) has pointed out, however, that it is emotions that enable different factors to be integrated when it comes to decision making and that they have an important – previously underestimated – function when it comes to weighing up advantages against disadvantages and taking account of very different kinds of factors. Thus emotions are also involved when it is a matter of developing a feeling for a situation.

15 This is the provenance of the rule that a judge must not preside over cases in which he himself is biased, that is, in which he has interests of his own or declares certain inclinations or partiality.

16 Kant (2001: 173–74) writes: 'By "sensus communis," however, must be understood the idea of a communal sense, i.e., a faculty for judging that in its reflection takes account (a priori) of everyone else's way of representing in thought, in order as it were to hold its judgment up to human reason as a whole and thereby avoid the illusion which, from subjective private conditions that could easily be held to be objective, would have a detrimental influence on the judgment. Now this happens by one holding his judgment up not so much to the actual as to the merely possible judgments of others, and putting himself into the position of everyone else, merely by abstracting from the limitations that contingently attach to our own judging; which is in turn accomplished by leaving out as far as is possible everything in one's representational state that is matter, i.e., sensation, and attending solely to the formal peculiarities of his representation or his representational state'.

8 Time and the practical dimension of the concept of stock

Die Zeit zum Handeln jedesmal verpassen
nennt ihr 'die Dinge sich entwickeln lassen'.
Was hat sich denn entwickelt, sagt mir an,
wan man zur rechten Stunde nicht getan?

(Time and again you fail to act in timely fashion,
calling it 'allowing things to evolve'.
So tell me, what then has evolved
from not doing something at the right moment?)

From *Spätherbstblätter* by Emmanuel Geibel (1877)

8.1 Preliminary comments

Having talked about the faculty of judgement, we return in this chapter to the concept of stock, addressing its *practical dimension* in particular. We shall show that this dimension is particularly important when using the stocks framework. The main thesis we wish to elaborate in this chapter is as follows: the concept of stocks brings the temporal dimension of action to the fore. This being so, the term *stock* itself articulates a specific feeling, namely, a '*sense of time*'[1].

What we mean by this will become clear in the course of this chapter[2]. First, in Section 8.2, we define the practical dimension of the stocks concept in contrast to its theoretical dimension. In Section 8.3 we identify *three distinct conceptions of time* which lay the foundation for using the concept of stock in its specifically practical dimension. This use of the term serves not only to generate factual information about reality but also to help policy makers and others to develop a special awareness of temporal structures – a 'sense of temporality' as it were. This sense enables them to structure complex problems in terms of time and to express them in a form that is clear, comprehensible and workable in practice (Sections 8.3.4 and 8.4). In this way, stocks function as a heuristic that policy makers can use to structure the temporal issues they find in the actual, real-life environment with which they are dealing. At the end of this chapter (Section 8.5) we shall see that stocks – in the context of this heuristic – are in turn a key building block for the faculty of judgement examined previously in Chapter 7: consideration of stocks serves as a bridging principle for purposes of judgement in relation to time.

8.2 Theoretical and practical dimensions of the concept of stock

So far we may have given the impression that the concept of stocks is a perfectly ordinary concept that is used to describe reality in a certain way. Sets of objects (Chapter 4) as well as non-material and non-quantifiable things (Chapter 5) can be regarded as stocks. It is possible to determine, for example, whether a certain thing is a stock or not. It is also possible to study the way it changes through time and to identify stock dynamics. The concept enables us to emphasise the temporal dynamic of the objects under consideration and to draw on and meaningfully bring together knowledge from various academic disciplines to explain this dynamic. Concepts are the key elements in propositions – or, to use Kant's terminology, in judgements – and serve to articulate either knowledge about reality or the constitutive principles of such knowledge. Such propositions thus form propositional knowledge and are the elements of scholarly knowledge (cf. Section 7.2). This aspect of the stocks concept is what we call its *theoretical dimension*.

The theoretical dimension of the stocks concept is highly significant for any policy of sustainability. At the same time, though, the stocks concept has a practical, heuristic function – or, as we call it, a *practical dimension*. Here, the concept functions like the heuristic principles of judgement introduced in the previous chapter. The aim of this heuristic function is not so much to identify individual stocks or to examine their dynamics in detail but rather to look at things from an overall perspective in terms of their temporality. This perspective of stocks in terms of their practical dimension is not related primarily to knowledge but to action, specifically with regard to the temporal aspect of action. While acting is about doing the right thing, there is also a right time for doing so. In other words, just as the external circumstances of a problem or a domain of action possess a temporal structure, so too any successful solution will need to follow a suitable temporal succession.

The conceptual framework of stocks can help in recognising this 'right time'. However, it can only do so by placing different understandings of time in relation to one another. When we ask what the 'right time' to act is, we are conceiving of time differently from when we consider it merely a matter of duration. We now turn to look at three different understandings of time.

8.3 Time

Why can we or should we speak about having a specific sense of time? Our everyday familiarity with time and the constant presence of time suggest that such a special sense of time cannot be assumed to exist. We see and experience ourselves constantly as temporal beings. We automatically arrange events according to whether they occur earlier or later in time. We can measure time and we can compare segments of time with one another, having no fundamental difficulty with saying whether they are shorter or longer or equally long in comparison to one another. We see ourselves in the present. We remember the past and look into the future, often worrying about what it will bring. So seeing ourselves in terms of time comes more or less naturally.

Our experience of time, then, is determined by what is obviously and fundamentally a sense of taken-for-grantedness. And yet on further consideration we can see that something different is the case. In his 'Confessions', Augustine put it like this:

> What is time then? If nobody asks me, I know: but if I were desirous to explain it to one that should ask me, plainly I know not (Augustine 1988: 239).

Augustine confirms that we do indeed approach time unquestioningly, because it is precisely when we do not question it that we believe we know what it is. This means that we apparently never need to question the nature of time in the same way we question what kind of action is the correct one in any specific situation. Unlike when we act in specific situations, we only have a problem with time when someone questions us about it. And for Augustine this problem is a philosophical one[3].

8.3.1 The time of Newtonian physics: chronos

While Augustine addresses most of the issues entailed in the philosophical debate about time, unquestioned knowledge about time is undoubtedly also subject to a number of fundamental considerations. We outline these briefly here, beginning with an understanding of time that is taken as given in the classical sciences but that also corresponds to our everyday experience. This understanding is based simply on the idea of time as it presents itself to us directly – or appears to do so[4].

In this understanding, time – like space – is a continuum that encompasses all things and all events. Just as things and events exist or take place next to one another in space, so too time places them in the context of a sequence consisting of an earlier time, a same time and a later time. Things and events can be identified by a space-time location: events are 'dateable' (Heidegger 1996: 407). However, whereas space just sits there motionless, as it were, time 'moves'. It *passes*. Whatever is happening now – the present moment – is soon past, and whatever is in the future will sooner or later be here now, in the present and, later still, in the past.

We can represent time in a diagram as a timeline on which we can enter the individual dates as *points* in time. The representation of time using a timeline highlights yet more characteristics of time. Time seems to us to be *homogeneous*: every segment of time, wherever it lies on the timeline, can be compared in quantitative terms to every other segment. Each individual span of time – an hour, a minute or a second – is exactly as long as every other previous or later hour, minute or second. Whether we spend two hours today on a particular activity or one today and one tomorrow – in quantitative terms it remains the same span of time, namely, two hours.

This concept of time can be described as that of Newtonian physics – it is a concept of time which can be described and comprehended fully in mathematical terms. The variable t in equations always represents the homogeneous and quantifiable time that corresponds to this concept[5].

This time, however, is also the everyday time we share when communicating with one another. It is the clock time according to which we set appointments and arrange to meet, and so on. We assume that a job that will take half an hour today will, all other things being equal, take just as long tomorrow, and that half an hour today is just as long as half an hour tomorrow. We shall call this homogenous, uniform, dateable time by the Greek term *chronos*[6].

Time as *chronos* can be interpreted in a number of ways philosophically. We can understand time, as Newton himself tended to, as something that is objectively given, as an inevitable precondition of our existence and of our actions. In this view, time is there even if we are not. Kant, however, who wrote the first part of his *Critique of Pure Reason* to give Newtonian physics a philosophical foundation, interprets time subjectively. According to him, time is a representation, one that we cannot avoid making[7].

Time must always be perceived by a subject. But the various points of access to time imply different locations of the subject: the 'chronicler' of *chronos* lists events without studying their internal connection to one another (causality, interaction). His or her approach to time consists in allocating a temporal marker to events, and order is achieved by establishing a temporal sequence of facts.

8.3.2 The time of fulfilment: kairos

For Newton and Kant alike time is 'empty'. Thus in his *Critique of Pure Reason* Kant speaks of 'pure intuition' (1855: 22) which must first be filled, as it were – with things, events or 'phenomena'. This conception of time is readily apparent, yet it is also one-sided and abstract. It contains no reference to the subject in his or her actual everyday life or capacity to act. In contrast to this and with specific regard to action, there is an idea of time that is central to the philosophy of antiquity and especially to the New Testament, namely, the 'right time' for doing something; it is qualitatively different from other kinds of time. The Greek language calls this kind of time *kairos*, a term we wish to adopt here.

The expression *kairos* serves to emphasise that certain times stand out qualitatively from others. When we look at *kairos*, time is not homogenous as it is when we look at *chronos*, absolute time, which always stays the same. It is *kairos* we have in mind when we say: 'The time to sow is now and not in one or two months' time'. *Kairos* – the right moment[8] – is what is good or 'useful' about time, as Aristotle says in his *Nichomachean Ethics* (2014: I, 4; 1096a26 f.). Because the meaning of action always lies in goodness or in striving for goodness, the person acting must heed the goodness of time and always stay alert to the demands of this 'right moment' (2014: II, 2; 1104a8 f.).

Thus unlike the absolute time of *chronos*, *kairos* is always related to action. To this extent it always has a subjective component. If there is no person acting with certain goals or purposes, there is no *kairos*, no right moment. But *kairos* is not only subjective. When we speak of *kairos* we are speaking about the fact that when we establish purposes and pursue goals, human meaning encounters a world that is itself meaningful and objective. It is for this reason indeed that there is such a thing as the right or the wrong time. Either we act at the right moment or else too soon or too late; we do something for too short a time, or for the right length of time, or for too long. All these are determinations which make no sense in the absolute time of Newtonian physics.

The time we call *kairos*, then, is non-homogenous as it distinguishes between the right and the wrong moment. But it is more than this: different moments (*kairoi*) themselves differ qualitatively from one another to the extent that different times are the times for different actions. This is the meaning of the following lines found in the Book of Ecclesiastes (the words of 'the Philosopher'):

> To every thing there is a season (*chronos*), and a time (*kairos*) to every purpose under the heaven:
>
> A time to be born, and a time to die; a time to plant, and a time to pluck up that which is planted;
>
> A time to kill, and a time to heal; a time to break down, and a time to build up;
>
> A time to weep, and a time to laugh; a time to mourn, and a time to dance;
>
> A time to cast away stones, and a time to gather stones together; a time to embrace, and a time to refrain from embracing;
>
> [...] a time to keep silence, and a time to speak;
>
> A time to love, and a time to hate; a time of war, and a time of peace.
>
> (Ecclesiastes 3, 1–8)[9]

These times, or *kairoi*, are not comparable with one another, as they are the right times or moments to do different things: the time for gathering stones together is not the time to throw them away. What these right times *do* have, however, is a certain duration; they have their place within *chronos* and to this extent can be compared with one another, namely, in relation to their respective duration and to what occurs earlier and what later[10].

8.3.3 The time of Aristotle's physics: inherent time and inherent dynamics

Kairos is the right time, the 'right moment', for doing something specific. It is this that distinguishes it in qualitative terms from every other time and every other moment. But how can we recognise the right moment or know what is to be done at a certain time? This question poses a problem for the faculty of judgement, as it too is a matter of subsumption: *kairos* must be subsumed beneath a certain activity. As 'the Philosopher' says, there is 'a time to heal' and 'a time to kill'. Equally, *kairos* must be located within the all-encompassing universal time of *chronos*: the 'time to heal' is today, or tomorrow, or in a month, etc. That means we have to be able to date *kairos*.

There is no general way of saying exactly how this subsumption can be achieved. All we can do is look once again for bridging principles (cf. Section 7.6.2) that make it possible or easier to achieve such a subsumption and reach a correct judgement. In the following we seek to provide a sound rationale for two hypotheses:

1 The Aristotelian conception of time can be understood as such a bridging principle. We refer to this using the terms *inherent time* and *inherent dynamic.*
2 The stocks framework can be regarded as one aspect of this Aristotelian conception of time, which is related to action in a specific way. It is on the basis of this conception of time that we seek to elaborate the practical significance of the stocks framework.

Unlike Newton or Kant, Aristotle has no concept of an absolute time that is empty and has to be filled from the outside, as it were. His understanding of time assumes that we only become aware of time when we observe something moving or changing. Thus time for Aristotle is essentially related to motion. In his *Physics* he describes time as something that belongs to motion, as the (measured) number of the motion according to an earlier and a later time (Aristotle 1993: IV, 11; 219b2 ff.). Time relates relatively to motion because time is 'not apart from alteration' without motion and cannot exist without motion (ibid.: 218b21). This is why time and motion are mutually related to one another – or, to use Aristotle's words:

> Not only do we measure change by time, but time by change also, because they are defined by one another. The time defines the change, being its number, and the change the time. (1993: IV, 12; 220b15–18)

What is special about the Aristotelian theory of time is that Aristotle grounds time in motion. His *concept of motion* is rather unique, however. In comparison with today's commonplace understanding it displays two peculiarities.

- The first peculiarity is a terminological one. Motion for Aristotle refers not only to a localised movement but to any externally perceptible process of change, such as growth or decline, arising and passing – in other words, any change at all (cf. Spaemann and Löw 1985: 58 f.). In the debate about time Aristotle makes no distinction between motion and change (see e.g. ibid.: 111). According to him, then, any dynamic of change is to be regarded as motion.
- Unlike modern physics, Aristotle understands motion in consistently teleological terms, that is, in terms of a goal that is either immanent to motion or is posited for it from the outside. Every motion conveyed to a body from the outside has its goal in a state of rest. Arising and passing away likewise have a goal, as do growth and decline and any change in which something becomes something else and, in doing so, completes or perfects this change. Motions and changes are never endless[11]. At the same time, their end is not random – or rather, it is random only when the motions are ended by some outside influence. This means that all motions have a time that is *inherent* to them. They have a certain duration whose length can fluctuate more or less and which at times occupies a quite specific place within *chronos*, as when plants blossom or fruits ripen only at certain times of the year. We refer to this as the *inherent*

> *time* or the *inherent dynamic* of motions. A seed, for example, requires a specific amount of time to become a fully developed plant; grape juice always needs the same amount of time to become wine – and so on. To put it another way, in Aristotle's view all motions have their own temporal order, an inherent time which in turn has its place within *chronos*. Any action needs to be guided by this order because this inherent time determines the right time to act. This is why there is also a specific relationship between this inherent time of motions and the time of action related to the right moment, *kairos*.

Both the natural world and the social world are, for Aristotle, a world of motions which mutually influence one another. These motions, as we have said, are conceptualised in teleological terms, that is, in terms of their end point. They are all determined by the act of striving towards a goal, and they can be facilitated, impeded or even blocked by other motions. For Aristotle neither the social world nor the non-human world is a set of interrelationships that is strictly determined. This is why they display not only regularity but also contingency; everything can be other than it is. And this is why this world is accessible to action with its goals and purposes – action can change things within it. Among the motions mentioned by Aristotle is human action, driven by human striving for a good or for goodness per se. Human action can become incorporated into the motions of natural things or social relations in such a way that it relates meaningfully to the motions of things in nature and society. Or else it can fail whenever the good that is being sought or the way of striving for the good is not in accordance with these motions. It is not possible to sail directly against the wind, but it is possible to make use of an unfavourable wind direction by sailing diagonally to it ('tacking' in sailing terms).

As soon as the inherent dynamic or inherent time of motions comes into play, there is a right moment, a *kairos*. Fruits must be harvested when they are ripe, not before and not after they have become rotten. In contrast to this, there is generally no such *kairos* in completely uniform motions.

Kairos – the right time for the right action – thus depends on the inherent time of things or on the specific inherent dynamics by which they change; it also depends on the order in which these inherent times and dynamics are related to one another (on this point, cf. Section 11.2.2). What needs to be borne in mind here is that action itself possesses inherent time. Statements such as 'there is a time for everything [every action]' and 'there is a time for all things' express this notion of order.

8.3.4 The practical dimension of the stocks framework, or the stocks framework as a heuristic

The question that always arises in relation to taking action is the right time to do so. It is a question that concerns the faculty of judgement, as we noted above. The general principle on which judgement proceeds here is a proposition such as 'to every thing there is [...] a time'. This principle is initially a rather general one that consequently offers no real assistance when it comes to making a decision. After all, we will want to know when the right time is and which time is appropriate for this or that. If we are to be assisted in our decision making we need more than just a general principle: we need a specific heuristic. We will now show that the stocks framework provides just such a heuristic.

Let us return to the general principle 'to every thing there is a time'. We can understand this in two ways, depending on whether we are focusing on *kairos* or on the inherent dynamic of things. On the one hand it means that things have their own very specific point in time, their *kairos* – sowing has to be done in the springtime, harvesting in the autumn – and on the other that they have their (own inherent) *span* of time, as when the Riesling grape requires a hundred days from flowering to ripening in order to develop its full aroma. In this case we say that the development of the Riesling has a particular inherent dynamic or inherent time. As we have already noted, *kairos* and inherent dynamic do not exist independently of one another. Rather the right moment, *kairos*, always depends upon the web of relations among things and their own inherent times and dynamics. This insight emerged from Aristotle's discussion of time and it is why, in order to hit upon the right moment in time, these inherent times need to be estimated correctly. This is precisely what the stocks framework does: it focuses on these inherent times and on the inherent dynamic of things.

The stocks framework was initially introduced as a theoretical concept: this concept can be used to study and describe any objects, material or immaterial, in terms of their quantitative and qualitative dynamics over time. It is the general perspective we adopt when working with this framework that we shall now focus on. This perspective is directed at stocks and persistence, that is, towards the temporal dynamic of things. All stocks have their own inherent dynamic, namely, their own time which is beyond our capacity to control or manipulate. Perhaps we can influence the intractability of inherent time, but we cannot ignore it, let alone overcome it or eliminate it.

Conversely, however, the inherent time of stocks is of crucial significance in relation to our actions: not only does it determine what the right action at the right time is; it can also help or hinder that action and the process of achieving its purposes. In other words, the inherent times or dynamics of various things – be they material stocks of natural resources or pollutants, be they institutions or capital stocks – determine *kairos* by virtue of the web of relationships in which they exist; they determine when we need to do what in order to achieve a certain goal. The stocks perspective provides a kind of grid of coordinates in which such temporal structures become clear. For this reason it is especially well-suited to ascertain the conditions and the options for our action in temporal terms. It can thus be understood as a heuristic with a practical element. This is the essence of what we referred to above as the *practical dimension of the stocks framework*.

The proposition 'to every thing there is a time' expresses a perspective on the world which we might think of as being a *sense of time*. This sense of time or, as we might also say, this feeling is the prerequisite for being able to adopt the stocks perspective. Conversely, though, testing this perspective is one way to school and to develop this sense of time. In the following section we present two examples in which this sense of time (along with an implicit stocks perspective) can be recognised.

Box 8.1 Three different concepts of time and the practical dimension of the stocks framework

We identify three distinct concepts of time:

Chronos is a conception of time that guides us in our everyday lives and is the foundation of modern science. Time here is a homogenous continuum: it contains uniform moments and spans – in other words, an hour today is just as long as an hour at any other time. This continuous, homogenous time can be represented on a timeline on which events can be assigned a date.

Kairos refers to the time for action and means the 'right moment', the 'right time' to act. *Kairos* differs fundamentally from *chronos* in that it is non-homogenous and discontinuous: times and moments in time differ qualitatively from one another. The right time (or temporal structure) to act is distinct from all other times. Different *kairoi* for different actions are all unique. Each *kairos* can be dated on the timescale of *chronos*.

Inherent time and inherent dynamic refer to typical spans of time or temporal structures of processes of change relating to objects. This concept of time goes back to Aristotle, who links time inextricably with motion. It includes every form of change, e.g. the growth of a plant. In the Aristotelian view change is always also teleological, i.e. it is directed towards a goal. All 'motions' – processes of change – have their own times, natural sequences and spans of time. These are referred to as 'inherent time' and 'inherent dynamic'.

The stocks framework has a *practical dimension* which is related to the temporality of action. The important point when engaging in action is to find the *kairos*. To the extent that *kairos* always refers to the particular and *chronos* to the general aspect of time (all moments in time and spans of time are qualitatively the same), we are faced here with a problem of subsumption in relation to the faculty of judgement. In order to solve the problem, a *sense of time* which allows the person concerned to recognise the *kairos* is helpful. In other words, a sense of time is helpful for recognising when, how and within what time limits a set of actions needs to be planned.

A sense of time is developed by contemplating stocks. Stocks act as a heuristic and are a bridging principle for purposes of judgement in relation to time. Why is this so? *Kairos*, the right time to act, depends on the inherent times of the circumstances affecting an action, on the inherent dynamics with which these circumstances change, and on the order in which inherent times and dynamics are related to one another. If we look at the circumstances of an action or set of actions within the stocks perspective then these inherent times and dynamics become visible in terms of their relationship to a possible *kairos*. This is the practical dimension of the stocks framework.

8.4 A sense of time: two examples

How are we to imagine this sense of time? For the purpose of illustration we have selected two examples that lend themselves particularly well to examining the notion of a sense of time. One of them is taken from the world of literature, namely, the example of Marshall Kutusov from Leo Tolstoy's *War and Peace*. It illustrates particularly clearly what we mean by a sense of time. The second example comes from more recent German environmental politics but is far enough in the past to facilitate a kind of concluding evaluation.

8.4.1 Field Marshal Kutusov in Tolstoy's War and Peace

Leo Tolstoy's novel *War and Peace* (1952) describes the life of a number of Russian noblemen and women in the years between 1805 and 1813 when, apart from some short breaks in hostilities, Russia was at war with Napoleon Bonaparte's France. This description of individuals' destinies is intertwined in the novel with the description of the war itself, which forms not only a backdrop but is an object in itself to which Tolstoy devotes no less attention. The Russian campaign conducted by the French army in 1812 takes up the largest part of the story in this description. The novel portrays this campaign as a dispute between two men. On the one side we have the French Emperor Napoleon Bonaparte – a man for whom Tolstoy feels neither sympathy nor respect – hurriedly surging forwards; and on the other side we have the elderly Russian Field Marshal Mikhail Illarionovich Golenishchev Kutusov, supreme commander of the Russian army, who is despised by Napoleon and is subject to derision even in his own circles.

In Tolstoy's story neither Napoleon nor Kutusov himself are heroes in the conventional sense – that is, as individuals engaged in *action*. While Napoleon always seems to have the upper hand, in reality he is merely a man driven by events and is – unlike Kutusov – blind to the real situation. Meanwhile Kutusov who, unlike Napoleon, sees what is really going on, does not act at all: he neglects to do things which the situation seems to demand. And whenever he actually does do something, his intention is to make others *not* do these apparently obvious things rather than to actively do something. Kutusov's main preoccupation lies in keeping his generals from engaging in battle as far as he is able to. He 'employed his whole strength to restrain the Russian army from useless engagements' and 'to restrain his troops from attacking' (Tolstoy 1952: 565).

We are no historians and cannot really assess Tolstoy's descriptions and judgements about the warring parties. Neither is this important for our purposes here. Tolstoy's portrayal is, of course, stylised. And it is precisely in this stylisation that the things we are especially interested in with regard to Kutusov's behaviour come to the fore.

Kutusov constantly causes others to be disgruntled with him. And this disgruntlement appears well-founded, because his strange passivity seems not at all to suit a field marshal. When Napoleon marches with his troops on Moscow, the Russian army under Kutusov's command repeatedly withdraws, leaving Moscow at the mercy of the French. Unlike his generals, Kutusov does not want to do battle with Napoleon. The Battle of Borodino on August 26, 1812 just a few miles outside Moscow comes about against Kutusov's will: he stands and faces the enemy here – according to Tolstoy's portrayal – only because the Czar and the generals urge him to do so. After the battle, in which the Russian army at least manages to avoid defeat, he withdraws further and ultimately cedes Moscow to the enemy without a fight. When the French army eventually leaves Moscow, Kutusov limits himself to pursuing it with his own army, but so sluggishly that one could hardly call it a hot pursuit: 'when they reported to him that Murat's troops were in retreat he ordered an advance, though at every hundred paces he halted for three quarters of an hour' (1952: 570).

Kutusov's passivity meets with Tolstoy's unequivocal approval. Why? Kutusov sees something which eludes most of the officers around him and even the Czar himself. What he sees are temporal dynamics, their inertia and their resistance to influence. There is no way Kutusov can put up an army as strong as the French army which, according to Tolstoy, is 800,000 men strong at the start. The Russian army is far inferior to the French one in terms of numbers, discipline and experience. And Kutusov knows that nothing of this will change up to the end of the entire campaign – recruiting, arming and training so many men takes time. This inertia and slowness of processes which impedes action is up against unpredictable dynamics that are barely capable of being influenced. The huge French army can do no other than march on Moscow and eventually take it – not even a battle will prevent it from doing so:

> And meanwhile, the very next morning after the battle, the French army advanced of itself upon the Russians, carried forward by the force of its own momentum now seemingly increased in inverse proportion to the square of the distance from its aim. (ibid.: 471)

At the same time, Kutusov knows that the *Grande Armée* will be decimated by the difficulties of the march – disease, hunger and cold – and that it will lose far more soldiers that way than through any battles:

> Why fight, why block the road, losing our own men and inhumanly slaughtering unfortunate wretches? What is the use of that, when a third of their army has melted away on the road from Moscow to Vyázma without any battle? (ibid.: 587)

And he knows that time is against Napoleon and in his own favour. An attacker needs success in a relatively short period of time – either capitulation or at least an offer of peace from the enemy. Since neither is forthcoming Napoleon is not able to reap any benefits from taking Moscow. Ultimately he has to withdraw, leaving Russia defeated, even though he has not lost a single battle.

What ultimately defeated Napoleon was not the Russian army and not Kutusov, but time. And it is Kutusov – 'whose motto was "Patience and Time"' (ibid.: 620) – who recognises this and is therefore victorious in the end. Kutusov displays that sense of time about which we spoke above. It is this sense which distinguishes Kutusov from his generals (at least, if we are to believe Tolstoy's narrative):

> 'They must understand that we can only lose by taking the offensive. Patience and time are my warriors, my champions', thought Kutúzov. He knew that an apple should not be plucked while it is green. It will fall of itself when ripe … (ibid.: 584)

There are two aspects of the description of Kutusov in *War and Peace* that we would like to highlight:

1 The generals differ from Kutusov not in the fact that they judge the inherent dynamic of things any differently from him. They do not expect Napoleon to need longer to reach Moscow or to be able to hold the city for longer. It is not that Kutusov judges the temporal dynamic of the campaign correctly and the generals wrongly; in fact, they fail to judge it at all – they do not even consider these kinds of things. They have no 'sense of time', or else they make no use of it if they do. They think in terms of troop strength, equipment and weaponry. For them, victory and defeat depend on battles won or lost, on discontinuous moments, and not on the duration of time. They are not sensitive to time *as time*. But Kutusov is.
   It is possible to judge temporal dynamics rightly or wrongly. We can either make a correct judgement or be mistaken. But to be able to judge at all as Kutusov judges, one needs a sense of time. This sense – unlike a judgement made about temporal dynamics themselves – cannot be either true or false: either one has this sense of time or one does not[12].
2 The sense of time comprises an aspect of the faculty of judgement that we referred to in Section 7.6.3 as feeling. It is that part of the faculty of judgement that is pre-conceptual or non-conceptual and which therefore cannot be communicated directly. For this reason Kutusov cannot make himself properly understood to those around him. He does not tell them what he sees and knows. 'He could not tell them [his officers] what we say now' (ibid.: 587). Why not? And why do we 'say it today'? Kutusov could not assume that his officers would understand the notion that temporal dynamics are the decisive factor in a war against a far mightier enemy. And he was not able to prove that this is so. Yet we are able to say this today because history in the sense of real and contingent events has shown (according to Tolstoy's portrayal) that Kutusov was right. When it comes to issues that involve judgement, we are reliant on examples from which we can learn. Such examples are often the key to awakening our understanding of temporal dynamics.

8.4.2 German policy on water pollution control in the 1970s

We now turn from a work of 19th century literature to real-life environmental politics of the 1970s. During this period strenuous efforts were undertaken in the western industrialised countries to make marked improvements to the condition of soil, air and water – with varying results. The endeavours made in the US and in West Germany regarding water pollution control are particularly instructive in relation to our concerns here[13].

Environmental policy in the US had particularly ambitious goals. In 1972 the Clean Water Act came into force, its aim being to ensure that surface waters should be largely free of pollutants within a very short period of time. The regulations contained in the law, however, proved to be impracticable. Two things led to a failure to implement the law. One was resistance to the ambitious regulations put up by powerful interest groups. This resistance might have been overcome had it not been for the other factor, namely, that the necessary water pollution control technologies – a prerequisite for the law to be effective – were not available. The law was revised for the first time in 1977. This revision was so far-reaching that it effectively constituted a withdrawal of the original law: the original legal requirements were now so diluted they were barely recognisable.

German environmental policy was somewhat more cautious in its approach. In 1976 the *Wasserhaushaltsgesetz* (Federal Water Act) was revised, in the course of which the *Abwasserabgabegesetz* (Waste Water Charges Act) was adopted, which stipulated that pollutants emitted into water bodies would be subject to a financial charge. This charge was to be levied for the first time in 1981, however, after a gap of five years. Furthermore, the level of the charge was quite reasonable to begin with; it was gradually to increase, starting at 12 German marks per unit of pollution in 1981 and reaching 70 German marks in 1997.

The Waste Water Charges Act of 1976 prompted critique from many environmental economists, who demanded that the charges should be set on the basis of the polluter pays principle: those who emit pollutants should have to pay the actual environmental costs involved. The Act fell far short of this standard, however. One reason for this was that the pollutant charge did not follow the cost covering principle because the external effects of pollutant emissions on the environment were not included when calculating the level of the charge. Another was that this charge itself was initially not even levied to its full amount; and, finally, investments in purification plants could be set off against the charges owed. From an environmental economics point of view, then, the waste water charge was inefficient, as the polluter was not given sufficient incentives to reduce harmful emissions.

The widespread critique directed by environmental economists at the apparently tentative and half-hearted water pollution control policy of the West German government of the day might make the latter seem something of an 'environmental Kutusov', failing to take a decisive stand against water polluters and instead pulling back in the face of their lobby's onslaught. Yet the introduction of the waste water charge was by no means ineffective; in fact it led to a marked reduction in water pollution – even prior to the charge being levied. The 5-year period of grace proved to be beneficial: local authorities and industry undertook great efforts and invested considerable sums of money in the construction of purification plants so that they would have to pay as few charges as possible from 1981 onwards. Between 1975 and 1979, for example, Baden-Württemberg's industry reduced its emissions by 40 per cent (Faber et al. 1989: 56). The comparatively long period of grace and the initially moderate level of the charge also helped in overcoming resistance to the law and in fostering acceptance for a new economic instrument of environmental politics.

Taking a less favourable perspective, one could describe the water pollution control policy of the 1970s as a compromise among different interests that was achieved at the expense of the environment. And this is indeed what happened. However, it would almost certainly not have been possible to introduce a cost-effective charge straight away. As it was, water pollution control policy was a compromise that achieved a great deal in the long term and averted the failure that befell the US Clean Water Act.

Thus German environmental policy was successful at this point and was obviously the right one. Why is this so? This is not immediately apparent from the perspective of neoclassical environmental economics. Yet by applying the stocks framework it is possible to show why this policy was able to achieve its goals. The charge was designed as an economic instrument to create an incentive to reduce harmful emissions, yet it took effect even before it was introduced. The emitters built a *stock* of purification plants, due to which they were able to reduce considerably the amount of pollution emitted[14]. This in turn fostered acceptance of the charge. The policy can be further interpreted as reflecting the policy makers' realisation that, in creating a charge for pollution emissions, they were effectively creating a new institution which first had to prove its worth. Institutions take time until they are truly taken for granted and guide people's actions and behaviours in a habitualised way. From this point of view it was a clever move not to levy the charge in full at first and to keep resistance to a minimum.

Patience and time, Kutusov's two 'brothers-in-arms', also seem to have been the two main champions of German water pollution control policy. How so? We hesitate to put the relative success of German policy down to German politicians and environmental officials being cleverer than their US colleagues – this would surely be impolite and is hardly a workable research hypothesis. Nonetheless we can mention a few factors which proved favourable in terms of a *sense of time*. First, German administration officials across the board display considerable quality and expertise; this is essentially due to institutional circumstances and itself constitutes a kind of stock. In addition, though, another institutional stock can be seen as having contributed to this success: German politics is characterised by a high degree of interpenetration between different levels of decision making (Petersen and Faber 2000). This means that whenever policies are formulated, the process includes representatives of all the relevant interests involved, both public and private, in some way. This leads to two outcomes:

- The ministerial administration, which occupies a central position in the structures of political/policy coordination (*Politikverflechtung*), has access to all the relevant information.
- When policy is formulated (a task largely accomplished by the ministerial administration) the potential objections of other stakeholders are anticipated and taken into account. This results in preliminary policy documents which are generally capable of commanding a consensus; this in turn makes resistance to them as difficult as possible while at the same time ensuring that the capacity for consensus is stretched up to its limits.

The complex structures of *political/policy coordination* in Germany obviously favour policy making that proceeds patiently and hesitantly, rather like Kutusov the 'falterer'. Equally these structures of policy coordination encourage politicians to wait for the right moment to undertake certain initiatives. Viewed from a less favourable standpoint, however, they can also be held responsible for a certain ponderousness and a relatively static mode of politics.

8.5 Conclusion: the stocks framework and judgement

The two examples just discussed outline a mode of action which is guided above all by circumstances and persistent factors relating to time. When a situation demanding action is affected by such circumstances and resistance, the response is one guided by the virtue of patience. Patience does not simply mean putting things off or hesitating. A patient individual is prepared to act, but he or she will wait for the right moment to do so, for the *kairos*. Recognising this moment demands attentiveness especially towards those things which the stocks perspective brings to the fore. When this perspective is adopted, questions such as the following suggest themselves in relation to the situation at hand: Where is there persistence or stability that is durable enough to constitute a decisive factor within the time horizon of one's own actions? What kind of time spans, what kind of duration should we reckon with for certain processes and changes? Can we influence this duration in any way? Or do we need to go along with these processes and the pace at which they occur, and merely try to adapt to them?

Of course we are not claiming that Tolstoy's Kutusov or the officials responsible for German environmental policy were explicitly adopting the stocks perspective. But we can say that, through their actions, they provided answers to questions that would also have been suggested by a stocks perspective. At any rate it ought to have become clear that, within the practical dimension of the concept of stocks, the stocks perspective is not a scientific model; rather, it is a kind of prior principle which guides both action as well as scholarly research, much as Kant speaks of a 'heuristic principle' (2001: 280). It is a principle pertaining to judgement and would, in the terms of Karl Popper's *Logic of Scientific Discovery* (2005), be considered a part of epistemic psychology.

The concept of stock, the stocks perspective and the stocks framework thus play a dual role in sustainability policy, namely, as a kind of instrument and as an internal principle, a *bridging principle* for purposes of judgement (Section 7.6.2) in relation to time.

- In its theoretical dimension the stocks framework is an instrument of judgement. In this regard judgement considers which aspects of a given situation are the ones to which the concept of stock can be applied. These might be pollutants, resources, goods or possibly institutions and patterns of behaviour. Equally, judgement must determine which of these aspects-as-stocks are relevant to the actions required to achieve a given purpose – in other words, which of them are conducive (or not conductive) to this purpose. The theoretical – one might say scientific – stocks framework is then applied to these stocks. Judgement draws on scientific analyses of stocks in order to determine the temporal dynamics involved as precisely as possible and then to make the right decisions; judgement itself does not play a part in these analyses, however.

- The situation is different with regard to the practical dimension of the stocks framework. Here, as we have seen, the stocks framework explicates the sense of time. Using this sense we can select an appropriate temporal horizon within which we can relate our own goals of action to objective temporal processes and developments in a meaningful way. For example, the temporal horizon of German water pollution control policy with regard to establishing the waste water charge was based not on years but on decades; it was this that enabled the policy to be successful. By contrast, the US environmental policy that produced the 1972 Clean Water Act and was based on much shorter timescales encountered severe setbacks.

Thus the stocks perspective is capable of developing and schooling a sense of time. In doing so it clearly leads to better decision making. The examples we present in Chapters 9 and 10 can offer only a practical illustration of this. This being so, in Chapter 11 we attempt to generalise the insights that arise from the stocks perspective, as far as this is possible, and develop them into a formal heuristic.

Notes

1 This serves as the conceptual and methodological foundations for the subsequent case studies and, in particular, for the sustainability policy heuristic described in Chapter 11.

2 The studies on time contained in the present book and encapsulated in this chapter are based on a longstanding tradition of research on the concept of time conducted under the auspices of Professor Malte Faber at Heidelberg University, where the authors spent an important part of their academic careers. To mention just a few publications from this tradition: Faber (1986), Faber and Proops (1998), Faber et al. (1999), Schiller (2002) and Winkler (2003).

3 It includes the difficulty, as yet unresolved, of how to comprehend the act of measuring time. To put it simply, the difficulty lies in the fact that we measure time by means of a clock, be it an egg-timer, a pendulum-driven clock or a clock whose function is based on the vibrations of an atom. Thus all clocks basically possess some kind of movement that we have to think of as being *regular*, as otherwise the clock would not be able to provide any reliable measurements. But how do we know that the movement of a clock is regular? This could only be confirmed by another measurement using another clock, of whose regularity we again require assurance, and so on *ad infinitum*.

4 Martin Heidegger spoke derogatorily in this regard of a 'vulgar concept of time' (Heidegger 1996: 404).

5 Relativist physics has relinquished the Newtonian assumption of time being the same everywhere. Here, time is no longer an independent variable but is dependent on movement and gravitation. But even the time of relativist physics is homogenous and mathematically ascertainable. Otherwise the various times in coordinate systems moved against one another would not be able to be related to one another using the formulas of the Lorentz transformation.

6 This concept of time, '*chronos*', is the same one we used in our definitions and explanations regarding the concept of material stocks in Chapter 4.

7 'Time is a necessary representation, lying at the foundation of all our intuitions' (Kant 1855: 28). We have to imagine anything we imagine at all as existing in time (and in space). We cannot say that time exists outside our faculty of knowledge and representation. This is why Kant calls 'time [...] the formal condition à priori of all phenomena whatsoever' (ibid.: 30). Time is *transcendental* because it is not an empirical given and therefore its concept is 'not an empirical conception' (ibid.: 28); thus we have to assume time as a 'pure intuition' in every (empirical) experience.

8 It should be noted here that acting in complex situations, as is the case with problems associated with sustainability, generally occurs in a process-oriented way, in other words, over an extended period of time. In such cases, *kairos* refers not so much to a single point in time as to a series of distinct actions.

9 The Septuagint, the Greek translation of the Hebrew Bible from the second century B.C., uses the contrasting terms *chronos* and *kairos*.

10 *Kairos* has a particular meaning in the New Testament, referring to the fullness of time brought about by Jesus Christ. The Apostle Paul in particular called upon people to allow their actions to be determined entirely by this kairos and to 'redeem' the time of *kairos* (*exagorazein*; Ephesians 5, 16).

11 According to Aristotle, one exception to this is the circular motion of stars and planets (Spaemann and Löw 1985: 59).

12 That is why a judgement based on such a sense of time is only partly wrong, even if it is in error. The error is, as Wieland (2001: 122) notes, only partial. This is because a judgement is already true by virtue of being a judgement at all.

13 For the following discussion, cf. Brown and Johnson (1984).

14 Gawel et al. (2011) show that this mechanism is effective even if the level of the charge is not optimal. This is important because often it is not possible to know what the optimal level is. The long-term cost burden provides an incentive to innovate, which leads over the long term to greater cost savings than are possible using the available technologies. Gawel et al.'s argument differs from that found in the usual environmental economics textbooks in that the factors ignorance and dynamics are taken explicitly into account.

Part III

Applying the stocks framework

Introduction to Parts III and IV

We use the term sustainable development to refer to the long-term positive development of a system, where 'positive' is defined according to the context-specific meaning of 'sustainability'. Thus looking at temporal trends over long periods of time is therefore essential to the notion of sustainability. In the course of this book so far we have elaborated the stocks framework, which can be used to describe long-term developments in nature and society in order to obtain information useful for designing sustainability policy. As we have seen, the stocks framework consists essentially of three elements, namely, the key concepts of stock (*Bestand*), time and judgement:

- *Stock*: A stock is something inert, persistent and stable. It is precisely this durability that suggests the suitability of studying stocks when it comes to establishing the sustainability – or otherwise – of a system. As we elucidated in detail in Chapters 4, 5 and 6, a stock may consist of something material, such as a stock of pollutants, or it may be of a non-material nature, such as the Energy Tax Act or other institutions.
- *Time*: In the stocks framework we make a distinction between three different concepts of time – *chronos*, *kairos* and *inherent dynamic* (Chapter 8). By *chronos* we mean time which passes continuously and can thus be measured. Stocks are characterised by their own typical duration and their own characteristic development. Taken together, we refer to these as the *inherent dynamic* of a stock. The best opportunity and the right time (or time structure) for action – which we refer to as *kairos* – emerges from the dynamic of a system, which in turn is essentially determined by the inherent dynamics of the stocks involved. Taken together, these concepts provide an opportunity not only to analyse the way policy processes develop but also to generate information that can facilitate targeted intervention – action – in the course of things.
- *Judgement*: The concept of 'judgement' draws attention to the fact that policy makers need certain faculties if they are going to make use of knowledge about complex situations and dynamics for their decisions and actions in order to

pursue objectives such as sustainable development. The stocks framework is geared towards honing precisely these faculties in the context of sustainability problems, and it does so by providing a heuristic.

These three components come together in the practical dimension of the stocks framework to form a sense of time (Section 8.3.4).

Philosophical considerations are crucial in developing and elaborating the stocks framework, and indeed these were the subject of the second part of this book. Now, in the third and fourth part, we seek to draw out clearly the concepts we have developed by looking at a number of practical problems relating to sustainability policy in Germany. We do so first by examining two case studies.

The first exploratory case study in Chapter 9 is an example of successful sustainability policy studied in retrospect and over an extended period of time, namely, the remediation of large-scale contaminations in Saxony-Anhalt since the peaceful revolution of 1989. The way in which the problem of brownfields has been dealt with in this federal state can in many respects be regarded as a success story. A set of regulations was established that provide conducive conditions for the successful remediation of contaminated land over the long term. The case study follows the development of this area of policy over a period of some 20 years and analyses the factors that succeeded in prompting institutional change. The key factors here were the will and the capacity of key individuals to recognise opportunities for a good solution and to find a way of implementing it. It can be said that these individuals possessed judgement and a sense of time. The concepts that make up the stocks framework help us to understand why sustainability policy was successful in this example.

The second exploratory case study in Chapter 10 deals with German land management policy. Starting out from the German government's objective, stated in its sustainability strategy from 2002, to reduce the amount of new land designated for residential and traffic uses from 100 hectares per day in 2007 to just 30 hectares a day from 2020 onwards, this study is more clearly oriented towards the future. Using the stocks concept we examine whether this objective can be achieved and, if so, how. The study looks at a few important material stocks and institutions, analysing on the basis of their history the inherent dynamic of the individual stocks and of the system itself and drawing conclusions from this in terms of intervention options and windows of opportunity to reduce land use. Specifically, we explore what action is currently required and what options for action currently exist. In the context of this case study a number of elements are developed, based on the stocks framework, for a generalised approach that makes it possible to develop sound sustainability policies.

In Chapter 11 we reflect on the experience gained from the two exploratory case studies. The elements of the stocks framework are drawn together and generalised to form a *heuristic*, i.e. a general (theoretical and practical) approach to sustainability problems. The aim of this heuristic is to generate an overall picture of a given sustainability problem, to define it clearly, to establish what action is required and to identify the available options for action. In consideration of the long-term nature of sustainability problems, the heuristic helps decision makers to develop a sense of time. It consists essentially of a series of steps that take the user through the analysis. Each step is accompanied by guidelines and rules for how to approach it.

The heuristic developed here is necessarily abstract. For this reason, in Chapter 12, it is applied by way of example to inland shipping policy in Germany. Chapter 13 summarises the nature of the heuristic (and the stocks framework) and discusses what contribution it might make towards more sustainable policy making.

9 Shaping institutional change in the course of contamination management in Saxony-Anhalt

with Mi-Yong Lee

9.1 Introduction

The 'real existing socialism' of the German Democratic Republic was notorious for neglecting environmental issues. The task of fulfilling the economic plan aimed at providing goods for people's daily needs took priority over effective environmental protection. Dangerous substances were often handled in inappropriate and negligent ways, waste was disposed of haphazardly and much-needed investments in environmental protection were neglected for decades. As a result of this it was no surprise when, after the peaceful revolution of 1989 leading to Germany's reunification, large amounts of pollution in the form of complex soil and water contamination came to light in the large industrial sites such as Bitterfeld and Leuna. A large number of these sites were immediately shut down after 1990 – not only because it proved to be uneconomical to keep them open but also in order to prevent any worsening of the environmental damage already done (Hentrich et al. 2000: 35).

Upon German unification the Federal Republic of Germany became the legal successor to the former East German state-run industries and so-called 'people's enterprises' (*Volkseigene Betriebe*). The German government wanted to privatise these firms quickly but found itself faced in particular with the problem that potential investors were exposed to the risk of the high costs of the remediation and prevention activities required, as property owners in (West) German environmental legislation are liable for the risks and damages caused by contamination even if they themselves have not caused it (SRU 1989: 204–205). This meant that it would not have been possible in practice to privatise those East German industrial and manufacturing facilities that contained contaminated waste. The institutional stock from 'the West' that was now applied to the new federal states – environmental legislation in its traditional practical form – was thus not suited to solving the problems that existed satisfactorily. Accordingly the remediation and privatisation of these contaminated sites occurred slowly during the first few years after 1989, despite formal exemption from liability and despite support funding from the government.

What was needed, then, was an effective means of organising remediation activities, securing government funding for them and, at the same time, ensuring that investors would be exempted from liability for the contamination. In Saxony-Anhalt a way was found to resolve these issues which involved a range of individuals and organisations, not least the environment ministry, and required several stages of development. In many respects – not least with regard to sustainability – the mechanisms developed can be regarded as a satisfactory institutional solution to the problem of inherited contaminants. Indeed it can be said that a solution was found whose structure fits well with the inherent dynamic of the problem, not least regarding the persistence of pollutant stocks and the expected long-term nature of remediation activities.

In this chapter we adopt a stocks perspective to examine this 'success story' and its origins over a period of about 20 years. Our aim is to discover which factors for success and broader conditions contributed to the institutional change that was required. We then seek to extrapolate some general conditions and guidelines from this for successful sustainability policy.

What becomes clear from this case study example is that certain individuals or groups of individuals with relevant interests and capabilities played an important role in achieving successful institutional change. For an individual or a group to be capable of prompting such change in institutional stocks, one necessary ingredient is the presence of certain external preconditions, namely, a particular combination of stocks. Another is that these individuals need to possess certain personal capabilities. In this regard, Faber et al. (1997: 459) mention the capacity to utilise their own expertise[1], Sabatier (1988) and Olsson et al. (2006) emphasise the ability to win over a political majority, while Baumgartner and Jones (2002) as well as van der Brugge et al. (2005) highlight the fact that these individuals need to be able to establish exactly what the problems are and to be creative in developing new options for solving them.

In this chapter we would like to discuss another capability that is important in prompting institutional change, one that is especially relevant in the context of – typically long-term – sustainability problems. This is the ability to anticipate temporal developments, i.e. the inherent dynamic of stocks and institutions, and to discover windows of opportunity (the *kairos*) for taking action. In Chapter 8 we called this specific form of judgement a 'sense of time'. The case study, which focuses on the problems surrounding inherited contaminants, shows how a group of individuals from political and administrative settings had just such a sense of time. They recognised the necessity of institutional transformation and had the will and the power to enact change. They utilised their sense of time to assess the inherent dynamic of the situation and to identify and make use of the right moment to intervene. To use the terms of the stocks framework, we could say that these individuals possessed a pronounced sensibility for stocks, for their inherent dynamics and for the resulting *kairos*.

The present case study evaluates a broad range of empirical material, including statistics, legal texts, grey literature and the websites of state authorities. The most important source, however, were conversations with the individuals who were directly involved in the developments. Extensive qualitative interviews were conducted in order to identify precisely how the institutional change occurred and what drove it. These interviews made it possible to gain an insight into the individuals' perceptions, motivations and ideas. Given the large amount of material collected (especially from the interviews) and the space available in this chapter, we can provide only a very limited selection here[2].

The present chapter is structured as follows. We begin in Section 9.2 by outlining the background details and history of the problem of inherited contamination in eastern Germany. Having explained how the soil and the groundwater in the former GDR came to be contaminated, we go on to elucidate how, following reunification, investors were exempted from their liability for inherited contamination and what problems this approach initially entailed. In Section 9.3 we conduct an inventory of stocks relating to the situation of contamination in Saxony-Anhalt and describe the improvements that have arisen from the most significant institutional changes. Based on interviews conducted with key figures during 2008 and 2009, we discuss in Section 9.4 the important factors in successful institutional change. Finally, in Section 9.5, we draw some conclusions.

9.2 The problem of inherited contamination in eastern Germany

9.2.1 Background information: environmental problems in the former GDR

The former GDR had inherited a diverse industrial infrastructure from the Third Reich. Parts of this infrastructure had originated in the mid-nineteeth century and included engineering facilities, broadcasting technology, electronics and aerospace industry facilities as well as large-scale organic chemistry industries (Ritschl 1995: 17). After the Second World War, heavy industry and the chemicals industry in particular were dismantled. During the 1960s and 1970s the remaining industries were subject to far-reaching processes of concentration and centralisation, manifested in the creation of large government-owned combines (ibid.: 26).

During the 1980s the former GDR's stock of industrial capital assets was based largely on technologically outdated facilities which could not be restored to international technical standards, not even by refitting them (Komar 1992: 116). The production methods used were inefficient and involved extensive inputs of raw materials, energy and labour. Dangerous substances were often dealt with inappropriately. Contaminated factory waste was dumped with no regard for safety. Accidents and so-called 'handling losses' (*Handhabungsverluste*) were common practice so that soils and groundwater were widely contaminated (Behrens 2007: 3; IFU 1990: 69). Pollution of this kind which arose in the past but still exists today is known as inherited contamination (*Altlasten*)[3]. This is comprised of stocks of substances which – depending on the extent of the contamination and the properties of the substances as well as on the geological and hydrological conditions – can only be removed over longer periods of time.

9.2.2 Exemption of investors from liability for environmental damage

Due to the seriousness and urgency of the environmental problems, a joint environment commission was set up by the two German environment ministries as early as February 1990 – shortly after the first free and democratic elections to the 'national chamber', or *Volkskammer* (former GDR parliament). On June 29, 1990, as the German Democratic Republic entered its final days, the Environmental Framework Act (*Umweltrahmengesetz*, URaG) was passed into law. This act contains a range of basic regulations on nature protection and also addresses the issues around inherited contamination. The institutional barrier to privatisation that such contamination represented for investors was presciently recognised at this stage. In order to counter this, a clause in the URaG was included to open up the option for exempting investors from liability for inherited contaminants:

> Purchasers of facilities serving commercial purposes or used in the context of business enterprises are not responsible for the damages caused by the operation of the facility prior to July 1, 1990 as long as the relevant administrative authority exempts them from responsibility in consultation with the supreme administrative authority of the *Land*. (URaG §4, Clause 3: Unification treaty, Appendix II, Chapter XII, Section III)

This exemption clause was intended to facilitate investment in cases where it would otherwise have not been undertaken due to the existing risk from inherited contamination. This was partly in order to boost economic development and partly to promote the reuse of land that had become derelict. The investigation and remediation costs for the property now owned by a private investor were paid for out of the public purse. Applications for exemption from liability had to be submitted by March 30, 1992.

Two years after reunification, on December 1, 1992, a regulation was established for dividing up the costs between the federal government and the new *Länder* in an 'Administrative agreement concerning the regulation of financing for inherited ecological contamination'. As an additional part of this agreement, so-called 'large-scale ecological projects' were introduced as a project category. These are characterised by the following features:

- On the suspect land there is a high probability of large-scale ecological risk caused by large-scale industrial activity in the past, with high potential for contamination. (Examples include the petroleum industry and chemicals industry.)
- The overall costs of remediation are estimated to be at least 100 m Germans marks (i.e. more than 50 m euros).
- The location is of great significance to the region's economic development.

While the federal government covered 60 per cent and the *Länder* 40 per cent of the costs for 'ordinary' remediation projects, they covered 75 per cent and 25 per cent respectively of the costs of the large-scale ecological projects (Seibel 2005: 392)[4].

In the first few months and years following reunification the 'Institute for the administration of national property held in trust' ('Trust' for short) took on a special role in the management of inherited contamination in the new federal states of the former GDR. From 1990 to the end of 1994 the main task of the Trust was to privatise the assets that had previously belonged to the GDR state (*volkseigenes Vermögen*), and this included providing real estate and land for economic purposes[5]. Due to the close connection between exemption from liability and privatisation the Trust was obviously entrusted with the administration of the federal government's financial contribution to the exemption[6]. Once the trust ceased operating, at the end of 1994, this task was taken over by the 'Federal Agency for Unification-Related Special Tasks' (*Bundesanstalt für vereinigungsbedingte Sonderaufgaben*, BvS)[7].

9.2.3 Problems associated with implementing the exemption from liability

Despite the rapidly agreed financing arrangement, it was not possible at first to encourage investment to a satisfactory extent or to conduct remediation measures. A key reason for this was that the federal government had to give its approval in all financial matters regarding exemption from liability. In practice this led to a dysfunctional administrative mix-up. Coordination between the central and regional state authorities responsible for these issues proved to be time consuming and prone to conflicts. The inspection and approval procedures operated by the public administration made a more flexible allocation of financial resources impossible. Greater flexibility of this kind would have been necessary, however, to respond appropriately to changes in ongoing remediation projects that typically occurred at short notice. Additionally, the exemption from liability for inherited contamination was a legislative novelty at that time and there were no precedents whatsoever regarding its practical implementation. The public administration in the new *Länder* was still in the process of being established and had insufficient capacity in terms of both human resources and specialist knowledge.

9.2.3.1 Difficulties with implementation at Länder level

The decision regarding whether or not exemption for inherited contamination should be given at all was taken by each federal state's government. After the application deadline of March 30, 1992 had passed the relevant state authorities had received a total of more than 70,000 applications (Eisenbarth 1995: 34; Wolf 2003). Exemption was granted by means of a so-called 'can' ordinance, which in turn was based on each *Land* weighing up the burdens and benefits that would accrue to the general public through such an exemption (Faensen-Thiebes and Müller 2008). In each case, then, it was up to the state authority to establish whether or not a hindrance to investment actually existed. If the costs of removing the damages were low in comparison with the volume of investment, no such hindrance was deemed to exist. But the state authorities were not prepared – in terms of either human resources or organisation – for this particular challenge. The existing administrative structures with their relatively inflexible budgetary management and hierarchical system of decision making and approval were ill-suited to deal with the complex management tasks posed by exempting investors from liability for inherited contamination (LAF 2010: 8).

9.2.3.2 Coordination by the Trust/BvS

Decisions regarding the funding of each remediation project were taken individually and by consensus by the Trust/BvS-*Länder* commission. The law does not stipulate clearly what the remediation objective for any given inherited contamination should be. Since the federal government and the *Länder* had divergent interests, this lack of clarity became a source of conflict. Whereas the federal government wanted to avoid so-called 'luxury remediation' in particular (that is, elaborate remediation activities that went beyond neutralising the dangers) the new *Länder* were interested in careful and thorough remediation measures in which the risk of later threats to human and environmental health were to be kept to a minimum (Seibel 2005: 392). In many cases it was hard to reach a compromise between these two positions.

The Trust/BvS occupied a more favourable position in the negotiations. The *Länder* were represented on the commission by their mediating authorities (regional government headquarters, district authorities, etc.), which did not have the same level of financial resources, specialist staffing or longstanding administrative experience (Seibel 2005: 392, Preuschoff 2000: 30). They did not negotiate on equal terms with the Trust/BvS (LAF 2010: 8), which led to the federal agency having a much greater influence. This unequal triad of interests represented by investors, federal state authorities and the Trust/BvS gave rise to an inefficient and time-consuming administrative process that was only exacerbated by the demands of the unanimity rule (Seibel 2005: 394, Preuschoff 2000: 30).

From a stocks perspective, then, one could sum up by saying that after the peaceful revolution of 1989 the existing institutional stocks were initially transferred to the new federal states of the east and were not adequately modified in the process. In particular, the key building block in land remediation and reuse, namely, exemption from liability for investors combined with governmental responsibility for remediation, was laid but could not be satisfactorily implemented due to unsuitable or non-existent institutions (unsuitable: lack of administrative clarity, unanimity rule; non-existent: appropriate administrative and decision-making competencies in the new *Länder*, experience with the instrument of exemption from liability for inherited contamination). In order to illustrate how important a change in institutional structure is for resolving problems satisfactorily, we focus in the following on the federal state of Saxony-Anhalt.

9.3 Exemption from liability for inherited contamination in Saxony-Anhalt

9.3.1 Taking stock of the problem of contamination in Saxony-Anhalt

The problem of inherited contamination in Saxony-Anhalt is an especially severe one. Some 5.5 per cent of the entire state area is contaminated or suspected of being contaminated (cf. Table 9.1). Roughly half of this area previously hosted industrial facilities. The main harmful substances are heavy metals, chlorinated and aromatic hydrocarbons (CHCs, AHCs), mercury, mineral oils, fuels, tar, phenols, acidic resins and benzene (LAF 2010: 23–26). Investigations are still ongoing regarding the areas suspected of containing contaminants as is the remediation of confirmed contaminated sites (Table 9.2).

With seven large-scale ecological projects within its boundaries, Saxony-Anhalt has more such projects than any other federal state. The large-scale projects there are also among the largest in terms of area. The kinds of contamination found there are typically 'cocktails' consisting of various dangerous substances that can seep down vertically into the subterranean layers and can expand horizontally across several kilometres of groundwater aquifers. The overwhelming majority of the remediation projects are to be completed (with the exception of long-term monitoring and associated measures) by 2020.

Table 9.1 Contamination in Saxony-Anhalt

Total area of federal state of Saxony-Anhalt	20,446 km^2
Inherited contamination and areas suspected of containing contaminants	5.5% of state area, i.e. more than 1,000 km^2
Remediation expenses 1993–2009	953.2 m €
Area covering the seven large-scale ecological projects	47.83 km^2
Estimated total funding requirements for remediation in large-scale ecological projects	2.2 bn €

Sources: LAF 2002: 8; LAF 2010: 22–28; personal communication from Division for Soil Protection and Inherited Contamination of the Saxony-Anhalt Environmental Conservation Agency.

Table 9.2 Status of investigation of areas in Saxony-Anhalt suspected of containing inherited contamination, February 2014

Status of investigation	*Number of plots of land*
Suspected contamination (i.e. close investigation not yet undertaken)	15,846
Investigation carried out	4,198
of these, contamination ruled out	1,989
contamination discovered	2,209
of these, remediation completed	1,808

Source: Statistics on inherited contamination February 2014, Saxony-Anhalt Environmental Conservation Agency, www.sachsen-anhalt.de/fileadmin/Bibliothek_Politik_und_Verwaltung/MLU/LAU/Bodenschutz/Altlasten/Dateien/altlastenstatistik.pdf, 19.5.2016.

The largest case of damage in Saxony-Anhalt and in the whole of eastern Germany is the large-scale ecological project at Bitterfeld-Wolfen. Here numerous widespread and highly toxic contaminants have been discovered, including an area of more than 400 hectares contaminated with chlorobenzene at a level that is 100,000 times higher than the permissible level (LAF 2010: 6). The costs of cleaning up the Bitterfeld-Wolfen site have so far amounted to some 230 m euros (LAF 2010: 25). Due to the complexity and extent of the contamination, remediation is set to last until at least 2050.

9.3.2 Targeted institutional change leads to breakthrough in exemption from liability for inherited contamination

A considerable proportion of the remediation carried out on contaminated land in Saxony-Anhalt is state financed because the investors have been exempted from liability for the costs arising. The difficulties mentioned in Section 9.2.3 regarding the federal states' capacity for dealing with exemption modalities were also encountered in Saxony-Anhalt. This meant that in the 1990s the inspection of sites suspected of containing contaminants and the remediation of sites containing confirmed contaminants began very hesitantly at first.

However, the situation improved markedly when a number of far-sighted institutional changes were made after the year 2000. It is these that we wish to examine more closely in terms of how they came about. The improvements were especially marked in relation to the administrative process associated with exemption applications. The three key changes in institutional arrangements were as follows:

- *Lump sum agreement*: The administrative agreement according to which remediation financing was divided between the federal government and the federal states was now replaced by an agreement which provided for a generous lump sum payment of 1 billion euros by the Federal Republic of Germany to the federal state of Saxony-Anhalt. This meant that on the one hand the German government discharged its financial obligations once and for all, while on the other the state of Saxony-Anhalt was granted full financial and administrative autonomy to deal with the problems relating to contaminated sites.
- *Creation of a special public fund*: The money was used to set up a special public fund to be used solely for dealing with remediation of inherited contamination.
- *Founding of the state agency for exemption from contamination liability (Landesanstalt für Altlastenfreistellung, LAF)*: This agency was set up in order to deal with all procedural matters associated with compiling an inventory of and remediating contaminated sites. The LAF is a full legal entity under public law which handles all activities concerning the exemption rule. It is the main point of contact for investors, property owners and local government authorities.

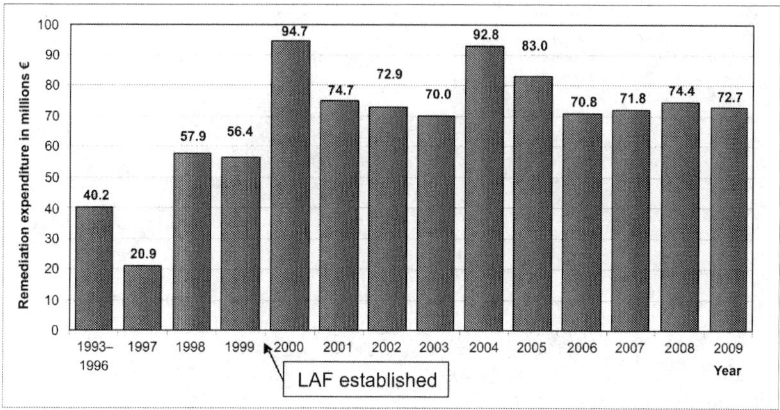

Figure 9.1 Expenditure on remediation of contaminated sites in Saxony-Anhalt, 1993–2009, in millions of euros.

Source: Landesanstalt für Altlastenfreistellung Sachsen-Anhalt (LAF 2010: 28).

One significant indicator of the extent to which these institutional changes have actually led to an improved situation is the flow of funds, i.e. the financial resources put to effective use in remediation efforts (cf. Figure 9.1). This flow of funds saw a marked rise when the LAF was set up and has remained steady ever since.

9.4 Success factors

Let us now look more closely at how the key institutional improvements came about: what impacts did they have? To which political actors can these achievements principally be attributed? What were their motivations and what special personal capabilities did they possess? We show which factors were crucial to the success by referring to a number of extracts from interviews with key individuals (cf. Table 9.3)[8].

The following quotations illustrate that first and foremost it is the commitment of specific individuals that is key to any successful restructuring of the institutional framework: these individuals must have the genuine intention to improve the situation and take responsibility for doing so. Also key is the coming together of like-minded individuals. The individuals in question also need to have the power to influence political decision-making processes.

> And I also have to say that I was actually lucky [...] enough to come across people like my department head at that time, Ms. Gäde-Butzlaff and also Mr. Gassner, who were very committed, as well as others who were all pulling together in the same direction. These activities, which we had developed within the department, and the ideas we had could have been easily choked

Table 9.3 Interviewees in Saxony-Anhalt and their positions

Vera Gäde-Butzlaff	Independent politician
	1998–2001: Head of division for 'Contaminated sites, waste management, energy, emissions protection law'
	2001–2002: Secretary of state in environment ministry of Saxony-Anhalt
Klaus Rehda	From 1992 onwards: Head of department in the regional council of Dessau responsible for water, waste and contaminated sites
	1995–2008: Department head in environment ministry of Saxony-Anhalt responsible for special waste/contaminated waste, latterly responsible for the implementation of the Water Framework Directive and Soil Protection
	Since 2008: President of the federal state agency for environmental protection

> off if the senior management [ministry] had said 'We're not interested in any of this. Let him write his proposals. We'll throw them in the waste basket or just not follow them up.' Then the process would have quickly come to an end. And that would actually have been a shame. Basically, you need people at all levels who are willing to accept changes and who will play along. That definitely was important. (Rehda, interview conducted 22 June 2009, lines 923–934)

> You basically need a certain combination of people to get things through, both in the political sphere, and the senior management has to be behind it – minister, secretary of state, head of division. The whole hierarchy has to want it. (Rehda, interview conducted 22 June 2009, lines 718–721)

> That was the first time that something really emerged just from inside the department. [...] But it all just [...] really came together nicely. First of all [there was] the lump sum agreement which was accompanied by a process of taking stock [of the brownfield situation] and of what needs to be done, together with an estimate of how much it will cost over a period of decades – a prognosis for many years ahead. And then there was consideration of how this task could be accomplished properly, also in the interplay with others involved. [...] And then getting the legal form established. I think that was the first and probably the only time [...] we had the opportunity to have all these things and to see it all through to the end. (Gäde-Butzlaff, interview conducted 18 November 18 2009, lines 224–225)

In the latter quotation it becomes clear that these individuals need to have the ability to recognise an 'opportunity', that is, to assess temporal developments and predict windows of opportunity for action. Recognising the *kairos* requires both experiential knowledge of the dynamics of the political system as well as sound judgement regarding the broader circumstances and the conditions within which action is to be taken.

> It's also a matter of whether there's continuity in the people involved, whether you can get the ministers on board, what the political situation is at the time. Often these kinds of processes are used for politicking, because after all you mustn't do it at the wrong point in time and risk them not getting ahead in the election campaign. So in effect a few things came together. (Gäde-Butzlaff, interview conducted 18 November 18 2009, lines 360–363)

> So for that reason you can never tell what the right moment is beforehand. [...] Let me give you an example from my current work context [head of Berlin city sanitation services]: I would never go into a public hearing with such a big project, where I know people have differing opinions (say, a waste incineration plant), five months before an election. Because you can bet your bottom dollar it'll be used. [...] No matter what people think – politics just comes into play too much, and that's what we managed [back then when we organised the contamination management in Saxony-Anhalt] quite well, I think, keeping it out of day-to-day politicking [...]. It's not enough for a project to be good. You have to sell it too. You know, the idea that other people have to understand what you're doing, I think that's something you can't really rely on in that kind of political arena. (Gäde-Butzlaff, interview conducted 18 November 2009, lines 368–406)

Some of the broader requisite conditions could not be influenced directly. In order to be able to act, random opportunities had to be recognised and exploited.

> And at many points it was [...] a lucky strike. But that's always the way it is in life. It often happens that certain windows of opportunity open up and then certain things become possible. And if you take advantage of these opportunities you can get things done. And if you don't make the most of them, then you lose your chance. [...] And we were just lucky in the sense that we, well, took advantage of certain opportunities. (Rehda, interview conducted 22 June 2009, lines 896–901)

To sum up, then, the following factors for success were decisive:

- The involvement of people who are prepared to assume responsibility and who are genuinely interested in making improvements is crucial.
- These individuals should also have the power to influence political decision-making processes.
- Finally, they need the ability to assess temporal developments and recognise windows of opportunity for action (i.e. a sense of time).

9.5 Summary: the importance of a sense of time

The peaceful revolution in the GDR in 1989 provided a unique opportunity for the two German states to reunite. In the first democratically elected people's chamber (*Volkskammer*) there were a number of political representatives who were committed to environmental issues and used the opportunity to set down environmental regulations that were inconceivable in West Germany at the time. These include, for example, the decommissioning of the two East German nuclear power plants and the setting up of large national parks and nature conservation areas. The far-sighted environmental framework act (*Umweltrahmengesetz*) that stipulates, among other things, how the exemption from liability for inherited contamination was to be dealt with, was also adopted in this brief window of opportunity between the first free elections in the GDR on March 18, 1990 and German reunification on October 3 of the same year.

The reunification treaty provided for the adoption of important regulations from the environmental framework act into German legislation for the reunified country, such as the exemption clause which makes it possible for investors to be exempted from liability for inherited contamination and thus removes a significant impediment to investment as well as remediation activities. During the first few years after reunification, however, it became apparent that the exemption modality in and of itself was not sufficient to push forward the remediation of contaminated sites or to attract investors. In Saxony-Anhalt a few key individuals recognised this and seized the opportunity to introduce improved and, in some cases, innovative new regulations. In this context the switch to lump sum payments from the federal government for investigation and remediation purposes, the setting up of a special public fund for inherited contamination and the founding of the LAF occurred in close association with one another, not only in terms of the issue itself but also in terms of the time frame.

The interviews conducted with the key figures involved in these changes enabled us to get an insight into how this (particularly with regard to sustainability) satisfactory institutional regulatory arrangement came about. In our conversations we were able to discover what the motivations, considerations and strategies of those involved were. Their statements provide numerous indications of the fact that recognising and taking account of temporal structures played a significant role in the success of their actions.

In order to identify the right moment, or *kairos*, for action, people need a sense of time (cf. Section 8.3.4). This sense of time is revealed not least in the fact that they keep an eye on the inherent dynamics of the material stocks and durable institutions relevant to their practical purposes and are able to judge them correctly. In the case study of remediation in Saxony-Anhalt these included the typical rates of decay of harmful substances, the typical duration of an approval procedure, the duration of existence of the Trust (and then the BvS), and political cycles. Evidently the key decision-making individuals in policy and administration possessed such a sense of time. This ability, along with the capacity to analyse problems, find creative solutions and weigh up what is politically feasible enabled them to recognise the signs of the time – the *kairos* – and to prompt key improvements in the institutional regulation of exemption from liability for inherited contamination.

Notes

1 The ability to put one's own expertise effectively to use refers to using all available legitimate means of achieving a given purpose, such as commissioning external expert reports, commissioning recognised experts, using formal and informal channels of communication, producing preliminary documents, defining agendas for meetings, taking an active role in consultations, readings, and so forth.
2 Lee-Peuker and Klauer (2010) present a comprehensive account of their case study on the problem of inherited contaminants in Saxony-Anhalt.
3 In German, an *Altlast* is legally defined (according to §2, Section 6 in connection with §3, Section 5, Clauses 1 and 2 of the Federal Soil Protection and Contaminated Sites Ordinance, BBodSchG) as a 'harmful change in the soil' on property containing disused facilities and on other properties on which environmentally harmful substances have been handled.
4 Administrative agreement concerning the financing of inherited ecological contamination, December 1, 1992, Appendix 1, No. 5.
5 Trust Act of 17.6.1990, Gesetzblatt der DDR 1990, I p. 300, introductory preamble.
6 See administrative agreement of 1.12.1992 between the Federal Republic of Germany and the *Länder* Berlin, Brandenburg, Mecklenburg-Western Pomerania, Saxony, Saxony-Anhalt and Thuringia, Annex, Part 1.
7 www.bvs.bund.de/003_menue_links/03_portrait/index.html, last accessed February 22, 2014.
8 A more detailed analysis of the interviews about the development of contamination management in Saxony-Anhalt can be found in Lee-Peuker and Klauer (2010).

10 Ways of achieving sustainable land use in Germany

A stocks-based analysis

with Beate Fischer and Frank Jöst

10.1 The German government's sustainability target

Current land use in Germany – particularly the marked trend towards urban sprawl – is associated with a range of environmental problems. The spread of areas dedicated to human settlements and transport infrastructure (*Siedlungs- und Verkehrsfläche*) entails the loss of fertile soils for agricultural use. Road building and soil sealing more generally are part of the reason why animal and plant habitats are being destroyed. Decentralised spatial structures (towns and villages scattered throughout the countryside) lead to high volumes of traffic and cause considerable noise pollution and harmful emissions. This is why more sustainable land use is crucial to implementing an environmentally sound form of agriculture as well as preserving biodiversity and combating climate change.

It is in this situation that the German government, in its 2002 sustainability strategy 'Prospects for Germany', set itself the target of limiting the growth of areas dedicated to human settlements and transport infrastructure. In 2008 some 100 ha of additional land on average was designated every day for this purpose[1]. From 2020 onwards the aim of the German government is to achieve a rate of 30 ha a day at most (German Federal Government 2002: 288, 2008). This target relates to a stock, namely, the stock of land dedicated to human settlements and transport infrastructure. It does not, however, stipulate any absolute proportion of the total area of Germany but just sets an upper limit for the rate of growth.

In this chapter we wish to examine – with the help of the concepts developed in Chapters 3 to 8 – whether or not the government's target is realistic. For this purpose our analysis is necessarily limited to just one aspect of the issue of 'sustainable land use'[2]. Thus we do not look here at issues concerning sustainable agriculture or the carving up of the countryside.

We proceed in our analysis as follows: first, we look at past trends in land dedicated to human settlements and transport infrastructure compared to other kinds of land use (Section 10.2). Areas of land used in a certain way can be regarded as a material stock. In order to be able to estimate the future development of these stocks of land we need to look at the so-called drivers. These too possess qualities of persistence, durability and inertia in relation to change. Accordingly, in Section 10.3 we examine those material stocks which influence the dynamic of land uses, and in Section 10.4 we analyse the institutional structure associated with them. Statistical data and information about legal regulations form the empirical basis for this. The inherent dynamics of these material stocks and durable institutions reveal much about the predicted development of land dedicated to human settlements and transport infrastructure in Germany. Thus if we put together the various stock dynamics to create an overall picture, it becomes possible to assess the extent to which the German government's sustainability target is realistic (Section 10.5). It is then possible to identify where the options for policy action lie and where not. And it is possible to get a sense of the *kairos*. Finally, we reflect on the potential benefits of the stocks perspective.

10.2 Past development trends in land dedicated to human settlements and transport infrastructure

The land use statistics produced by Germany's Federal Office of Statistics provide various data that can be used as a basis for describing the temporal structures of land use (StaBa 2008a)[3]. The current situation and thus the starting point for political action is the following: land dedicated to human settlements and transport infrastructure[4] in Germany currently comprises 13.2 per cent of the country's total land area; roughly half of this is actually sealed. More than half the total land area of Germany – 52.5 per cent – is in agricultural use; 30.1 per cent consists of forested areas (StaBa 2009b)[5].

This structure of land use is the result of a lengthy process of development. Figure 10.1 shows the development of these three stocks of land for the period 1950 to 2000 for the so-called 'old' federal states (i.e. former West Germany).

The graph illustrates two things in particular. First, it shows that changes in land use are occurring slowly but surely. Within the typical time horizon faced by a political decision maker – that is, over one or two legislative sessions or 4 to 8 years the relative changes in land use are almost negligible. This raises the question of what responsibility the relevant policy makers have in a certain legislative session, given that the problem only emerges over several such sessions. Second, though, the trend shown in the graph is clearly heading in a particular direction. There are no turnarounds; rather, the amount of land dedicated to human settlements and transport infrastructure has grown continuously and the amount of agricultural land has steadily fallen[6]. This indicates a high degree of persistence and inertia in the drivers behind these trends.

The only fluctuation was in the *rate* of growth of land dedicated to human settlements and transport infrastructure, as illustrated in Figure 10.2. If we look at

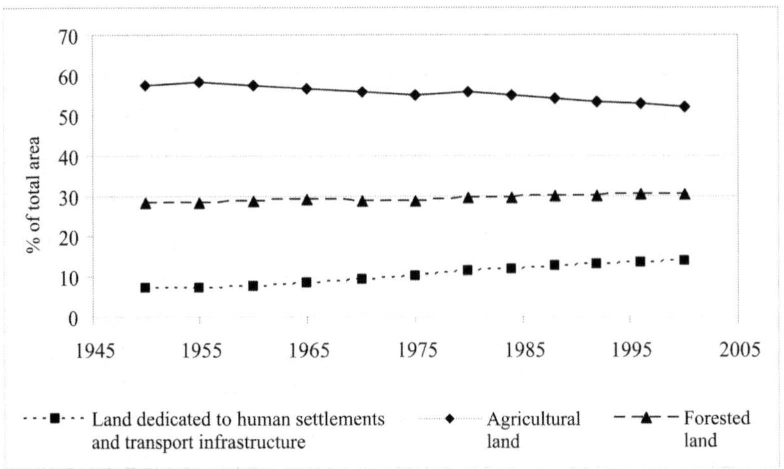

Figure 10.1 Trends in the most important types of land use in former West Germany, given in per cent of area.

Source: StaBa 2008a.

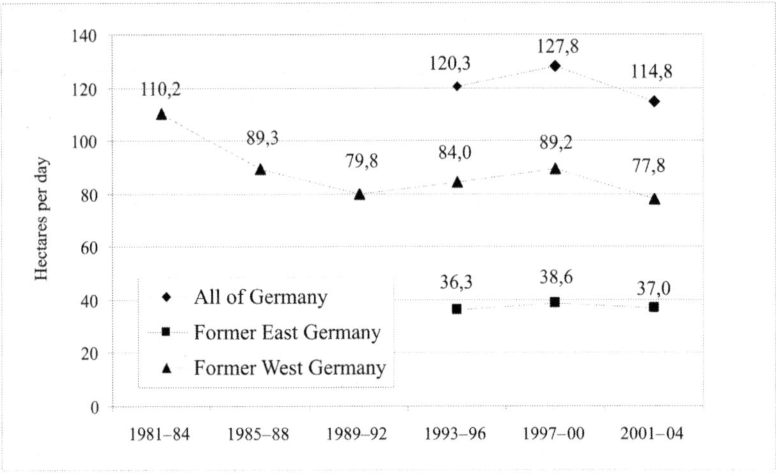

Figure 10.2 Growth in amount of land dedicated to human settlements and transport infrastructure.

Source: authors' calculation based on StaBa 2008b.

the average rates of growth separately according to the former West and the former East Germany, we see that the rates of growth in West Germany have fallen noticeably since the 1980s. When measured against the 30 ha target, however, the amount of land made available for development is still very high.

This macro perspective on the development of the stock of land dedicated to human settlements and transport infrastructure can be complemented by a micro perspective, which provides an insight into its inherent dynamic. The transformation of agricultural land into land dedicated to human settlements and transport infrastructure generally occurs much faster than the other way around. The speed at which new areas are designated for development is determined by the consultation processes conducted with higher levels of planning (land use plan, targets for regional and federal state development plans) and typically takes place on a timescale of between one and five years. The minimum duration is given by the legally prescribed processes of decision making and administration entailed by overall construction planning and by construction times.

There are two different cases in which land dedicated to human settlements and transport infrastructure is transformed back to agricultural use. In the first case, the land is no longer being used, buildings are standing empty, or land once used for industry is derelict. Since the landowners cannot be obliged by law to cover the costs of removing the buildings or remediating the soil, derelict land is often not cleared but is left to a natural process of decline and to processes of succession. Investors are rarely found who are willing to reuse the land, which is why remediation – if it occurs at all – is usually undertaken by the state authorities (cf. Chapter 9), whose financial resources are far from plentiful. Realistic time horizons here are ten or more years.

In the second case, whatever kind of land use is in operation, it is to be changed back to agricultural use. In this case, powerful incentives (price differential between residential and traffic use and crop land!) in combination with property rights serve to protect building developments. In statistical terms such reversions of land use occur only over very long periods of time – realistic time horizons are in the order of 50 years or more[7]. This means that, in a macroscopic perspective and on mid-range timescales, the change of land use from agricultural to human settlements and transport infrastructure is virtually irreversible (cf. also Box 10.1)[8].

Box 10.1 Example: construction boom in Spain

The virtual irreversibility of the designation of new land for construction purposes can be illustrated vividly using the examples of the development of Spain's Mediterranean coastline. In 1998 the conservative government of Spain under José María Aznar liberalised building legislation. Local municipalities were now permitted to designate land for building purposes as they saw fit. Approvals for the building of hotels, apartment blocks and villas directly on the coast were granted generously, which brought in large amounts of money to the municipal coffers and led to a veritable construction boom (*Der Spiegel* 31/2012, p. 49). Today, some 700,000 homes in Spain stand empty[9], but it is inconceivable that the buildings that are only occasionally in use or not at all might be demolished.

To sum up, then, land use in Germany is characterised essentially by the following three dynamics:

1 Compared to the short-term decision-making horizons of policy makers (some 4 to 8 years) the growth of land dedicated to human settlements and transport infrastructure is characterised by a long-term, sluggish dynamic[10].
2 The developmental dynamic displays a clear trend: land dedicated to human settlements and transport infrastructure has increased continually in the past; only its rate of growth has fluctuated.
3 The process of changing land use from agriculture to human settlements and transport infrastructure occurs on a much shorter timescale (1 to 5 years) than the reverse process (typically more than 10 years for derelict land and more than 50 years for land still in use). On mid-range timescales this leads to the virtual irreversibility of a change of land use to human settlements and transport infrastructure at the macro level.

10.3 Factors influencing the development of land use

The reasons for the growth in land dedicated to human settlements and transport infrastructure are many and varied. The European Environmental Agency (EEA 2006b: 17) has listed the following factors:

- *Macroeconomic factors*: economic growth, globalisation, European integration
- *Microeconomic factors*: rising standards of living, land prices, availability of agricultural land, competition between local municipalities
- *Demographic factors*: population growth, changing size of households
- *Housing preferences*: increasing per capita housing space, living in the countryside
- *Inner-city problems*: poor air quality, noise, small houses/flats, lack of safe surroundings, social problems, lack of green spaces, poor quality of schools
- *Mobility*: motorisation, road stock, low fuel prices, poor public transport systems
- *Institutional setting*: little regional planning capable of being implemented, poor horizontal and vertical cooperation between public institutions, financial incentives for local municipal governments

The development trends of these different factors are in turn determined crucially by stocks. The following discussion does not claim to capture and analyse exhaustively the complex relationships between these factors and their impacts on land use. Rather, it represents an attempt to paint an overall picture of the complex situation using the stocks concept, one that captures just a few of the key factors in broad brush fashion. Various statistical information about the development trends of relevant stocks in the past is brought together in order to assess likely future developments.

In order to enable the relevant stocks to stand out, we first discuss what key specific types of land use comprise the overall land use category 'human settlements and transport infrastructure' and which uses can be ignored in quantitative terms. A detailed analysis of land use statistics suggests that the analysis can be limited to the following three land use types:

1 Transport developments (34 per cent of land dedicated to human settlements and transport infrastructure)
2 Housing developments (25 per cent)
3 Commercial developments (15 per cent)

These three land use types together make up 74 per cent of land dedicated to human settlements and transport infrastructure (authors' calculation based on StaBa 2008a, cf. Dosçh 2008: 42[11]. All three types of land use have been growing steadily since the early 1990s, even though housing and commercial developments grew much more markedly than transport infrastructure developments (authors' calculation based on StaBa 2008a and 2008b, see also EEA 2006a: 37).

We now want to discuss a few stock dynamics of influencing factors that are relevant to all these land use types – the trend in population growth (Section 10.3.1), economic development (Section 10.3.2) and trends in the growth of road traffic (Section 10.3.3) – in order to be able to formulate (in Section 10.3.4) estimates regarding future trends in land use.

10.3.1 The trend in population growth and the associated demand for land

The demand for housing land depends on a variety of factors, including the size, age structure and regional distribution of the population, people's incomes, the price of rented and privately owned homes, people's housing preferences and the strategic planning instruments available to the federal government. In the following analysis we concentrate on two factors that can be considered to represent some of those just mentioned and are seen as crucial to trends in the demand for housing land: demography and average per capita housing land. We analyse time-based data relating to the developmental trend of these two factors in order to derive information about future demand for housing land.

Germany's population reached an apex in 2002 with some 82.5 million people. The Federal Office of Statistics predicts that the country's population will shrink in the future (cf. Figure 10.5). According to a mid-range scenario[12] the population will decline by 1.9 per cent (to 80.4 million) by 2020, by 6.4 per cent (to 76.7 million) by 2040 and by 14.5 per cent (to 70.1 million) by 2060 (StaBa 2009a: 40). This trend – the inherent dynamic of the population stock – will generally weaken demand for housing land. Whether the declining population does actually manifest in reduced demand for such land or not, however, depends among other things on the regional distribution of the population. This is because domestic migration from structurally weak to structurally strong regions will lead to additional demand for housing land in growing regions. This is why population predictions need to be regarded in a differentiated way according to region.

In order to obtain an overall picture of how things are set to develop in the future, 97 spatial planning regions in Germany were divided into growing, shrinking and stable regions according to their predicted development (BBR 2006)[13]. The result of the prognosis is shown in Figure 10.3. It shows that the number of growing regions is set to decline continually in the future, and after 2030 there will be no longer be any growing regions. The majority of regions will have a stable population, and after 2030 the proportion of shrinking regions will increase.

If we consider that the change in land use from agriculture to land dedicated to human settlements and transport infrastructure occurs much faster than the other way around (cf. Section 10.2) then it seems reasonable to predict a number of developments in relation to trends in available housing land in the regions, as follows. Due to the persistence of settlement areas there will not be any mass demolition of empty houses and apartments in the shrinking areas. Rather, it can be assumed that these regions will try to establish favourable prices for building land by designating new land for housing, thereby attracting new residents. Due to the trend in preferences (cf. below) there is likely to be a moderate level of newly designated land for housing in the stable regions. The growing regions will continue to designate new areas for housing in a big way in order to meet the demand for living space. All in all, then, it is unlikely that the demand for housing land in growing regions will be offset by demolitions and land use changes in shrinking regions by 2030.

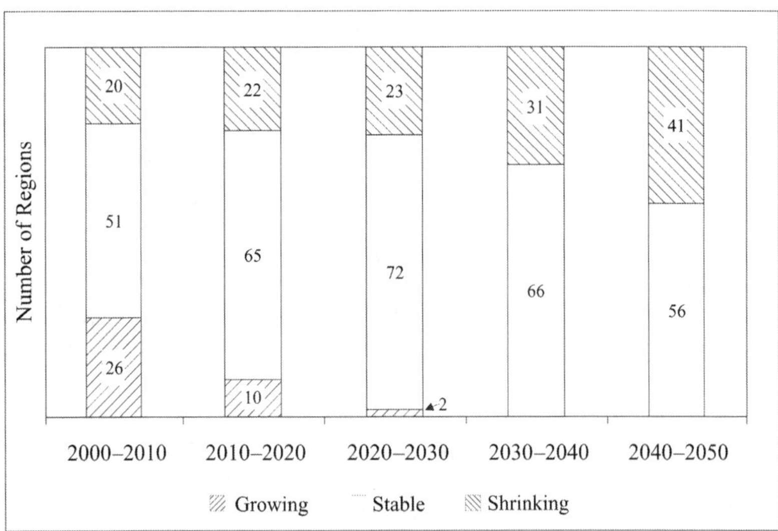

Figure 10.3 Developmental trend of regions with varying growth dynamics.

Source: BBR 2006.

Yet it is not only population growth that influences demand for housing land; people's housing preferences do so as well. By housing preferences we mean size of household, size of house/apartment, type of building, location, etc. We can conceive of housing preferences as an immaterial stock that is subject to slow change. The indicator 'per capita housing land'[14] forms one part of this stock and has developed rather impressively in the past (Figure 10.4).

In the federal states belonging to the former West Germany, per capita living space increased from 22.3m² in 1965 to 42.8m² in 2002. In the federal states belonging to the former East Germany, a catching-up process occurred after reunification so that per capita living space stood at 36.2m² in 2002. This means that per capita living space here saw an average increase of some 0.5m² every year between 1965 and 2002.

What trend can we expect for the future? A number of factors suggest that there will continue to be an increase in per capita living space. Population predictions indicate that the populace will continue to age overall (StaBa 2009a: 40), which will lead to even smaller average household sizes. For shrinking regions it is realistic to assume that there will be growing numbers of empty properties, declining rents and falling house prices, which can equally be expected to encourage a further increase in per capita living space. However, a sharp increase should be counteracted by rising energy and maintenance costs along with rising rents in the growth regions.

We now examine two scenarios on this basis. Scenario *A* assumes that per capita living space will increase by just 0.25m² per year. In 2020 average living space would be 46.5m² and in 2050 54m². Scenario *B* assumes that the previous trend will continue, that is, that there will be an increase of 0.5m² per year. This

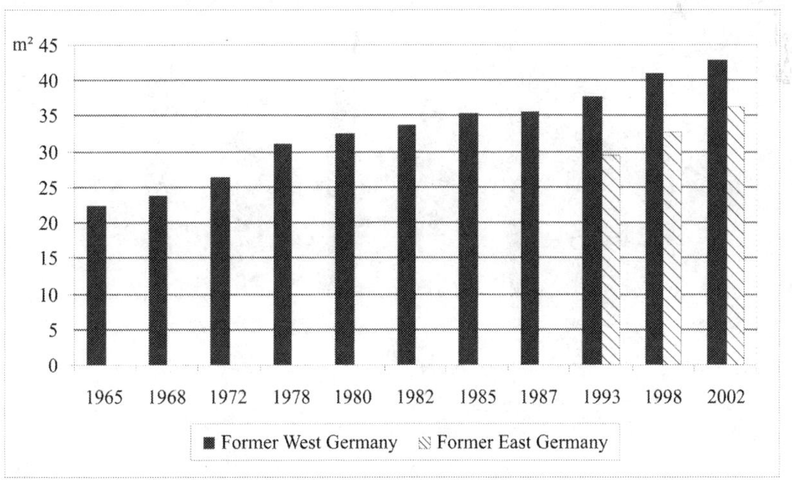

Figure 10.4 Development of per capita housing land.

Source: StaBa 2008c.

would mean that, in arithmetic terms, average living space would increase to 52m² by 2020 and to 67m² by 2050. High figures such as these do not appear unrealistic when we compare them with contemporary dwelling sizes of one-person households.

Figure 10.5 shows how aggregated land for housing – the total area of all apartments/houses[15] – would develop in each scenario if the population declined as predicted. To show this, per capita living space has been multiplied by the population. The figure illustrates very clearly that the increase in per capita living space cancels out the effects of population decline even in the more favourable Scenario *A*. It also illustrates that the future trend will depend heavily on the development of people's housing preferences. Thus the difference between Scenario *A* and Scenario *B* amounts to 442km² in 2020 and to 957km² in 2050.

Even this rather rough-and-ready analysis is very instructive. If we assume, quite plausibly, that an increase in (total) living space also entails an increase in housing land in terms of land use statistics (that is, the amount of land dedicated to housing), then this means overall that, given a shrinking population, we cannot automatically expect a turnaround in the trend regarding housing land. Although the massive decline in population and the fact that there will be no more growing regions after 2030 will limit the growth of housing land, further pressure towards growth will arise, especially from the predicted trend in housing preferences. Finally, the high degree of persistence of existing housing land means that, even at the regional level, it is not likely to revert back to agricultural land in the near future, despite a shrinking population.

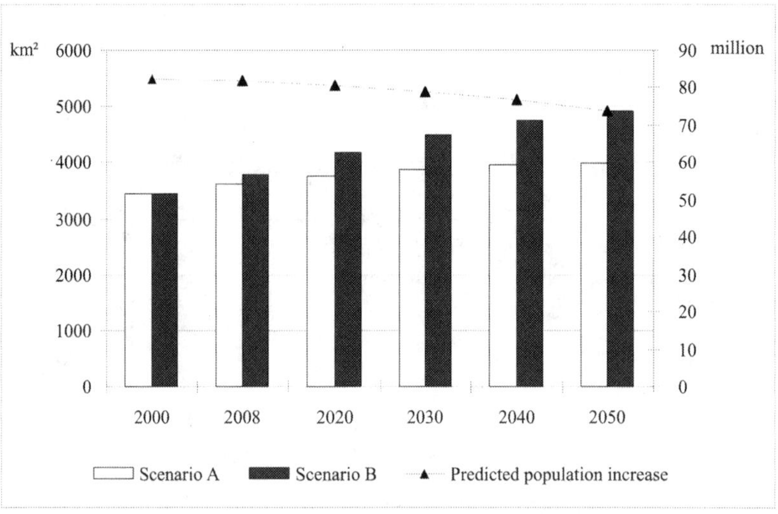

Figure 10.5 Predicted trend in total living space.

Source: authors' own calculation.

10.3.2 Economic trends and associated demand for land

Predictions regarding economic development are difficult, indeed actually impossible over the period up to 2050 that we are looking at here. What is more, there are few statistical data for past trends of, for example, the stock of companies, from which – analogous to population trends – it might be possible to draw conclusions about future commercial land use. It may be, however, that trends in commercial land use by sector can provide a point of orientation. It is widely argued that sector-based transformation – from an economy based largely on industry to a service-based one – ought to lower the pressure on the growth of commercial land use, as the service sector generally needs less land. Figure 10.6 shows a short time series for trends in commercial land use by sector.

The graph illustrates that the service sector is growing strongly in terms of land use while agriculture and manufacturing commerce are not replacing areas dedicated to human settlements to the same extent, so that the economic sector as a whole is contributing to the growth of these areas. It is likely that this is due to a similar reason as in the case of housing land. Unused building land and associated open spaces in agriculture and manufacturing commerce are generally not converted back or given over to other uses within a short period of time. Instead they initially lie fallow while agricultural land elsewhere is converted to new uses. With regard to future trends, therefore, it seems sensible to assume a further growth in the service sector on the one hand and not to assume, on the other, that this growth in land use will be offset by processes of shrinkage in relation to building land and associated open spaces in agriculture and manufacturing commerce.

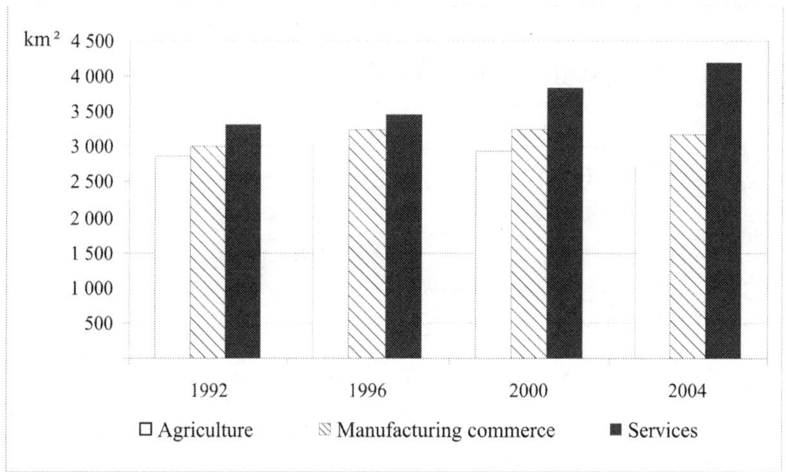

Figure 10.6 Trends in commercial land use by sector.

Source: StaBa 2008d.

10.3.3 Trends in road traffic and associated demand for land

It is estimated that just below 90 per cent of transport-related land use is dedicated to road traffic[16]. For reasons of simplification, therefore, we wish to disregard other kinds of transportation in our analysis. Generally speaking, two sets of reasons can be identified in relation to the growth in land dedicated to road traffic.

On the one hand, road building is closely related to the development of areas dedicated to housing and commerce. Estimates indicate, for example, that some 45 per cent of all new roads are those that provide access to new housing developments. 21 per cent of new road building occurs in the course of extending the long-distance road network and 31 per cent is given over to providing access to agricultural land and forests (Penn-Bressel 2005: 130). The future growth of land dedicated to road traffic is thus driven largely by the development of areas dedicated to housing and commerce.

The second set of reasons has to do with the volume of traffic. An increasing volume of traffic leads to an increasing need for road infrastructure. Current predictions regarding the trend in traffic volume assume an increase in traffic in every respect: more goods and people will be transported over longer distances (Prognos AG 2001; Intraplan Consult 2007). Traffic itself is not a stock, so in this respect it could theoretically be reduced at any time, as the traffic-free Sundays declared in the Federal Republic of Germany in 1973 impressively demonstrate. However, behind the observed traffic flows are material stocks (stock of cars, stock of heavy goods vehicles, stocks of infrastructure of various kinds etc.) as well as immaterial stocks (transportation habits, business relationships, production structures based on the division of labour, such as 'just in time' processes, etc.), which give the flow of traffic the quality of persistence. By way of example, Figure 10.7 shows how the stock of cars developed between 1950 and 2000.

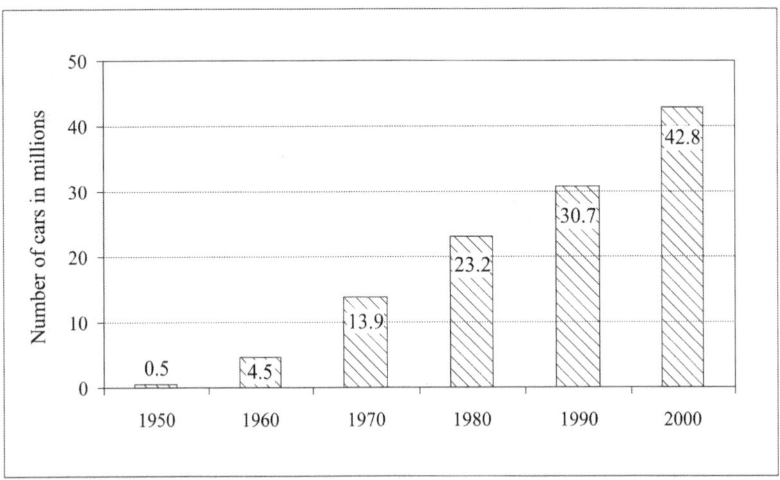

Figure 10.7 Development of the stock of cars 1950–2000.

Source: KBA 2007.

Whereas in 1950 there were just half a million cars, by 2000 there were more than 42.8 million. Although the growth in the stock of cars can be expected to ease off once a certain degree of motorisation has been reached and the stock reaches saturation point, this point does not yet appear to have been reached. It is expected that by 2025 the stock of cars will have increased to 51.1 million. This would mean that for every 1000 people over the age of 18 there are 737 cars in use (Intraplan Consult 2007: 3). Gehlen's theory of institutions (cf. Section 6.3) draws our attention to the fact that cars do not only fulfil a need for mobility but rather that driving a car becomes an *institutionalised* behaviour. In the course of this, the original purpose of a car may be transformed from means of transport to status symbol.

Environmental policy is now forced to take account of the 'requirements' of this growing stock. From the perspective of sustainable land use, the stock of cars is linked to certain spatial requirements: a growing number of cars will require associated parking space and roads.

10.3.4 Expectations with regard to future land use trends

The above discussion shows that due to the inherent dynamics of population trends, economic activity, and road traffic together with road building requirements, it is likely that there will continue to be considerable pressure towards expanding the amount of land dedicated to human settlements and transport infrastructure in the future. These trends are pre-empted in part in existing plans, such as the German government's Federal Transport Infrastructure Plan (BMVBW 2003) and local municipal authorities' land use plans. In order to get an indication of the policy action required to achieve the 30 ha target, we analysed by way of example three current land use plans[17]. While the neighbouring urban regions of Mannheim and Heidelberg and the city of Friedrichshafen are predicted to see a growth in population, the population of Flöha is expected to decline.

Figure 10.8 contrasts the new designated areas currently planned in these three planning regions with the possible amount of designated area that would conform to a linear adaptation to the 30 ha target. The dark grey columns stand for the new designated areas currently planned. The shaded columns depict possible new designations up to 2015 and 2020 if adapted to the 30 ha target. In order to break this target down to the local municipal level and the planning horizons of the land use plans, the following assumptions are made for purposes of simplification[18]:

1 The temporal adaptation trajectory for the current new designation of some 100 ha to 30 ha per day in 2020 is linear.
2 The amount of new designated area remaining if the national sustainability target is achieved is distributed among all three municipal areas in proportion to their area.

Figure 10.8 illustrates that the rate of new land designation in the growing regions deviates considerably from the 30 ha target adapted to the regions concerned. The shrinking regions typically do not offset the growth in the growing regions, however[19] – illustrated here by the shrinking municipality of Flöha, which uses up

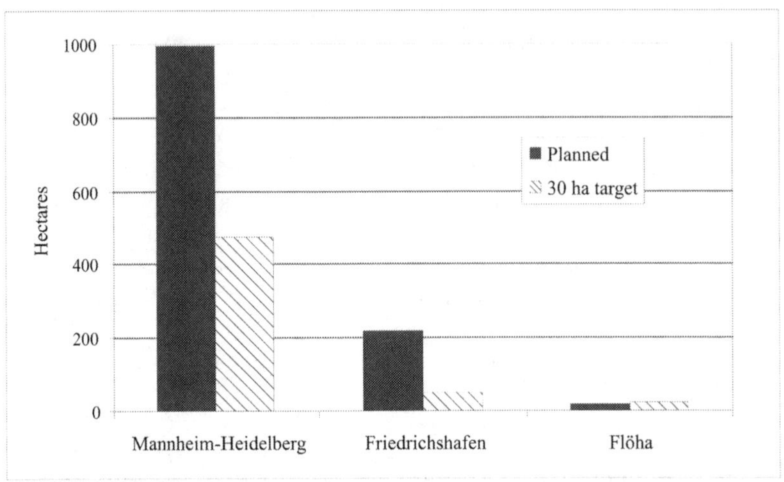

Figure 10.8 Planned new land designation in comparison to potential designation if the 30 ha target is implemented.

Source: authors' calculation, using *Nachbarschaftsverband* Mannheim-Heidelberg 2006; *Verwaltungsgemeinschaft* Friedrichshafen-Immenstaad 2006; *Verwaltungsgemeinschaft* Flöha 2006.

its quota of new designation almost completely despite a declining population. It is worth bearing in mind here that these predictions are not uncertain: the land use plans are already in force legally speaking and could only be altered with considerable political effort.

10.4 Discovering windows of opportunity for land use governance

In order to identify the periods of time over which land use governance can take effect, it is necessary to analyse not only the factual circumstances that exist within a policy field (as we did in the previous two sections) but also the relevant institutional structures. To put it in terms of the stocks concept, what we are looking for are the inherent temporal dynamics of institutions that are particularly relevant in relation to the governance of land use. The following questions need to be answered:

1 Which political actors have what interests and powers and are thus able to exert an influence on land use?
2 Which institutional structures need to be changed, and in what way, in order to achieve a more sustainable form of land use?
3 How quickly – over what periods of time – can these institutional structures be changed?

10.4.1 Which actors influence land use?

When new land is designated for human settlements and transport infrastructure this generally occurs at the expense of agricultural land. Those who offer this land directly for sale – farmers – tend to have a strong interest in its rededication to a different use, due to the large price differential between land approved for building purposes and arable land (in most cases a tenfold difference). In principle, however, it is not possible in Germany for land dedicated to human settlements and transport infrastructure to be designated as such without this being approved by the state authorities. Thus the *amount of land available for sale* is essentially determined by the amount designated for the relevant uses by state authorities, so that it ought to be possible for land use to be regulated effectively by means of state governance. We pursue this idea here by analysing the institutions that are broadly involved in approving new land dedicated to human settlements and transport infrastructure and thus in determining the availability of land per se[20].

Approval of new land dedicated to human settlements and transport infrastructure is entrusted to the more than 12,000 local municipalities (*Gemeinden*) in Germany: they are responsible for establishing guidelines for town planning. This planning autonomy is an important element of a municipality's *right to self-administration* as guaranteed in Germany's Basic Law. The actions of municipal authorities are constrained by the formal stipulations set out in Germany's Federal Building Code (*Baugesetzbuch*) and the Federal Regional Planning Act (*Bundesraumordnungsgesetz*) at the national level, as well as by federal state–level (*Länder*) planning laws. In addition, the targets formulated in state-level development and regional plans limit the decision-making options available to municipalities in that federal state. The finance system also exerts a key influence on the way municipalities designate land for different uses. In sum, then, the relevant actors are the government at the federal (national) level (*Bund*), the federal state authorities and the local municipalities. It bears emphasising, however, that land use governance occurs first and foremost through the decentralised local municipal administrations – though these are not bound formally to the 30 ha goal set by the federal government.

10.4.2 Which institutions should be changed with a view to achieving sustainability?

As far as their sovereignty in matters of planning is concerned, local municipal administrations have the option of setting effective limits on the designation of new land dedicated to human settlements and transport infrastructure. Standing in the way of this, however, are huge incentives and powerful interests. One key concern of municipalities is to promote local prosperity. The dominant strategy for achieving this in German municipalities is to strengthen the local economy. Policy measures are devised to attract companies to the area and thus 'create' jobs and incomes for the local population. Attempts are also made to attract high-income residents whose purchasing power boosts the local economy (Bizer et al. 2006: 25–26).

This mode of reckoning is reinforced by the structure of local municipal financing: the options available to a municipal administration – e.g. when it comes to taking on discretionary tasks – are largely dependent on their financial situation. Local municipal administrations have three main sources of financing available to them: the so-called trade tax (*Gewerbesteuer*), income tax and the municipal fiscal equalisation mechanism (*kommunaler Finanzausgleich*)[21]. Since the revenues from trade taxation depend on the profit levels of locally based companies, the tax system provides an incentive to try to attract companies by designating land for commercial development. The same is true when it comes to designating land for housing construction in order to bring in new residents. New residents mean higher income tax payments; they also tend to increase the claims a municipality can make within the fiscal equalisation scheme[22]. In this way, the local government system of finance effectively pits local municipalities against each other in a competition for companies and residents (Bizer et al. 2006: 24 ff.; Bizer and Gubaydullina 2008: 36).

From a local government perspective, then, manifest economic interests stand in the way of a policy of reducing new land use, and these interests derive, in part, from the institutional design of the local municipal finance system. This creates an undesirable situation (from the point of view of sustainability) in which, on the one hand, local municipal authorities formally possess executive powers for land use planning while, on the other hand, due to the broader institutional setting and manifest interests, few incentives exist to devise policy aimed at reducing new land use at the local municipal level.

It bears asking, therefore, what the situation is with regard to the options available to actors at the state and federal (national) level. First of all, it is conceivable that the federal and state governments might work towards changes in the system of local government finance. They could try to weaken the incentives for local municipalities to designate more land dedicated to human settlements and transport infrastructure. However, the local government finance system has to accomplish a range of highly diverse tasks regarding allocation and strategic planning and to reconcile many different – often contrary – interests. As a result, proposals for change that are focused on solving only one part of a problem generally tend to engender other problems (quite apart from the predictable resistance of those affected).

Another governance instrument that might be used to implement quantitative targets for limiting the growth of land dedicated to human settlements and transport infrastructure is regional planning, although the governance impact of this instrument is also limited. In the context of federal state–level and regional planning the principle of countervailing influence (*Gegenstromprinzip*) applies, i.e. plans existing at the higher, federal state level are not placed hierarchically above the local plans of municipal administrations. Instead, the development, organisation and protection of the region as a whole must take account of the conditions and requirements prevailing in its component regions (Gawron 2007: 145 ff.).

These remarks should suffice at this point to illustrate that the governance impact of plans that exist at higher administrative levels is limited; so too, then, is the capacity of federal government and state policy makers to use their powers of enforcement to work towards achieving sustainable land use. Regardless of whether or not such institutional changes would have the hoped-for impact on the designation of new land dedicated to human settlements and transport infrastructure in practice and of whether the political will actually exists to carry out such changes, we want to look in the next section at the kinds of timescales on which such changes typically occur. This will help us in our assessment of whether the 30 ha goal can realistically be achieved by 2020 as planned.

10.4.3 How long does it take to change institutions?

In order to find out how long it takes for institutions to change in the ways required by the 30 ha target, we looked at the way the relevant institutions have developed since the Second World War (for a detailed account, see Fischer et al. 2010). The institutional foundations for today's regional planning were laid in the Federal Regional Planning Act of 1965, after long years of dispute over the distribution of powers between representatives from federal and state (*Länder*) governments. The Act's chief significance lay in the fact that it obliged the states to set targets relating to regional planning and state-level planning (Brohm 2002: 33). This was followed in the 1970s by ambitious efforts on the part of the federal government to establish a regional planning framework for the entire country by means of the Federal Regional Planning Programme. This ultimately failed, however, due to resistance from many actors at both the state and federal level (Hübler 1991). In 1989 the Regional Planning Act was updated in response to the requirements of the 1985 European directive relating to the environmental impact of projects. A reform undertaken in 1998 finally led to the principle of sustainable development being included as one of the guiding ideas of regional planning. In addition to this, the governance demands of federal regional planning regulations were relaxed, the binding nature of planning statements was reinforced by juridical means, and new instruments of regional planning (priority areas, conditional areas and unitary areas) were introduced (Gnest 2008). Thus past trends in regional planning suggest that substantial institutional reforms are likely to occur roughly every 10 years.

After 1949 the municipal finance system continued operating with the institutions from the pre-war system. At the time the Basic Law was adopted, land and trade taxes generated roughly one third of local municipal revenues. Over subsequent years, however, economic development, legal amendments and the increasing obsolescence of unitary values for plots of land all led to the trade tax becoming an increasingly important component of municipal revenues (Waldhoff 2006: 32). Three key changes essentially describe the institutional change in the local municipal finance system:

- In 1955/56 local municipalities' sovereign rights of self-administration were safeguarded in financial terms as well, with municipalities being guaranteed the funds generated from trade and land taxes by law (in its original form, the Basic Law made no provision for local municipal administrations to have a direct share in the yield from tax revenues).

- The next significant stage of reform, in 1969/1970, saw local municipalities being granted a share in the revenue from income taxes.
- Finally, in 1997/1998 local municipalities were also granted a direct share in the revenue gained from value added tax (Werner 2008: 94–109).

More substantial reforms of local municipal financing have thus occurred at intervals of about 15 or 25 years. A commission established by the German government in 2002 to oversee reform of local municipal finances completed its work without achieving any positive outcomes, due in part to conflicting interests, again giving an indication of the persistence of current institutions. The rate of local municipal finance reforms (roughly every 20 years) is much slower than that of regional planning. Substantial changes to institutions relevant to land use thus occur on timescales expressed in decades rather than in months or years.

10.5 Conclusion

10.5.1 Prospects for achieving the 30 hectare target

We have examined stocks and durable institutions in the realm of land use in terms of their inertia and inherent dynamics in order to assess whether or not the 30 ha target is realistic. Our analysis shows quite clearly that the 2020 deadline for achieving the 30 ha target, set out in the German government's sustainability strategy, appears unrealistic. Let us summarise once again the reasons for this assessment:

1 Land use statistics reveal only a slight decline in the designation of new land dedicated to human settlements and transport infrastructure, which is currently still a long way off the 30 ha target.
2 It is apparent from our analysis of the key reasons for the expansion of land dedicated to human settlements and transport infrastructure (in Section 10.3 above) that the population decline in large parts of Germany does not automatically lead to a sufficient decline in the designation of new land for this purpose. The reasons for this are, first, the trend towards larger homes and, second, the asymmetry between the ease with which new land is designated for specific uses and the difficulty of demolishing settlements and converting the land back to agricultural use or woodland areas. The economic trend towards a proportionally larger service sector and the expected ongoing growth in road traffic also ultimately increase the need for land dedicated to human settlements and transport infrastructure.
3 There are interest groups within both the business community and the wider society that exert direct or indirect pressure on policy makers to designate new land dedicated to human settlements and transport infrastructure. As a result, it is difficult to form political majorities in favour of a more restrictive land use policy. The federal government, state governments and municipalities can all influence land use to varying degrees. Local municipal authorities in particular and, to a lesser extent, the federal states are almost forced to engage

> in a competition to attract businesses to locate within their boundaries, and this triggers incentives for new land to be designated for human settlements and transport infrastructure. Although the federal government may be capable, in principle, of restricting this competition between states, regions and municipalities to attract companies and residents, there is a danger that such interventions may come into conflict with local municipal self-administration or with the local municipal finance system. Both are institutions that enjoy constitutional status and to this extent pose a powerful obstacle to change. Thus substantial reforms to the broader institutional conditions that influence the designation of new land for human settlements and transport infrastructure seem to be possible only over periods of time best measured in decades.

If the period to 2020 seems too short to achieve any decisive change, what can we expect to find if we look further into the future? If we were to extrapolate the trend in new land designation from the past into the future, the amount of land dedicated to human settlements and transport infrastructure would be 15 per cent of German territory in 2028, one quarter in 2100 and a third of Germany's total area in 2170[23]. This simple projection illustrates that sooner or later the need to limit dramatically the designation of new land for development will become obvious. Even today the proportion of land dedicated to human settlements and transport infrastructure in some heavily built-up areas, such as the region around Stuttgart, is as much as 20 per cent. In urban agglomerations such as these the resultant problems exert greater pressure than elsewhere and so the need for action is perceived more clearly in these places.

Sooner or later, then, the expansion of areas dedicated to human settlements and transport infrastructure will automatically come to a halt. If, however, our concern is for sustainable land use, the key issue is ultimately not only that of growth but also of the desired absolute amount of land dedicated to human settlements and transport infrastructure as a proportion of total land area. How much space do we need to live and go about our daily lives? How much do we need to cover our food requirements, to grow biofuels and to generate other renewable forms of energy? How much space do we need for our economic activities and for transportation, and how much space is left for nature? A policy of sustainability should set not only 'deceleration targets' but also targets for the absolute amount of land used – and should guide us towards those targets.

The shrinking population – no matter how deleterious its impact may be on many areas of economic and social life – gives cause for hope that the pressure to designate new land for development will ease, measured against the high levels to date, and that windows of opportunity will open up for concrete measures to restrict 'land consumption'. However, our analysis also shows that broader institutional conditions – people's preferences and behaviours as well as regulatory structures – change very slowly and that the physical, material structures also display a large degree of persistence and inertia in the face of change. This being so, a shrinking population will not be sufficient on its own to curb new land use designation within a sufficiently short space of time. Instead, given the typical pace of institutional change, various additional institutional reforms would have to be introduced now in order to take effect in the period after 2030.

10.5.2 Potential of the stocks framework

The way land is used nowadays is the result of numerous historical factors, institutional conditions and more or less deliberate political and individual activities. Any analysis of the prospects of achieving the 30 ha target and of the need for policy action must necessarily reduce the complexity of these interrelated factors and carve out a few rough-hewn areas of understanding. To do so, it is necessary to get to grips with the relevant information, look at statistics, evaluate background material, research statutory regulations and conduct conversations with experts.

Strictly speaking the stocks framework, as elaborated in the second part of this book, is not really needed to do this. In retrospect, though, we can see that as we worked on the case study the framework helped us significantly not to lose our orientation amidst the sheer amount of information with which we were dealing. First and foremost, it acted as a compass, pointing us towards those aspects that are especially important and those that are less so. By 'important' we mean 'important for a policy of sustainability'. Specifically, the concept of stocks prompted us to look not only at the material aspects of development – particularly the land use statistics – but also the non-material aspects – institutional arrangements, incentives and statutory regulations as well as preferences – and to link the two to one another (cf. Figure 10.9).

In addition, the stocks perspective repeatedly draws our attention towards time: it demands that our analysis take a long-term view when looking into the past as well as into the future. In the debate about options for action it encourages long-term thinking.

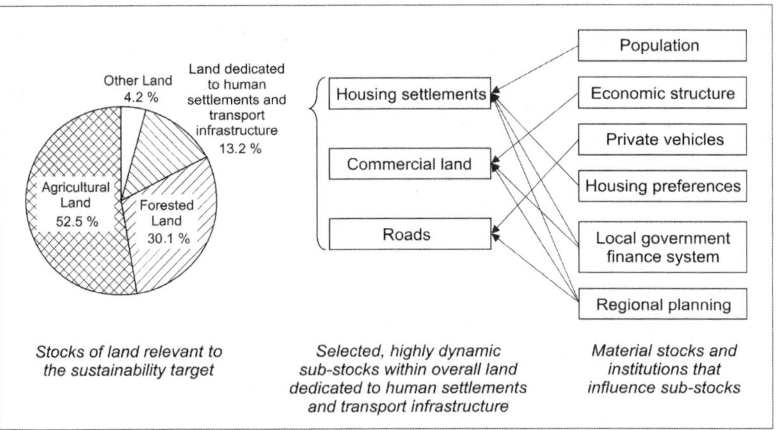

Figure 10.9 Overview of the key material and non-material stocks looked at in our analysis.

The analyst's power of judgement is especially called for when it comes to the process of distilling large amounts of interconnected information and linking together individual pieces of information into an overall picture. The stocks perspective and the concepts of 'stock' and 'institution', addressed in Chapters 3 to 8, were helpful to us in carrying out this task.

Precisely how these analytical aids helped us, though, is hard to say specifically. For this reason we attempt in the next chapter to specify in detail how the concept of stocks can be developed into a heuristic – a collection of guidelines, questions and rules of thumb that can help focus political action on sustainability.

Notes

1 By way of illustration, 100 ha correspond roughly to 140 football pitches.
2 Fischer et al. (2010, 2013) provide a detailed presentation of this case study on the problems associated with sustainable land use in Germany.
3 Unfortunately, however, there are no long time series available. The prior collection of land use data up to 1975 utilised a different data gathering system than the one used after 1980, which was based on the actual land use type.
4 Land for residential and traffic purposes is the sum of several different land-use types whose functions, whether directly or indirectly, predominantly serve local economic needs.
5 These values relate to 31.12.2008. Water bodies and other types of land are additional to those named.
6 The dip between 1975 and 1980 can be traced to a change in the way data was gathered (see Note 3).
7 The ecological aspects of (ir)reversibility should also be mentioned here. Soil formation processes occur at extremely slow rates, lasting over a period of centuries. However, certain soil properties can be re-established over much shorter periods of time (e.g. fertility).
8 This macroscopic 'virtual irreversibility' is not cancelled out by the fact that at certain points individual parcels of land certainly can be – and indeed are – reverted to agricultural or other uses.
9 www.gevestor.de/details/das-bittere-ende-des-baubooms-in-spanien-503231.html, last accessed 19.5.2016.
10 The German Advisory Council on the Environment (*Sachverständigenrat für Umweltfragen*) refers to this issue using the term 'persistent environmental problems" (SRU 2004: para 1176 cont.).
11 As at 31.12.2004. These values are estimates, as not all federal states designate land for particular uses in the same way. In addition, due to mixed uses not all land can be allocated to a single use type.
12 These figures refer to the mid-range scenario (Version 1-W2: upper limit of 'middle-range' population, assumptions: almost steady frequency of births, base assumption regarding life expectancy, migration gain: 200,000) (StaBa 2009a: 40).
13 The following classifications were used: 'growing' = population increase of 3 per cent in 10 years, 'stable' = population increase between –3 per cent and +3 per cent in 10 years, 'shrinking' = population decrease below –3 per cent in 10 years. Of course, this classification is somewhat random, but is nonetheless helpful for illustrative purposes.
14 The Federal Office of Statistics speaks here of per capita housing land but means the average housing/living space of a person. In contrast to this, the 'housing land' of land use statistics denotes the *area of land* allocated to housing as a type of land use.
15 It should be recalled at this point that these are aggregated figures for living space and not the housing land referred to by land use statistics (building land and associated open spaces).

16 Authors' calculation based on StaBa (2008a).

17 Land use plans are proposals that are not necessarily put into effect; in this respect they should be interpreted here as being just an indication of local municipal authorities' approach to designating land for specific purposes. Since land use plans are highly variable in terms of their current relevance and planning horizons, it is only possible to provide examples at this point.

18 No consensus has been reached to date regarding the adaptation trajectory to be pursued and the allocation formula that should apply for permissible land use nationwide (Siedentop 2008: 31-32; Köck and Bovet 2008: 97ff.).

19 Empirical studies confirm this finding: despite shrinking population figures, there has been an expansion of land dedicated to human settlements and transport infrastructure in the urbanised and, especially, the rural areas of West as well as East Germany. It is only in the growing urban conglomerations that the positive allocation of new land dedicated to human settlements and transport infrastructure correlates to rising population figures (BBSR 2011: 5).

20 For reasons of simplification, we will not consider here those institutions that are assumed to have an (indirect) effect on demand for land, such as income tax legislation or the commuter tax allowance (*Pendlerpauschale*).

21 In 2007 an average of 21 per cent of revenues received by western German municipal authorities came from trade taxes, 16.5 per cent from income taxes and 30 per cent from the fiscal equalisation mechanism. In the eastern German municipal authorities, by contrast, the most significant source of financing came from the fiscal equalisation mechanism (53 per cent of revenues), while revenues from trade taxation accounted for just 12 per cent and from income taxes for 7 per cent (BMF 2008:1).

22 In conversations, many local government officials said that, as a rule of thumb, one new resident brings in roughly 1000 euros a year in additional revenues.

23 Authors' own calculations.

Part IV

The art of long-term thinking

11 The stocks framework as a heuristic for sustainability policies

with Beate Fischer

11.1 The stocks framework as a heuristic

The stocks framework serves to render visible long-term trends in nature and society in order to articulate possible ways of shaping sustainability policy. The key features of this framework were presented in Chapters 3 to 8. Two case studies were then used to show how it can be used to analyse specific policy fields in terms of their sustainability. The aim of the present chapter is to show how important the stocks framework can be when used by decision makers in politics and administration and, even more so, by their (academic) advisers, to reach a precise definition of a sustainability problem and to identify potential options for action. The stocks framework is used as a basis to develop a *heuristic* (cf. Section 7.6.2) that enables the individuals involved to structure their knowledge of the policy field and associated problems in a clear way and to focus it on the decisions that need to be taken.

The heuristic consists of a series of steps. Its principal purpose is to depict an initially confusing situation in terms of a clearly formulated sustainability problem, to ascertain what needs to be done to address this problem and, in doing so, to identify potential options for action. The aim of the heuristic, then, is not so much to solve the problem directly as to enable it to be defined in a way that facilitates a solution. An important aspect of this is to avoid overlooking or suppressing key factors by narrowing down the problem too soon.

The nature of the heuristic and what it can help achieve is described in Section 11.3. Prior to this, in Section 11.2, the key characteristics of the stocks framework are recalled succinctly. Finally, in Section 11.4, the heuristic's potential is discussed along with its limitations.

11.2 A reminder: the core elements of the stocks framework

The concept of stock (*Bestand*) enables objects to be depicted in terms of their temporality, changeability, persistence and inertia. The stocks concept is embedded in a stocks framework consisting of the three key concepts of time, stock and judgement. The framework is designed to facilitate action that is guided by judgement and oriented towards achieving sustainability. When policy makers and others use the key concepts of the stocks framework to gain a comprehensive view of a specific sustainability problem, we say that they are adopting a stocks perspective.

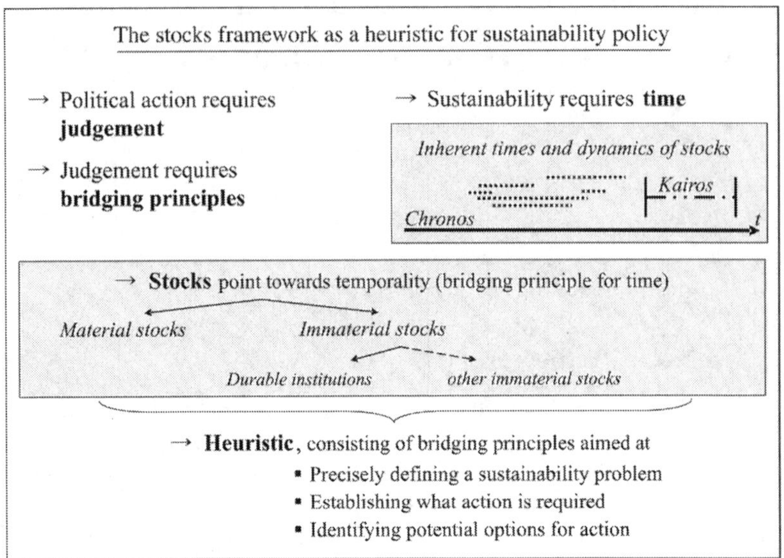

Figure 11.1 The core elements of the stocks framework

The core elements of the stocks framework (cf. Figure 11.1), namely, the concepts of *time*, *stocks* and *judgement*, will be explained again briefly below. First, though, we will consider an important distinction between two ways of looking at problems that are a combination of ecological, economic and social issues: the systems perspective, in which things are always regarded as being part of a system, and the stocks perspective, in which ecological/economic/social systems are perceived first and foremost as being a conglomeration of stocks.

11.2.1 Understanding ecological/economic/social interconnections: systemic knowledge and the stocks perspective

Understanding nature, society, the economy or aspects of these in terms of a system means not merely looking at things in isolation from one another but taking an interest in the particular way these things are interconnected with one another. An omniscient individual wishing to devise policy action for sustainability would take into account the interplay between all the interactions that occur in nature and society in order to reach the best of all possible decisions based on this knowledge. The notion of achieving a full and complete understanding of the world and acting on this basis seems to be the (unachievable) ideal of scientifically grounded policy making. One could call such a depiction of the entirety of interrelationships and interactions an 'ecological/economic/social comprehensive system'.

Since such a comprehensive depiction is not possible, disciplines such as ecology, economics and sociology instead develop ways of representing those parts of this interconnected whole that are empirically available to each disciplinary perspective and can be described using their conceptual and methodological apparatus. Although interdisciplinary and transdisciplinary programmes exist for bringing the separate disciplinary systems together into a unitary overall picture, these programmes do not themselves constitute scientifically robust methods in the strict sense. Compiling an overall picture of a problem based on the results of isolated disciplinary studies is not itself the task of a scientific discipline (in the sense of developing a falsifiable theory); instead, such a task is already part of practical (scientific) policy and policy advice. This means that those involved in devising sustainability policy typically have access to systemic knowledge which, measured against the task of producing an overall picture, is necessarily piecemeal.

The stocks perspective is an attempt to find an answer to the tension that exists between the diffuse totality of each actual problem and the (more or less) precise partial analyses produced by the disciplines concerned. Given this situation, the stocks framework and the heuristic based on it (to be presented in the next section) constitute a tangible means of gathering together knowledge relevant to sustainability policy, ordering it according to a common set of terms, and rendering it comprehensible to policy makers and their advisers.

Studying the way various elements are interconnected with one another is initially not so important for the stocks perspective. The aim first is to identify the elements relevant to a certain sustainability problem and to depict them in terms of their temporality. In other words the stocks perspective sets aside the available systemic knowledge for a moment in order to highlight the aspect of time in relation to its objects of concern. This perspective assumes that the available systemic knowledge has already been reviewed and verified. The aim of temporarily bracketing out the systemic perspective and adopting a stocks perspective is to generate new knowledge at a higher level of cognition which can then itself be ordered systematically.

It is not possible to analyse a problem from the stocks perspective without first having adopted a systemic perspective. The starting point for this is preliminary knowledge that has been arranged in a more or less systematic manner – we might describe it as an 'initial system'. Building on this, the stocks perspective seeks to identify the temporality of things. These insights are then embedded in a comprehensive systemic perspective in order to be rendered useful in terms of sustainability policy (cf. Figure 11.2). Thus the stocks perspective and the systemic perspective are not competing views; rather, they are two ways of identifying and depicting a sustainability problem, and it is possible – and necessary – to move backwards and forwards between the two. The schematic comparison between the systemic and the stocks perspective, shown in Table 3.1, provides an overview of the various approaches.

The new knowledge gained from the stocks perspective should likewise not be construed as an attempt to construct a comprehensive system. Rather, the aim of this analytical process is to generate practical knowledge that is structured systematically and is tailored to address a specific sustainability problem. In addition to scientific knowledge, experiential knowledge and judgement should also feed into this process, and ignorance and uncertainty should also be given consideration alongside inconsistencies and contradictions.

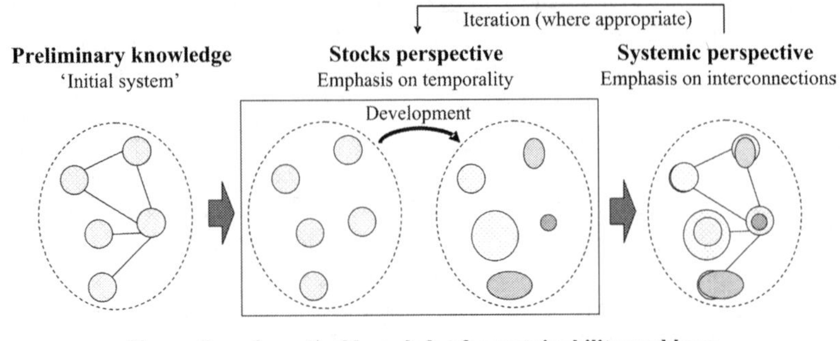

Figure 11.2 Switching between the systemic perspective and the stocks perspective.

11.2.2 Time

The notion of time is central to the concept of sustainability: it is a matter of securing the *long-term continuation* of life in its diverse forms and in a humane way – in other words, it is a matter of phenomena that exist in time.

Sustainability in general requires a long-term temporal horizon, because the impacts of today's actions need to be considered not only in relation to the basic resources for life of those alive today but also to those of future generations. For this reason, we need to be concerned with the temporal structures of things which are either durable in themselves or which give rise to long-term effects. Terms that refer to the persistence and long-term nature of things include enduringness, inertia, stability, persistence, dynamic, change, upheavals, arising and passing away and, in the case of living things, living and dying. While such phenomena are addressed by the concept of stock, there are a number of concepts relating to the aspect of time which are preliminary to the stock concept. These concepts are *chronos, inherent time* and *inherent dynamic*, and *kairos*. These are concepts that illuminate different aspects of time and simultaneously constitute different ways of addressing things in relation to time.

11.2.2.1 Chronos

Chronos refers to time in its plain and empty progress. *Chronos* is the time that is counted in units of measurement and is measured using a time measuring device (chronometer – clock). This time is imagined to exist independently of what happens within it. Time is measured as follows: certain vibrations and movements of, say, a pendulum, quartz crystal or an atom are defined as regular, and all other temporal occurrences are set in relation to these regular movements. Everything that happens can be understood using a time index. This index makes it possible to:

- attribute a duration to a certain occurrence or course of events, expressed in numbers (lasts 3 minutes, 54 years etc.); and
- date events or occurrences, that is, various occurrences or courses of events are set in a temporal relation to one another – before, afterwards or at the same time.

Depending on the approach taken toward time, it is perceived accordingly by a particular subject: *chronos* corresponds to a 'chronicler' who lists occurrences and arranges them in a temporal order. Both physical and historical events and processes can be entered into the numerical framework of *chronos*.

The following definitions of time presuppose *chronos*, but in contrast to the latter, inherent time, inherent dynamic and *kairos* are not an empty measure but rather time filled with content. For this reason the role of the subject when identifying inherent dynamic and *kairos* is different from that when measuring *chronos*.

11.2.2.2 Inherent time and inherent dynamic

Objects possess a duration between their beginning (emergence, birth) and their end (disappearance, passing away, death). We refer to the *typical* duration of sequences of events, processes and life cycles as *inherent time*. It is the 'internal' time of things, so to speak – in the case of non-living things, their typical duration and in the case of living things, their normal lifetime. Inherent time is one of an object's characteristics.

The inherent time of objects is a part of their *inherent dynamic*, i.e. the dynamic that is inherent to them. Inherent dynamic describes, in rough terms, the 'natural course of things', in other words, typical developmental trajectories of observed objects. The scenario assumed here is one in which no deliberate intervention occurs to influence the dynamic. The operation and normal upkeep of a coal-fired power station, for example, is described by its inherent dynamic. This includes maintenance and, where necessary, the replacement of individual parts of the facility. Changing the facility into a gas-fired power station or decommissioning the entire plant and transforming it into an industrial monument would go beyond this inherent dynamic, as the character of the object would be fundamentally changed in the process.

There is a certain degree of leeway when it comes to distinguishing inherent dynamic from the dynamic driven by some kind of external influence on an object. The half-life of uranium, for example, can be defined precisely (the half-life of the uranium isotope ^{238}U is 4.468 billion years), but such precision is more the exception than the rule. In a causal, dynamic theory that seeks to describe a given system in detail, it is not generally possible to separate the two elements of dynamic strictly from one another. The inherent dynamic referred to here, however, relates (from a phenomenological point of view) to *typical* temporal sequences of events in which non-typical external influences are bracketed out. Judgement is required to make this distinction.

Determining inherent dynamic requires a subject with experience or knowledge of the set of circumstances in question, over and above the role of chronicler. For those who need to act, knowledge of the inherent dynamic of things within their domain of action is indispensable and often also taken for granted. The farmer is aware of the rhythms of the seasons, the crops and the animals he keeps; he will take these into account when making decisions in order to obtain good yields. The concept of inherent dynamic can be rendered more specific and tangible when it is applied, for example, to changes in stocks.

Inherent dynamic includes, in addition to the duration of things (inherent time), typical *rhythms* as they develop as well as the typical dynamics of stock variables. The term duration can be applied usefully to stocks: in Section 4.3 we addressed the duration of a material stock as an important characteristic and, in Proposition 4.1, established a relationship between persistence and remaining duration of a material set. Williamson (2000: 596 ff.) discusses immaterial stocks and suggests the typical duration of institutions, mentioning periods of years, decades and indeed centuries (cf. Section 6.2.3). Typical rhythms can often be found in the dynamic of natural systems, e.g. in forest succession, but also in the life cycle of a product in the economic sphere, for example. The exponential decay of radioactive material, mentioned above, is an example of the typical progression of a stock variable.

11.2.2.3 Kairos

For people who want to achieve something and to act, *kairos* is of utmost importance. *Kairos* is the right moment, the suitable opportunity. Those who manage to find the *kairos* do not act at an inopportune moment but rather at the right time. *Kairos* matches a subject who not only registers things (such as the chronicler) or acquires knowledge (like the observer of inherent dynamic) but who also has goals and the will to achieve them. A person who has such a will always observes a field of action with regard to potentially intervening in it. In doing so, she takes account of the inherent dynamics both of the objects themselves and of the ways they are interlinked. She looks for a window of opportunity in which she can take action and can influence the course of events. Looking at the inherent dynamics helps her to surmise or perceive an upcoming window of opportunity before it occurs and, if necessary, perhaps even to work towards it.

In order once more to illustrate by way of summary the differences between the three concepts of time, let us look at the example of the meaning of the word 'year'. In the sense of *chronos*, a year is simply the period of time taken up by 31,556,952 seconds. The inherent dynamic of a year can be described as the succession of the four seasons or of the feast days in the church year. In the sense of *kairos*, spring is the right time to sow and late summer the right time to harvest.

One might justifiably say that reading the time off a clock requires less judgement than comprehending inherent dynamic or discovering the *kairos*. Whereas *chronos* is something absolute, inherent dynamic and *kairos* are relational. Inherent dynamic is a property of an object, and *kairos* is related to an action.

11.2.3 Stocks

We introduced the concept of stock in order to address objects from the point of view of their temporal development (enduringeness, change, arising, passing away) – i.e. their inherent dynamic – and to distinguish between them accordingly. The inertia and stability of things point to their persistence. A stock is always something that exists for (a certain) duration. It is precisely this property that makes stocks an interesting object of study when it comes to analysing long-term developments and seeking to achieve sustainability.

Every stock is accompanied by change. The arising and the passing away of stocks constitute extreme changes. In between the two lies the lifetime, or duration, of a stock. Even during its lifetime a stock is typically subject to changes which, however, do not completely alter its essential nature. Something which is 'eternal' – e.g. the sun in relation to human timescales – should not be described as a stock, and neither should something that is volatile in relation to a problem-related timescale in the sense that it arises and instantaneously disappears – e.g. noise. Thus stock is an intermediate term between the eternal and the present moment. To the extent that a typical lifetime or typical rhythms of change can be identified for stocks, one can speak of their inherent time and inherent dynamic. Stocks can be categorised as material or immaterial.

11.2.3.1 Material stocks

We describe a set of material things (cf. Section 4.3) that exists over a certain span of time as a material stock. The precise nature of this set is established according to a property of appertainment. This says which elements belong to the stock and which do not. The set is described as persistent if it never completely disappears for the duration of its existence. Duration is measured on a timescale that depends on the individual observer's or policy maker's cognitive interest.

In the context of sustainability policy we assume that the individual concerned will be guided in her cognitive interest by her interest in pursuing sustainable development. Accordingly she will define the stocks concerned by means of the relevant properties of appertainment in such a way that she can gain an insight into the options for and limits to action.

11.2.3.2 Immaterial stocks

Non-material objects also possess persistence, duration and inertia as major temporal properties. Among the things that have the character of stocks in this sense are institutions, values, norms, convictions, preferences, habits, traditions, technologies and so on. These objects cannot always be clearly defined apart from their setting, and their stock-like character is not directly observable. Values and convictions, for example, can be articulated and preferences in consumer behaviour can become manifest, but this does not say anything about their persistence.

These objects – not least among them, institutions – are especially important in relation to the question of how to support sustainable development. On the one hand, institutions constitute pre-given (short- and medium-term) conditions for individual and collective action while, on the other hand, they can be influenced directly by political action (unlike values, preferences, knowledge and technologies). Thus they are – albeit generally only in the medium and long term – the object of political action aimed at influencing people's future behaviour. Institutions impact upon values, preferences and interests both individually and collectively. The use of technologies is also influenced by the relevant institutional setting. Desired changes in values, preferences, knowledge, interests and technologies can be brought about politically – if at all – only by shaping or influencing institutions. It is crucial to understand institutions in their stability and persistence in order to influence them in particular ways, and this in turn is hugely important for any sustainability policy.

By 'institutions' we mean rules-in-effect *[Regeln in Geltung]* which are manifested from an external perspective through repetitive patterns of behaviour (on this, cf. Section 5.5). As such, rules and patterns of behaviour are in some respect two complementary ways of representing the same object from two different perspectives. These two aspects belong together like the two sides of a coin. One important difference between them, however, is the following:

- Patterns of behaviour can be observed directly: they thus constitute the 'outside', as it were, of institutions.
- Whether or not a rule – be it formal, such as a law, or informal, such as a convention or mode of interaction – is effective cannot be observed directly but can only be discerned by reflection. The rules and their factual validity are thus the 'inside', as it were, of institutions. For example, whether or not a rule is in effect can only be ascertained indirectly from people's behaviour, from surveys, from introspection or from a shared lifeworld ('that's the way it is').

A complete description of institutions always encompasses both the 'inside perspective' of the rule and the 'outside perspective' of the behaviour. Neither of the two aspects on its own is sufficient. As discussed in Chapter 6, there are various concepts of institution in the social sciences. The term used by us here can be viewed in the context of both philosophical institutional theories, such as that of Arnold Gehlen, and economic institutional theories. By looking at (persistent) institutions as immaterial stocks, however, we are emphasising the element of time in a particular way.

The persistence of institutions is manifested in a repetition of behavioural patterns that is subject to particular rhythms, in behaviour that regularly appears and disappears. The source of this persistence lies not only in what the institutions specifically do to fulfil the purpose for which they came into being. Rather, institutions can continue to exist even if they do not fulfil their original purpose. This is because people may perceive their persistence as a value in itself, namely, whenever a large number of people in a society have a pronounced preference for security and stability in their life, towards which institutions for their part contribute.

11.2.4 Judgement

Judgement refers to the faculty for relating general principles (e.g. scientific theories and laws, legal norms or ethical postulates) to specific individual cases and practical situations. Thus judgement is the ability to handle these general principles correctly in concrete situations, i.e. to apply them in the appropriate way and to render them meaningful for the here and now. In addition to directly applying the general principles ('This is a case of …'), this can also mean that they need to be modified and extended in order to do justice to conflicting aspects and to avoid succumbing to dogmas. Judgement is needed by all those who are contemplating an arena of action and who want to – or should – understand it and possibly intervene actively in it.

Judgement always relates to concrete situations; its domain is the particularity of these situations. Furthermore, judgement proceeds heuristically, i.e. it is guided by general procedural rules, so-called bridging principles, which it uses to work on the situation in question. What needs to be established in the course of this is whether or not the general procedural rule actually fits the particular case in question, whether or not the premises are really fulfilled and whether or not there are other particularities which render its use problematic. In reality one can never be completely sure *a priori* that these conditions are actually given. In addition to suitable heuristics, judgement also needs a flash of creativity, a way of approaching its object playfully. For this, the person concerned needs to have a feeling for the situation – something that can (at least in part) be learned and practised over long years of practical experience.

When hearing evidence in a court case, for example, judges have certain procedural rules that guide them through the complicated circumstances presented in the case. Nonetheless there often comes a point in the process of deciding upon the guilt or innocence of an accused person where this cannot be settled with ultimate clarity by mechanically applying the trial rules. Thus there is no readily available universally valid procedure for judgement in the sense of an algorithm that consistently leads to completely reproducible outcomes or results. Exercising judgement always involves an awareness of the limited nature of the human mind and of its fallibility.

However, in order to ensure that the exercise of judgement does not lead to arbitrary outcomes, it works with the heuristics mentioned above. One example is the rule 'In case of doubt, in favour of the accused'. Additionally, though, the feeling for a situation mentioned above acquires intersubjective validity by the fact that the person judging has to justify and defend her judgement (either explicitly or implicitly) in discourse, thereby taking account of the imaginary positions of the others involved.

11.3 Weaving together a heuristic for sustainability policies

The more complex the terrain – the less standardised the problem to be solved and the greater the lack of knowledge involved – the less it helps to apply standardised schemes in a mechanical way to solve the problem; it is here that the faculty of judgement acquires its considerable significance. Sustainability policy constitutes precisely such terrain, being highly complex and involving a large number of unknowns. It therefore calls for especially well-honed judgement.

This appeal to judgement should not be taken to mean that a person should merely point to their intuition or gut feeling (something they either have or do not have) when making a decision. Rather, the outcomes that emerge from applying the faculty of judgement should also adhere to certain criteria – points of orientation, guidelines and procedural rules, heuristics – which help to provide a rationale for judgements and to make them comprehensible and communicable. Points of orientation and guidelines help to ensure that the goal always remains in view during the process of problem solving while procedural rules give an idea of how to proceed on terrain that is initially complicated and seemingly impenetrable. A procedural rule differs from a law of nature or an algorithm in that it represents a rule of thumb and explicitly allows for exceptions.

In the following we propose a heuristic which is based on the core elements of the stocks framework and offers guidelines, questions and procedural rules to help the sustainability policy maker get a reasonable overall picture of a given sustainability problem. This picture should be neither too simple nor too complex. The aim of the heuristic is to achieve an accurate and workable definition of a sustainability problem, to establish what needs to be done in response and to recognise or discover potential options for action. Applying the heuristic requires judgement while, conversely, it provides information on which judgement can draw to determine what is to be done. The heuristic cannot be used like a recipe, however; it is more like a general guideline that enables a problem to be 'unpacked' so that is then amenable to potential practical solutions.

Defining a problem is the prerequisite for selecting specific instruments and measures to deal with it. Our motivation in developing the heuristic is our experience that *defining* problems is given far less attention than *solving* them – in both academic and policy settings. This is despite the fact that identifying the issues involved is usually no trivial matter and constitutes an important step towards solving the problem itself. Economic theories of decision making as well as technical decision support procedures nearly always presuppose that the problem has already been properly and conclusively defined. Yet defining the problem in a 'quick and dirty' way regularly leads to wrongheaded policy recommendations, to policies that remain merely symbolic and to the use of the wrong policy instruments.

The heuristic we propose is comprised of a series of steps, as follows:

1 Become aware of existing knowledge, and review prevailing opinions, conjectures and insights.
2 Develop ideas for sustainability and frame the problem.
3 Identify relevant stocks.
4 Describe the inherent dynamic of these stocks.
5 Sort through and order knowledge about the relevant stocks and their inherent dynamics and integrate it into an overall picture.
6 Formulate tangible sustainability objectives.
7 Identify the sustainability problem and what needs to be done.

Although these steps prescribe a linear progression, it is certainly legitimate to diverge from it if circumstances require. For example, some steps or sequences of steps may need to be gone through several times in an iterative manner, and it may be advisable to look back over the steps already taken in order to ensure they have been dealt with properly.

The seven steps are described in more detail below. In each case we provide some general information (in italics) at the start before describing how to proceed specifically; finally, we mention certain guidelines, questions and rules that may be helpful during the process.

11.3.1 Step 1 – Become aware of existing knowledge, and review prevailing opinions, conjectures and insights

There is no such thing as 'starting from scratch' when it comes to understanding something. Every act of understanding involves a prior understanding that needs to be clarified. Existing knowledge needs to be verified and placed in a provisional order; pre-judgements need to be articulated and thereby subjected to critical examination. As the process of knowledge acquisition moves forward, all preconceived views and evaluations as well as all apparent knowledge needs to be tested and confirmed, modified or rejected. Pre-judgements that cannot be dropped are obstacles to understanding.

Before a sustainability problem is even formulated, there is a justified assumption – an 'initial suspicion' – that something needs to be done in relation to achieving sustainability. This assumption may come about as a result of scientific information, media debate or coincidental political constellations or through information put out by environmental organisations or politically active citizens.

In order to grasp the problem, the first step consists in gathering together all the available information (one's own experience, others' experience, 'certain' knowledge, conjectures etc.). This may well involve working with heterogeneous fragments of knowledge from different sources – from practical and theoretical contexts, for example. An attempt is then made to draw up an initial, provisional representation of the facts. This representation (which we describe as the 'initial system') links up the available heterogeneous bits of knowledge to create an overall picture of the situation, one that is clear in parts and blurred in others and also contains blind spots and contradictions. This is then brought into association with possibly conflicting ideas about how the system ought to develop.

Generating an initial overall picture is, despite its fundamental flaws, necessary because it renders transparent the element of 'pre-judgement' that exists prior to any action (Gadamer 1975). This transparency is important because in many instances unspoken and unconscious presuppositions guide decisions and yet are not subjected to critique or correction. It is not until the 'cards are on the table' that it becomes possible to ask whether there may be other ways of depicting and understanding the overall situation, apart from this pre-judgement.

The overall picture and the ideas associated with it are provisional. The actor concerned should be aware that in some respects – possibly even in key ones – the initial system may be an incomplete, one-sided or even false representation. It may then be sensible to work with several representations simultaneously. The path towards understanding involves gradually detaching oneself from the grip of pre-judgement and critically clarifying all the factors that are part of the initial picture.

11.3.1.1 Guidelines and rules

- It is important to make oneself aware of existing knowledge and pre-judgements and to convey them clearly to others. This does not necessarily mean having to fill the knowledge gaps, as this is often not possible. Contradictions should not initially be resolved, as they often reflect various points of view that cannot be reconciled with one another.
- At the stage of gathering together existing knowledge it may be necessary to sort and select from it in order to prevent information overload. Nonetheless the basic approach should be one characterised more by openness and curiosity than by a focus on objectives or on narrowing down the available information.
- One ought to be willing at all times to question, correct or even let go completely of one's assumed knowledge and firm convictions.

11.3.2 Step 2 – Develop ideas for sustainability and frame the problem

In order to know what kinds of changes ought to be brought about, we need an idea of what we are aiming to achieve – of what is not yet a reality but can possibly become one if we act appropriately. Utopian visions can help us to develop such ideals. Utopias are ideas about how the world ought ideally to be. They are not usually put into practice but they do provide orientation for articulating ideals and for shaping reality accordingly.

The second step has to do with working out what the desired conditions are in which the problem in question can be regarded as being resolved or at least as having been dealt with appropriately. Even if some aspects of these desired conditions are utopian or visionary, they should bear at least some relation to reality. Ideas about sustainability in a given case can be developed in relation to existing sustainability policy objectives, such as the 'good status' of water bodies contained in the EU Water Framework Directive, the UN's Millennium Goals (e.g. to halve the number of people without access to clean drinking water), the 30 hectare target for land use in Germany (cf. Chapter 10), or the goal to limit global warming to 2°C proposed by the IPCC.

Thus Steps 1 and 2 serve to frame the problem. The task to which the faculty of judgement must be applied here is to create an initial, as yet relatively indeterminate connection between the general (desired conditions and sustainability goals) and the particular (the way the problem is represented in the initial system).

11.3.2.1 Guidelines and rules

- Ideas should be developed about what a sustainable world might look like. This requires creativity: unusual ideas are expressly permitted. Utopias and visions are allowed and may prove fruitful. Whenever it appears certain, based on the analysis conducted in previous steps, that the goal is unachievable, the point to remember is that things which appear impossible in the short or medium term may nonetheless succeed in the long term.
- As well as developing new objectives, existing sustainability goals should be reviewed and questioned to see whether they are adequate or whether they need to be amended.
- One should make oneself aware of which conditions *cannot* be regarded as sustainable and thus know what must be avoided at all costs.
- A provisional description of the problem is gained by forming an initial idea of the desired sustainability goals and setting it against the provisional picture of the overall situation generated in Step 1.

11.3.3 Step 3 – Identify relevant stocks

Relations of cause and effect are often apparent to only a very limited extent – especially when it comes to human interactions and the relationship between humans and the environment. In addition to this, it is often unclear how much significance should be attributed to certain causes and how far they contribute to certain effects, while the host of causal relations gives rise to an extremely complex set of problems. In this context the stocks framework offers an alternative perspective that initially shifts this host of (not entirely certain or clear) causal relations into the background. This serves to reduce the complexity involved. At the same time the stocks perspective enables us to get a clear view of the temporal and long-term trends relating to factors that are regarded as essential.

The initial overall picture formulated in Step 1 is now analysed, extended and, where necessary, reformulated. Analysis here does not mean 'studying causalities' but rather 'dividing into constituent parts'. These constituent parts – natural, economic and social givens – are examined in terms of their persistence and, where appropriate, are described as stocks. It is usually the case that both material stocks and durable institutions as well as other immaterial stocks are part of such a description from the stocks perspective.

Identifying and determining the material stocks involved is done by formulating the property of appertainment. This can be done by referring to existing conventions, such as scientific or legal definitions, or to German industrial standards (*Deutsche Industrienormen*, DIN) or else to European norms (ISO) and so on. In most cases it will not be a problem to identify the individual stocks in question – but it will not always be possible to use existing definitions.

As far as institutions are concerned, it is important to bear in mind that whereas formal rules are normally written down, it may be more difficult to describe informal rules – perhaps because to date nobody has seen the need for a conceptual definition, so that there is no groundwork to build on. Recognising informal rules typically requires an intimate knowledge of the object in question along with determining judgement (cf. Section 7.6.1).

Whether or not the material or institutional objects mentioned here are persistent – and, if so, to what extent – depends on the timescale under consideration, and this emerges out of the provisional description of the problem made at the end of Step 2. Care should be taken that the number of stocks under consideration is not too great and that the representation of the field does not become too confusing and complex; at the same time, no relevant factors should be overlooked. Judgement is needed in order to identify and define the relevance of stocks in relation to the problem at hand. Analytically speaking there are two distinct steps involved in identifying the relevant stocks, even if in practice they often coincide:

3a: First of all we need to establish which stocks come into play in the context of the problem at hand – or, to put it differently, which things are to be regarded as stocks.

3b: The significance of the stocks identified in Step 3a is assessed with regard to the sustainability problem being looked at, and a decision is made as to which stocks are relevant and should be examined more closely in the subsequent course of analysis.

11.3.3.1 Guidelines and rules

Rules and questions for identifying stocks (Step 3a):

- It is important to take account of environmental factors: which animal or plant species are affected? Which habitats are affected? Which renewable or non-renewable resources are affected and what trends are apparent in their future development?
- It is important to take account of economic factors: which goods and services are being produced? Which raw materials are used to do so? Which associated products are generated in the process? What kind of trade relations exist?
- It is important to take account of the institutional structure: what are the relevant legal or other formal regulations? Which informal rules exist which

appear to be set in stone in the short or medium term? Which traditions or conventions are affected? Which habits and customs are important?

- It is important to take account of debates in the society: which issues are currently 'fashionable'? Which ones give rise to conflicts? What are the topics that cannot be talked about? What taboos exist?
- It is important to take account of the options available in the political sphere: what are the key factors in terms of the power to maintain or change situations? How are decision-making structures institutionalised? Who is able to influence whom? Who is obstructing whom? Who has what interests?

Rules and questions for judging the relevance of stocks (Step 3b):

- A stock is relevant if the sustainability goal stands in relation to it (such as the stock of land dedicated to human settlements and transport infrastructure in relation to the 30 ha policy target for land use, or the stock of CO_2 in the atmosphere in relation to climate policy).
- A stock is relevant if it serves to achieve a sustainability goal. It is especially relevant, however, if it stands in the way of achieving that goal.
- A stock can also be relevant if, even though it may not be clearly judged to be either conducive or obstructive, it is nonetheless important in terms of determining the arena of action. For example, it may be important simply due to its sheer size, so that there is no getting around taking it into account.
- It is important to take account of processes of growth in this regard: even apparently insignificant and small stocks may be relevant if they grow rapidly.
- A stock may be relevant on account of its influence on the development of other relevant stocks. A certain understanding of the system or a systemic perspective is necessary to establish if this is the case (cf. Step 1).
- It is important to take account of the (economic) interests of stakeholders and the needs of those affected: which powerful interests are at stake with regard to preserving, changing or eliminating a stock? Whom do the stocks benefit? Whom do they harm?
- It is important to take account of risks: where might rare occurrences trigger massive change or damage? Which stocks would be affected?

11.3.4 Step 4 – Describe the inherent dynamics of stocks

Working on sustainability problems requires a long-term perspective. For this reason temporal processes play an especially prominent role in sustainability policy. Even if everything is subject to flux and change, stocks can steer our attention toward what exists over a longer period of time, and they enable us to speak about the future. They convey a feeling for the temporal structures involved – in other words, they give the policy actor a sense of time (cf. Chapter 8).

The stocks identified as relevant in Step 3b are now considered one at a time in terms of the dynamic of their development. Information is sought about the temporal development of the stock – this is often information relating to the past such as historical descriptions, statistics, time series, documentary materials and personal experiences. It can also include predictions derived from scientific theories, making it possible to establish the characteristic inherent time and inherent dynamic of a stock. The main reason for determining the inherent dynamics of a stock is to anticipate trends: how is the stock likely to develop (in terms of both quality and quantity) unless an intervention is made in its development to influence this dynamic[1]?

The inherent times and dynamics of the different stocks viewed alongside one another give rise to an aggregate of knowledge about policy-relevant dynamics, but they do not automatically come together to form an overall picture. Synthesising the different kinds of temporal information into an overall picture is the task tackled in Step 5.

11.3.4.1 Guidelines and rules

- First, the history of every relevant stock should be considered. What trends are typical in relation to the stock? How long has it existed to date? What is its typical lifetime? These questions may require looking at relationships between different stocks.
- At what points do inherent dynamics point to change or to the disappearance of a stock? Conversely, at what points do they suggest inertia or non-changeability?
- In what way is the stock typically amenable to change? How frequently has it been changed in the past? Have there been failed attempts to change it?
- It is important to take account of elements of inertia in stocks, although it should not be forgotten that change can come suddenly and unexpectedly.
- When assessing the elements of inertia that have been identified, the unpredictability of the 'human factor' should also be taken into consideration: people can intervene deliberately in the development of stocks or they can change them unexpectedly. This can include such diverse phenomena as human error and senseless destruction as well as selfless or creative acts.

11.3.5 Step 5 – Sort through and order knowledge about the relevant stocks and their inherent dynamics and integrate it into an overall picture

Once the particulars have been examined in and of themselves, the next step is to examine the whole and to look at the larger context. As far as is possible, the available knowledge from both scholarly and experiential sources should be integrated into the picture of the whole. At the same time, it is ordered and structured so that what is important is brought to the fore and what is less important remains in the background. Viewed through the stocks perspective, this overall picture is neither a 'snapshot' nor an isolated scenario but rather encompasses various trends and potential futures. In particular it should enable us to see what we will be bequeathing future generations if we do nothing (in relation to sustainability).

In Step 5 the aggregate of knowledge about stocks and their inherent dynamics is combined into an overall picture. Judgement is needed to enable a structured whole to emerge from the previously unconnected factors that appeared on the list of relevant stocks. In the course of this, knowledge about systemic interconnections that is available (easily accessible) is deployed in such a way that the interrelationships between the stocks become visible rather than their inherent dynamics simply being set alongside one another. At this point structures begin to appear within the aggregated information. Although this kind of overall picture includes scientific knowledge, the task of creating it is a creative act that requires judgement. It is the attempt to generate an understanding of the problem that is at once comprehensive and focused on relevant time lines. Although options for intervention are not yet being considered, the overall picture nonetheless points toward the need for action: it shows what will happen if we do *not* act.

The overall picture is a summary of currently available, critically verified knowledge. It will generally also become apparent that knowledge gaps, uncertainty and ignorance exist at certain points. The question then is whether these knowledge gaps should be filled and, if so, how. Ideally, at the end of Step 5 the preliminary understanding (the 'pre-judgement') formulated in Step 1 has been transformed into a well-founded judgement and a reliable understanding.

11.3.5.1 Guidelines and rules

- It is important to research the relationships and interconnections between the different stocks and their dynamics. Different kinds of both 'hard' and 'soft' sources of knowledge should be drawn on for this purpose: factual knowledge, certain scientific knowledge, experiences, assessments and even intimations etc.
- How can time be ordered on the basis of the different inherent dynamics of the stocks in question? At what points do the inherent dynamics proceed synchronically and where are they disparate or even contrary to one another? At what points are these dynamics influenced or even dominated by external influences? The following issues need to be investigated: How do ecological rhythms relate to economic rhythms? How do election cycles, the inertia of laws, irreversible developments in nature and society play into the dynamic of the overall picture? At what points do inherent dynamics and expected influences (or influences that need to be considered as risks) point towards change, destruction or the disappearance of large parts of the overall system? At what points do they point towards preservation, obstruction or inertia?
- The overall picture should be comprehensive but not overly complex. It is unwise to make do with the first picture that emerges: it may be appropriate to produce and compare several pictures with one another. In doing so, it is possible to experiment with different ways of representing the overall picture. Alongside textual representation one can also try out graphic, statistical, mathematical, pictorial, model-based and narrative forms. It is often helpful to work with scenarios.

- Don't jump to conclusions! Understanding the problem is more important at this point than solving it! The desire to intervene successfully should not mean that aspects of the overall picture are misrepresented in order to fit an image born of wishful thinking.
- How are we to deal with residual ignorance? Sometimes it is worth formulating research questions and seeing how knowledge can be obtained within a reasonable amount of time, i.e. before any final decisions are taken.

11.3.6 Step 6 – Formulate tangible sustainability objectives

The things we bequeath to future generations in terms of material stocks, institutions and knowledge will influence the way they judge us. How do we want to live on in their memory? What bequest of material and immaterial stocks do we think constitutes a fitting foundation on which future generations can build their lives? The notion of a 'fair' bequest, however, is initially just that – an idea. In order for this idea to guide us in our actions, it must lead to tangible sustainability goals for the set of problems under consideration.

The current generation cannot guarantee that in the distant future the world will exist in some kind of desirable state – this is beyond humanity's capacity to influence. Nonetheless current generations do bear responsibility for the state of nature, the economy, society and politics that they pass on to subsequent generations. This state, which we call 'bequest', is made up of stocks. We might say, then, that the responsibility of current generations to ensure sustainable development lies in passing on to their children a 'fair bequest package' (Norton and Toman 1997) to the extent that it is within their power to do so.

In this step, the sustainability ideas developed in Step 2 are taken up again and related to the relevant stocks identified in Step 3 as well as to the overall picture generated in Step 5. For this purpose, ideas about a desired state or about a sustainable mode of development need to be simplified and rendered workable. The fair bequest takes on concrete form by the naming of the key stocks that comprise it. A target state is defined for each of these stocks – where possible, in specific qualitative terms or else in quantitative terms using a key indicator.

11.3.6.1 Guidelines and rules

- To what good, i.e. sustainable, state should the overall picture lead as it develops? Which of the stocks that exist currently should be bequeathed to subsequent generations and which should not? To what extent should they be preserved, enlarged, reduced, changed or eliminated? In other words, what is a fair bequest package specifically? Are there stocks not yet in existence (new technologies, innovative institutions) that ought to be created? The ideals and utopias developed in Step 2 should be drawn upon to assess this.
- Can the ideals and goals be expressed by means of precise descriptions and definitions? Are there reliable (perhaps even quantitative) indicators capable of demonstrating progress towards achieving the goal?

11.3.7 Step 7 – Identify the sustainability problem and what needs to be done

The heuristic is brought to a conclusion in Step 7. Following a more or less diffuse articulation of the sustainability-related problem in the preceding steps, it is now delineated precisely and described in terms of its essential structures; the specific action required is then fleshed out. It may be that the mere process of describing clearly the need for action already points to ways of solving the problem. However, the task of actively developing options for action is not part of the heuristic itself but rather constitutes a stage beyond it.

Individual clearly defined tasks are specified on the basis of an overall picture and concrete objectives. These tasks need to be tackled in order to get closer to the goal of achieving sustainable development in the area under consideration. To this end scenarios relating to the development of the individual stocks and the overall picture are devised; the development that is likely without any intervention is then compared with the development required in order to achieve the sustainability goals. Ideally this comparison is one between different paths of development rather than between different (static) states or sets of conditions.

This comparison then leads to the question of what can and should be done. The heuristic presented here prepares the ground for seeking practical options and solutions; it enables the range of potential options to become clear. It is from this range of options that specific courses of action must be sought – or perhaps developed from scratch. This involves a certain element of creativity which, at this point, is needed as a complement to the faculty of judgement. Creativity is not something that can be conceptualised or structured into a scholarly analysis or a heuristic. Nevertheless, working diligently with the concept of stocks as part of the heuristic presented here can form a basis on which the individual's creativity can spring to life; it can help to ensure that the individual is firmly grounded in their approach and that creative actions do not occur randomly.

The range of potential options refers to actions that involve preserving and changing stocks as well as creating and eliminating them. This goes for material stocks and for institutions alike. Identifying this range of options is always linked to the search for the *kairos*, i.e. for the window(s) of opportunity in which they can be implemented. Anyone who wishes to seize the *kairos* will often need to be very patient. In addition to having the ability to wait, though, what is also needed is the determination, i.e. the willingness, to intervene without a moment's hesitation when the 'time is ripe'. Recognising and seizing the *kairos* demands both judgement and creativity.

This final step in the heuristic leads the way towards specific decisions which are not, however, addressed as part of it. Step 7 completes the task of defining the problem, brings to light what needs to be done and also provides clues as to where potential solutions might be found and when the window of opportunity for putting them into practice is likely to appear. What the heuristic does is prepare the ground for this. Among other things, it avoids a situation in which particular options for action are chosen too soon and on an incomplete basis. In addition, it enables options to become apparent that might otherwise be overlooked given the overhasty problem framing so common in everyday policy making.

11.3.7.1 Guidelines and rules

- In order to find out what action needs to be taken, it is necessary to compare the factual bequest (viewed dynamically) with the fair bequest (viewed dynamically). This involves going through the individual stocks and setting their future development – where this development is left to itself – in relation to the targets identified in Step 6.
- In order to identify the range of potential options for action it is helpful to think on a large scale: what is the main impediment to achieving the goals? What are the crucial potential obstacles? What are the main dangers of implementing measures overhastily? What unwanted developments might they trigger?
- It is important to take account of the inherent dynamics of the stocks to be changed. This stock analysis provides clues as to the *kairos* – the right time to act. But there is no need to stand back passively and merely observe: one can actively ask, what can and must be done in preparation right now in order to enable a window of opportunity to open?
- It is important to be prepared for the unexpected and to make the most of surprising changes in politics, society, the economy and the environment. Revolutions, environmental disasters or even a change in a society's mindset can open up windows of opportunity and present a chance that should be taken.

11.3.8 Outlook – Moving toward solutions

Once a specific sustainability problem has been formulated clearly as such, solutions need to be found and then approved and implemented politically. Using the stocks framework, the heuristic presented above has led us to the point at which a sustainability problem is formulated as a concrete task to be tackled by means of policy action. The next question that arises is this: which concrete measures and instruments are available? What kinds of attitudes currently prevail in the society? What are the chances of securing political majorities? Where might resistance to certain options be expected to arise and where might support be garnered? And finally: which of the various options for action is the best one and should be implemented?

Answering these questions, i.e. implementing sustainability policies, takes us beyond the heuristic presented in this chapter, as it involves the imagination and creativity of the policy maker; these can hardly be depicted by a heuristic in the sense of a set of instructions or the like. Nonetheless, three related issues will be mentioned briefly here though not addressed in any comprehensive way.

1. *Exploration* – Searching for a range of potential options and developing specific ones.

2 *Reflecting* upon the social discourse in which discussion of sustainability problems and objectives takes place.
3 *Deciding* which of the available options is the most suitable overall and should be implemented, taking into account all the advantages and disadvantages.

11.3.8.1 Exploration – Searching for a range of potential options and developing specific ones

The search for an appropriate range of potential, practicable options requires a prior clear identification of the problem at hand. Once a stocks perspective is adopted, it becomes apparent that workable options for action nearly always consist essentially in manipulating stocks, whether they are capital goods, supplies of various kinds, resources, institutions, technologies and so on: they are preserved or changed, created or eliminated. To this extent the heuristic, and the analysis of stocks in particular, offers an indication of what to look for when it comes to seeking solutions to sustainability problems.

The process of seeking solutions entails not only analytical issues but creative elements as well. Sustainability problems are typically characterised by a high degree of complexity, novelty and ignorance, so that good solutions can rarely be expected to emerge from standard approaches. What is needed instead is to try out new, unusual approaches. In the exploratory phase that involves devising potential solutions, the aim is to open up a variety of options and not to work too soon towards a solution that is supposedly the only possible one.

For abstract ideas for solutions to turn into realistic options for action, they need to be technically feasible – but also acceptable to society. Even if the extent of a sustainability problem seems to demand far-reaching and fundamental change in society, it is wise to be cautious in response to calls for revolutionary change or autocratically imposed measures. As a rule such changes are not desirable from the point of view of sustainability because they carry a high risk of adverse side effects. The model for sustainable development is instead a mode of policy action that works towards positive change using gentle but steady pressure and considerable patience.

11.3.8.2 Reflecting upon the social discourse about sustainability problems and objectives

For a chosen practical option to be successfully put into practice it is important that the search for potential options (as well as the subsequent decision about which is to be chosen) should reflect the discourse in the wider society. It is within this discourse that debates take place about sustainability problems and objectives. Communication on these issues requires the expertise of scientists and experienced practitioners. However, when it comes to deciding politically what is to be done, this is a matter for the whole society (i.e. its elected representatives). A far-reaching sustainability policy needs political majorities. When articulating proposals for suitable political measures it is crucial to take account of the dominant discourse with its conventions, fashions and taboos: how are problems spoken about in the public sphere (media)? How are the points of overlap and interaction between various aspects of a sustainability problem – protecting the natural environment, economic and social factors etc. – portrayed? What are the fears people have?

The extent to which it is appropriate to adapt to the dominant discourses and the points at which it is suitable to deliberately highlight differences or adopt a counter-position is, on the one hand, a matter of tenacity. It is important to remain true to the insights and objectives that have been identified in the previous steps as the right ones. On the other hand, judgement – understood here as the ability to entertain compromise on details – is indispensable. Potential compromises that entail watering down far-reaching demands are permissible as long as the substance of the sustainability objectives is not affected in any substantial way. A high level of judgement is needed when designing concrete sustainability measures: in some cases all it takes is a small step to irrevocably bring about the required 'turnaround' in sustainability policy. In other cases it may be that a policy becomes diluted to the point of ineffectiveness by 'lazy' compromises.

11.3.8.3 Deciding between different options

Decisions relating to sustainability are made in people's personal lives, in companies, and above all in the public space of politics. Not all public decisions are subject to public debate, however. Many decisions relating to sustainability are administrative ones that only in certain cases involve the public. Some decisions are reached with the support of academic policy advisers. A minimal degree of participation is guaranteed insofar as those who are affected by an administrative decision enjoy the protection of the law, which gives them the chance to resist such decisions. Naturally, this legal protection applies only to those who are currently living and not to future generations.

Academics usually conceptualise problems relating to decision making in terms of selecting the 'best' option (according to certain criteria) from a given number of options, and they provide a range of decision making procedures for doing so. For example, there are economic decision-making processes such as cost-benefit analysis or cost-effectiveness analysis as well as alternative procedures such as multi-criteria analysis. In all these procedures the decision making process is typically structured as follows (Klauer et al. 2006):

1 Criteria for assessment are identified.
2 The effects of various practical options are predicted in relation to these criteria – for example with the aid of scientific models or expert assessments.
3 The practical options are assessed using the assessment criteria.
4 The advantages and disadvantages of each option are weighed against one another; the option chosen is the one that will ultimately be implemented.

Applying scientific decision-making methods to sustainability problems comes up against both theoretical difficulties – such as dealing with uncertainty and complexity (dealt with in detail in the literature but not resolved[2] – as well as practical difficulties. This is why these methods are rarely made use of in actual political decision-making processes. A further key reason for the difficulties involved in bridging the large gap between academia and politics is, in our view, the failure to address the issue of judgement in relation to the practical application of scientific procedures and methods – e.g. in the context of decision support.

11.4 Possibilities and limitations of the heuristic

The heuristic presented here builds upon the stocks framework and thus upon the three core concepts of judgement, time and stock: political action requires judgement. With regard to sustainability problems, this is especially the case when dealing with long-term developments, that is, when dealing with time. By describing the factors involved in political action as stocks, temporal structures are rendered workable and are made accessible to those concerned; stocks, then, are a bridging principle for purposes of judgement in relation to time.

The heuristic based on the stocks framework serves as a means of taking vague notions that certain trends in politics, society, nature or the economy are not sustainable and compressing them into a clearly articulated problem. This in turn makes it possible to formulate the need for action and to identify a range of potential options for action. The stocks framework helps to generate a comprehensive and yet not overly complex picture of the situation, one that brings to the fore the temporal structures of the problem and of potential solutions.

One crucial concern of the heuristic is to avoid a situation in which particular options for action are chosen too soon and on an incomplete basis; this is in order to remain open to innovative solutions. The reason the authors wish to emphasise this element of openness is that, in their experience, the choice of approaches and methods used to predict and evaluate scenarios frequently predetermines the expert statements given to policy makers. In contrast to this, the heuristic presented here enables options to become visible which otherwise disappear out of sight if inadequate descriptions of the problem are taken unquestioningly as given.

We wish at this point to reiterate certain characteristics of the stocks framework and the heuristic that is based upon it:

- The heuristic and the stocks framework provide a way of fitting together into an overall picture the different building blocks of knowledge needed to describe a diffuse problem relating to sustainability policy.
- In doing so, they highlight the aspect of time, which is essential to sustainability and at the same time is especially difficult to deal with.
- They explicitly address the faculty of judgement of both the decision maker and his or her advisers, which is indispensable to ensuring that policy action succeeds. This makes the diverse nature of different kinds of knowledge explicit and available to debate.

Dealing with stocks and the faculty of judgement is not a science in the strict sense. The stocks framework is not a falsifiable theory. Instead it is more of an *art* in the sense of a skill or a capability. The framework and the heuristic developed on the basis of it provide a practical guide to transdisciplinary work. They show

how scientific knowledge and experiential knowledge relating to the temporal structures of a problem can be placed in a common context and rendered fruitful in the search for concrete solutions. As a heuristic, then, the stocks framework is not in competition with scientific approaches but rather complements them, helping decision makers to view them in the round and to render them useful for practical problems relating to sustainability policy.

It is in this way that the stocks framework acquires practical relevance: it highlights important factors that are needed to define a sustainability problem and to ascertain the need for action. At the same time, at a theoretical level it enables an analysis of interactions between academics and practitioners and thus contributes towards the conceptual robustness of transdisciplinary work.

Notes

1 Exogenous influences on stock dynamics or influences exerted by various stocks on one another are also important for purposes of anticipation, of course – even in the context of a 'business-as-usual' scenario. They require an understanding of the system and only become visible within an overall picture of the situation. For this reason we shall not address them at this point.
2 Sigel et al. (2010) offer an overview of approaches used to describe uncertainty and ignorance in decision-making situations.

12 Applying the heuristic

Key elements of a sustainable inland shipping policy

12.1 Applying the heuristic to inland shipping policy

We now apply the heuristic for sustainability policy developed in the previous chapter to a practical case study in order to illustrate how it works. In the following brief study we examine how political decision makers can manage inland shipping in Germany in a sustainable way – or at least in a way that is more sustainable than at present[1]. Our main focus at this point, however, is on method. Using this example, we want to demonstrate that the heuristic developed in Chapter 11 can be put to practical use to generate a rough overall picture of a given problem using relatively simple means, to outline the need for action and, where necessary, to gain pointers toward options for action and windows of opportunity for implementing them. The example is also provided by way of illustration in order to make the abstract and rather general description given in the previous chapter easier to understand. There are two things we wish to highlight in particular in this regard:

- We deliberately do not describe the process of the heuristic in relation to a real-life situation involving policy advice or decision making.
- Given that our main interest lies with the method, we give only a cursory account of inland shipping rather than a detailed one[2]. We attempt to show, in 'short sharp' fashion, how readily accessible items of information can be pieced together to generate a preliminary but fairly robust picture of inland shipping in Germany.

It is in the nature of a heuristic that the information it helps to generate is neither inevitable nor incontrovertible. Additionally, of course, it is always possible to arrive at the same information by another route, that is, without the heuristic. The heuristic, then, is merely a device designed to help the enquirer move systematically along a path toward sustainable solutions. It cannot, however, be applied in a purely schematic or automatic way but rather requires expert understanding and the faculty of judgement.

12.2 How can politicians manage inland shipping in Germany in a sustainable way?

Let us consider first the political background to the question of how German inland waterway transport might be managed sustainably. The 2009 coalition treaty between the conservative CDU/CSU alliance and the liberal FDP party states the following in a section entitled 'Nature conservation':

> Free flowing rivers are highly valuable in ecological terms. It is crucial to make rivers passable again for migrating fish. For nature conservation and flood protection purposes natural river meadows should be re-activated and river valleys, wherever possible, restored to their natural state. We will examine whether the German Waterways and Shipping Administration can be used to accomplish this task. (Coalition treaty between CDU, CSU and FDP, 17th legislative period 2009–2013: 23)

In this statement the German government highlights an important sustainability issue, namely, the use of the country's large rivers for inland shipping operations. Further on, beneath the heading 'Shipping policy', the coalition treaty states the following:

> We will continue, as recently begun, to give the national waterways greater priority when it comes to disbursing investment funding. We will also remove unnecessary bureaucratic obstacles to shipping and put forward a draft law aimed at reforming the Waterways and Shipping Administration. (ibid.: 31)

This agreement between the coalition partners exists against the background of a debate about how public funds can be deployed effectively and to the greatest possible benefit of society at large, and what kind of reforms are needed in order to do so. Evidently the government is pursuing different – and possibly conflicting – goals with regard to inland shipping. On the one hand more river meadows are to be returned to their natural state while on the other the waterways are to be further expanded.

Against this background we now want to use the heuristic, along with its guidelines and rules (cf. Chapter 11), to find out what the sustainability problems are in relation to German inland shipping policy and where there is a need for action. Our discussion is based on the political debate as it stood in October 2010. At the end of this chapter, in Section 12.2.6, we will briefly mention current developments.

12.2.1 Step 1 – Become aware of prior knowledge about German inland shipping

Waterway transport on Germany's rivers and canals goes back more than a thousand years. It enables goods to be transported in large quantities. For this to occur, of course, it has to use existing waterways. Centres of industrial production have consequently sprung up time and again in exactly those places where access to rivers is easy. Canals were additionally built in order to establish connecting routes between the natural waterways.

Important inland waterways in Germany include the rivers Rhine, Mosel and Neckar and the Midland Canal, which extends west-to-east across the northern part of Germany. The main bulk items transported along these waterways are gravel, coal, mineral ores and scrap metal. However, container shipping has become increasingly prevalent in the last few years. Inland shipping is important for the port of Hamburg and other large ocean ports in terms of linking them up with the 'hinterland'. The inland waterways capable of handling goods transportation are among the so-called federal waterways and are under the administration of a national agency rather than of individual federal states, unlike other water bodies.

Inland waterway transport on the federal waterways requires favourable and reliable navigation conditions, as far as is possible – in other words, waterways should be passable throughout the year wherever possible, with a sufficient depth and no significant obstacles. In order to do justice to these requirements and also to allow flood water to run off more easily, the waterways have been and are being 'improved' and continuously 'maintained'. As a result most waterways are non-natural, technically altered stretches of water containing very different species than they otherwise would and fulfilling a limited role as flood barriers. Rivers in a near-natural state – of which there are hardly any left in Germany – offer poor conditions for shipping. They are generally characterised by changing water levels, shifting riverbeds and shifting sand banks, potholes and shallows – all in all, then, a highly dynamic riverscape.

There has frequently been heated debate among experts and the general public in the past – some lasting for years or even decades – about the pros and cons of expanding Germany's rivers into navigable waterways and maintaining them over the long term as well as about canal building projects. Well-known examples include the controversy over the construction of the Rhine-Main-Danube canal (cf. Glas 1996), the expansion of the river Saale (cf. Petry and Klauer 2005) and maintenance activities on the river Elbe (cf. Petschow and Wlodarski 2009).

12.2.2 Step 2 – Briefly consider relevant aspects of sustainability and develop ideas for sustainable inland shipping

What does 'sustainability' mean in the context of inland shipping policy? Generally speaking, sustainability (cf. Chapter 2) is a normative model to which the German government has committed itself, in part in its national sustainability strategy entitled 'Perspectives for Germany' (German Federal Government 2002). Sustainability demands that the different interests of current and future generations be balanced in a fair manner and that the natural conditions necessary for human survival should be preserved. To do justice to this model it is necessary to adopt a long-term perspective and to take account, for example, of the impacts of demographic change, climate change, globalisation and the development of the economic structure from an industrial to a service-based economy when looking towards the future and deciding what policy action to take.

Sustainability, then, is initially an abstract demand which needs to be rendered specific in relation to inland shipping in order to be politically effective and to provide practical guidance in individual cases. This macro-social task entails formulating an idea about what structure our economic development in general and inland shipping in particular should have, what transportation ideals are important to us, what features functioning habitats, landscapes and infrastructures should possess and how strictly or loosely nature and environmental conservation should be handled. In other words, sustainable shipping policy cannot be designed in isolation from macro-social and economic development and certainly not from other domains of transportation policy – indeed it must be integrated into these.

Neither the above-mentioned coalition treaty nor the relevant legislation offers any clear answers to these questions. The national sustainability strategy contains the vague and currently rather unrealistic demand to decouple the development of motorised transportation from economic growth (German Federal Government 2002: 111). An ideal scenario (impossible to achieve) would seek to have both at the same time – inexpensive goods transportation that is environmentally sound and uses up fewer resources alongside (cultural) landscapes that are as close to natural as possible. However, because these options are mutually exclusive in a single location (at least given existing technologies), it is necessary to deal with the conflict that exists between creating the best possible shipping conditions on the one hand and preserving or re-creating river stretches in their natural state on the other. One important approach to balancing these different objectives is to establish spatial priorities for goods transportation and nature-like landscapes in such a way that both can be regarded as being met on a larger scale.

The policy strategies quoted above neither address the conflict between the different objectives nor do they take account of the possible approach to dealing with them just mentioned. This suggests that the debate about the different objectives of creating optimum shipping conditions and preserving natural rivers and river meadows has not yet been conducted to the point of resolution in Germany.

12.2.3 Steps 3 and 4 – What are the relevant stocks associated with German inland shipping and what are their (inherent) dynamics?

In order to avoid redundancies and too much complexity we will concentrate in the following on presenting a few stocks that are especially relevant to the issue of inland shipping (Step 3) and give an account of their dynamics (Step 4). We will describe the temporal development of the material stocks mainly using statistics and that of the immaterial stocks using a qualitative approach.

The Federal Republic of Germany is an industrialised country that depends upon an intact transportation infrastructure. Germany does indeed have a densely woven, properly functioning network of roads, railway routes and national waterways. There are airports, pipelines, multi-modal harbours (ocean and inland), freight centres, a large fleet of goods lorries, railway rolling stock and an inland shipping fleet. A network of private sector and publicly owned companies as well as government administrations organises goods traffic and keeps it running.

There are currently some 7,350 km of inland waterways in Germany, of which approximately 6,600 km are inland shipping waterways and some 750 km waterways for ocean-going vessels. Among the most important inland waterways for ocean-going vessels are the Lower Elbe, which connects Hamburg harbour to the North Sea, and the North Sea–Baltic Sea canal. 35 per cent of the entire network of inland waterways consists of free flowing stretches of river, 41 per cent are stretches managed using weirs, and 24 per cent are canals[3]. There are 54 of 80 urban regions connected to the network of waterways (BMVBS 2010: 290).

If we look at the role of inland shipping within the overall context of goods transportation the following picture emerges: whereas the volume of freight and thus the demands placed on the transport network have grown steadily over the years overall, the tonnes per kilometre transported using inland shipping has stagnated to an almost constant level over the last 10 years. By contrast, rail freight has grown slowly while road freight has grown rapidly (cf. Figure 12.1).

In the so-called modal split between the various forms of freight transport, inland shipping accounts for far less than 10 per cent of total freight transport, with a declining trend (cf. Figure 12.2). The German government's current prediction regarding the future of freight transport to the year 2050 (Ickert et al. 2007: 4) is that the proportion of freight accounted for by inland shipping will continue to decline in the modal split, whereas that of rail and road freight will increase slightly. In absolute figures, though, the prediction is for there to be a surge of growth in all forms of freight transportation. Inland shipping is predicted to see a

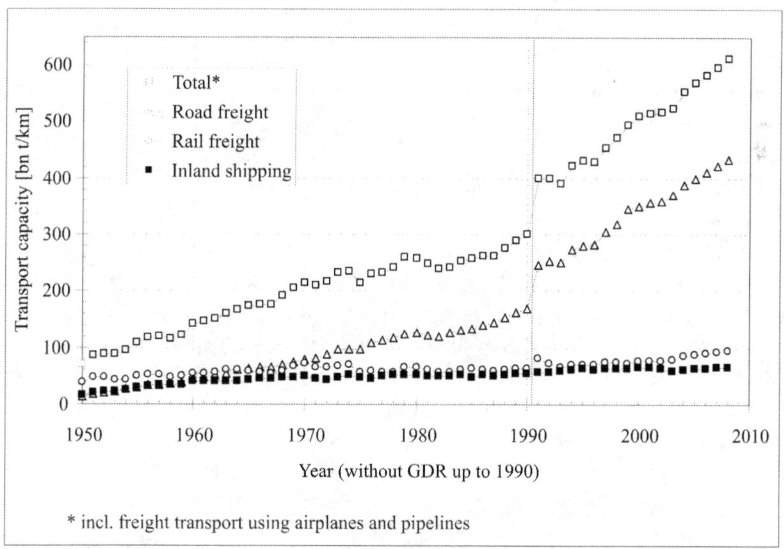

Figure 12.1 Freight transport in the Federal Republic of Germany, development of transport capacity 1950–2008 in billions of tonnes per kilometre.

Source: Bundesverband Güterkraftverkehr, Logistik und Entsorgung 2010[4], authors' diagram.

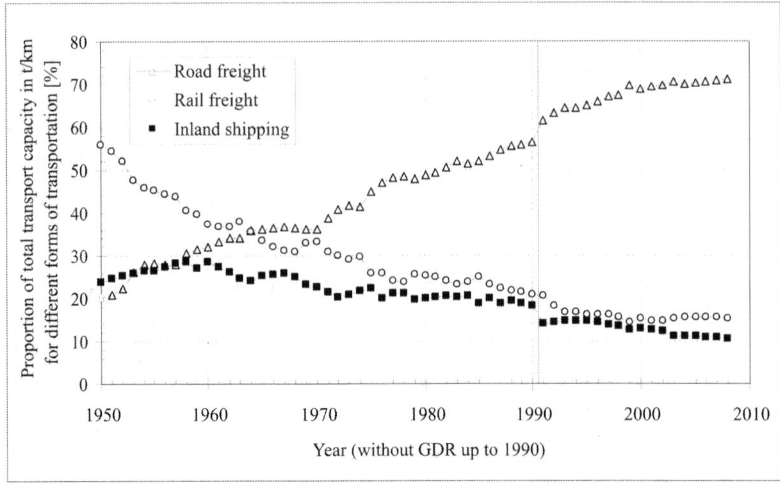

Figure 12.2 Freight transportation in the Federal Republic of Germany 1950–2008, modal split – tonnes per kilometre of selected forms of transportation as a proportion of total inland freight traffic.

Source: Bundesverband Güterkraftverkehr, Logistik und Entsorgung 2010[5], authors' diagram.

growth rate of 36.3 per cent up to 2030 and of 56.6 per cent up to 2050 (in each case using 2005 as the base year) (ibid.). Predictions over such a long period of time should be treated with caution, of course, given that they assume there will be no structural breaks along the way. Nonetheless it does not appear unreasonable to assume that all forms of transportation will see a marked increase in freight traffic even as the relative significance of inland shipping declines (cf. Petschow and Wlodarski 2009: 73–74).

Transport volumes are a good indicator of the potential development of the *material stocks* that comprise them, i.e. transportation infrastructures on the one hand and corresponding infrastructures in the economy on the other. Much harder to capture than roads, railways and waterways and the lorries, trains and ships that use them, though, are the *immaterial stocks* that give rise to these increasing transport volumes, or rather make them possible. Clearly, however, there is an uninterrupted growing need for transport capacity, which enables us to draw conclusions about the way our economy – based as it is on the division of labour and on growth – works as well as about consumer behaviour.

One important *institution* for dealing with the dynamic of this demand is Federal Transport Infrastructure Planning. Every 10 or 15 years the German government adopts a Federal Transport Infrastructure Plan in which investments in the transport infrastructure are set out for the following 10 to 15 years. The last Federal Transport Infrastructure Plan in 2003 foresaw an investment volume of approximately 150 billion euros (BMVBW 2003: 70). The plans are drawn up on the basis of extensive traffic predictions using an analytical method that is essentially based on cost-benefit considerations (BMVBW 2002). Decisions regarding the proposed transport infrastructure projects are taken individually – regardless of whether or not they are to be considered as priorities. There is no real overall planning across the different forms of transportation. In particular, investments in the road and rail networks are planned largely independently of those in the waterways network.

In 2004, for example, the government spent some 1.6 bn euros on investment, maintenance and administration for inland waterways (StaBA 2006: 22). According to the coalition treaty (see Section 12.2.1) this budget item is to increase during the current legislation period. The administration of Germany's inland waterways is organised as follows: the Federal Waterways and Shipping Administration (WSV) is answerable to the supreme authority of the Federal Ministry of Transport. The former is responsible for maintaining the country's waterways as well as for planning, authorising and implementing improvements and new construction projects. In 2009 some 13,000 people were employed by the WSV[6]. The work of the WSV is supported by strong divisional research institutions, namely, the German Federal Institute of Hydrology (BfG) and the Federal Waterways Engineering and Research Institute (BAW). With regard to the national inland waterways, the transport ministry and the WSV have seen their task in the past above all as one of ensuring that navigation conditions are maintained at a steady high level by implementing maintenance and improvement measures. Note that the WSV is – even today – simultaneously the authority responsible for planning, authorising and implementing such measures. An unsatisfactory aspect of this arrangement to date has therefore been the degree of consultation and coordination of tasks with those relating to nature conservation. Having said this, activities have generally been conducted in coordination with the tasks of dike construction and flood protection, and a number of improvements appear to be on the horizon regarding coordination with river catchment management in line with the European Water Framework Directive.

In addition to the formal institutions associated with the Waterways and Shipping Administration, nationwide transportation planning and the Water Framework Directive, there are a number of frequently recurring mindsets that are relevant in relation to sustainable inland shipping policy and can be regarded as persistent informal institutions. The WSV and its departmental research facilities, for example, are influenced by a tradition and culture steeped in hydrological engineering. This tradition and the skills and interests connected with it are themselves an important immaterial stock. Other mindsets of this sort which one encounters again and again in policy debates include the following:

- Inland shipping is the most environmentally friendly and most inexpensive way of transporting large quantities of goods.
- Investments in transport infrastructure are effective measures for boosting the economy and thus creating jobs.

Having looked first at some material and immaterial stocks in the transport sector, we now turn to stocks which are relevant to environmental protection and nature conservation. We focus here on two important factors, namely:

1 The stock of near-natural river meadows
2 The condition of German water bodies according to the criteria contained in the European Water Framework Directive

Near-natural river meadows and flood plains are important as retention areas for preventive flood protection and fulfil a variety of ecosystem functions – especially nutrient retention, self-purification and habitat provision for a large number of rare plants and animals. They are important leisure destinations for city dwellers and also constitute transregional axes for habitat connectivity.

The ecological situation of Germany's waterways can currently be described as critical. For example, the Federal Agency for Nature Conservation's report on the state of river meadows states that, particularly alongside the country's larger rivers, 'intensive use of river meadows, dike construction, the expansion of water bodies and dam facilities have led to considerable losses of natural flood plains and to extensive changes in the condition of river meadows', which is associated with a marked decline in biological diversity (BMU/BfN 2009: 10). Shipping requires the expansion of waterways, continual maintenance work and dam facilities and thus clashes with the preservation of near-natural river meadows. Only around 5,700 ha of near-natural hardwood woodlands remain along riversides in Germany, which is less than 1 per cent of the original stock. Swamp areas which, if left to themselves, would take up large amounts of land, constitute only approximately 2 per cent of floodplain meadows (10,000 ha) and much less than 1 per cent of ancient river meadows (ibid.).

One of the key aims of the European Water Framework Directive (WFD) is to achieve 'good water status' for natural surface water bodies by the year 2015. However, waterways are typically not regarded as 'natural' but as 'artificial' or 'heavily modified'. These are subject to the weaker ecological criteria of 'good ecological potential' (Article 4.1 WFD). The so-called inventory mentioned in Article 5 WFD and an initial evaluation of the present versions of economic plans show that the overwhelming number of water bodies will not achieve the objectives of 'good status' or of 'good potential' for several years yet, particularly when it comes to the large rivers (BMU 2010; Bathe 2010; Bathe et al. 2010, 2011). The main reasons for this – alongside the addition of nutrients from sewage plants and agriculture – are the morphological changes[7] which have been made to the water bodies in respect of, for example, flood protection, the drainage of agricultural land and shipping. A particular problem is the poor passability of rivers for migrating organisms. Barrages for vessels prevent salmon and eels from swimming over long distances up and downstream – unless, that is, facilities such as fish ladders or similar constructions have been provided. A lack of obstacles is necessary in order for the fish to reach their spawning grounds.

For a long time there appeared to be uncertainty around who is responsible for the practical implementation of the WFD on the country's waterways. Eventually, in 2009 it was decided that the WSV must pay greater heed to ecological criteria in the course of maintaining the waterways and that it must make dam gradients passable by means of fish ladders or similar arrangements for migrating fish.[8] Since that time a programme has been put in place to ensure passability in the case of 260 weirs with locks by the year 2027, entailing costs of up to 700 m euros[9].

12.2.4 Step 5 – Sort existing knowledge and integrate it into an overall picture

Steps 3 ('Determine relevant stocks'), 4 ('Determine their inherent dynamics') and 5 ('Sort existing knowledge and integrate it into an overall picture'), which are kept separate for analytical reasons in the heuristic, are not always easy to distinguish in practice. This is not a problem as long as the issues are taken into account and addressed. In our brief case study on sustainable inland shipping we have not presented our description of the relevant stocks separately from our description of their dynamics. Additionally, in the previous section relationships between the various stocks were identified either explicitly or implicitly so that the individual facts gradually came together to form an overall picture. In our account of Step 5 we will now identify explicitly a number of other relationships and attempt to bring a more systematic arrangement to the picture.

In Figure 12.3 we have grouped together some of the relevant stocks, indicated how they may develop over time, and placed them in relation to the sustainability goals with which these trends come into conflict. As indicated in Figures 12.1 and 12.2 as well as by the transport ministry's predictions (Ickert et al. 2007), Figure 12.3 also shows that the number of goods lorries is set to increase steadily and that there will be no shift from roads to inland shipping but rather, if anything, fierce competition between the railways and shipping. To this extent the need for waterways will not grow any further either. Nonetheless, investment in facilities such as fish ladders at barrages is still needed in order to achieve at least some degree of balance between the goals of 'protecting water bodies' and maintaining a 'good transport infrastructure', even if transport capacity remains stagnant.

The conflicts that arise between different sustainability goals cannot always be resolved by technical means, however. The maintenance measures undertaken along shipping routes usually have an adverse impact on the adjacent river meadows and thus indirectly on water status. Beneficial shipping conditions and near-natural rivers and meadows are extremely difficult to achieve along the same section of river. Given this sustainability conflict (which we mentioned briefly in Step 2) and on the basis of the inventory presented above, therefore, we wish to conduct a more detailed breakdown of the shipping routes and find out where goods transportation actually happens. This information was not included in the stock analysis contained in Steps 1 to 4, but it is important when it comes to formulating spatial priorities

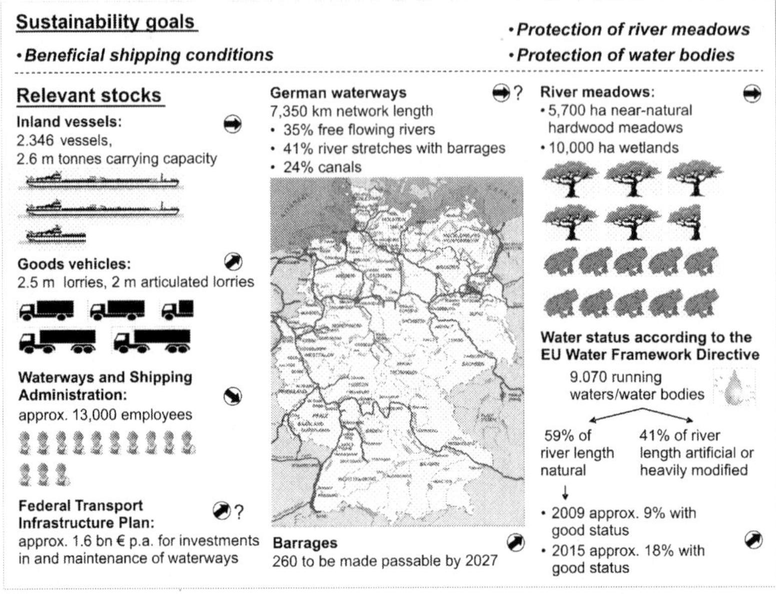

Figure 12.3 Overview of important stocks, their future trends and their relation to the conflicting sustainability goals in the sphere of inland shipping[10].

for achieving the different goals of sustainability – for goods transportation on the one hand and for near-natural rivers and meadows on the other.

For this purpose the entire stock of Germany's waterways is divided up into separate stretches of rivers and canals, and the amount of goods transported annually is ascertained for these sub-stocks. Figure 12.4 shows that the overwhelming proportion of goods transported on Germany's waterways is carried on the Rhine and on the Lower Elbe northwest of Hamburg (though the Lower Elbe is classified as a maritime waterway). Other oft-frequented inland shipping routes include the east-west Midland Canal, the Dortmund-Ems Canal, the Elbe Lateral Canal, the Mosel, the Main and the Neckar. In contrast to these, hardly any goods transportation occurs on many other stretches of the German waterways network.

It is likely that the spatial distribution of goods transportation in the future will not be subject to any great change and that at most the differences will grow larger. Studies conducted by the Potsdam Institute for Climate Impact Research, the Helmholtz Centre for Environmental Research and other research institutions show, for example, that as a result of climate change the shipping conditions on the Elbe over the coming decades will deteriorate markedly (PIK 2009). Conditions on the Rhine, by contrast, are affected less by climatic changes.

Let us now consider the combined effect of informal and formal institutions which regulate decisions about the waterways network. The complexity of factors involved in balancing the different requirements of the water bodies is often

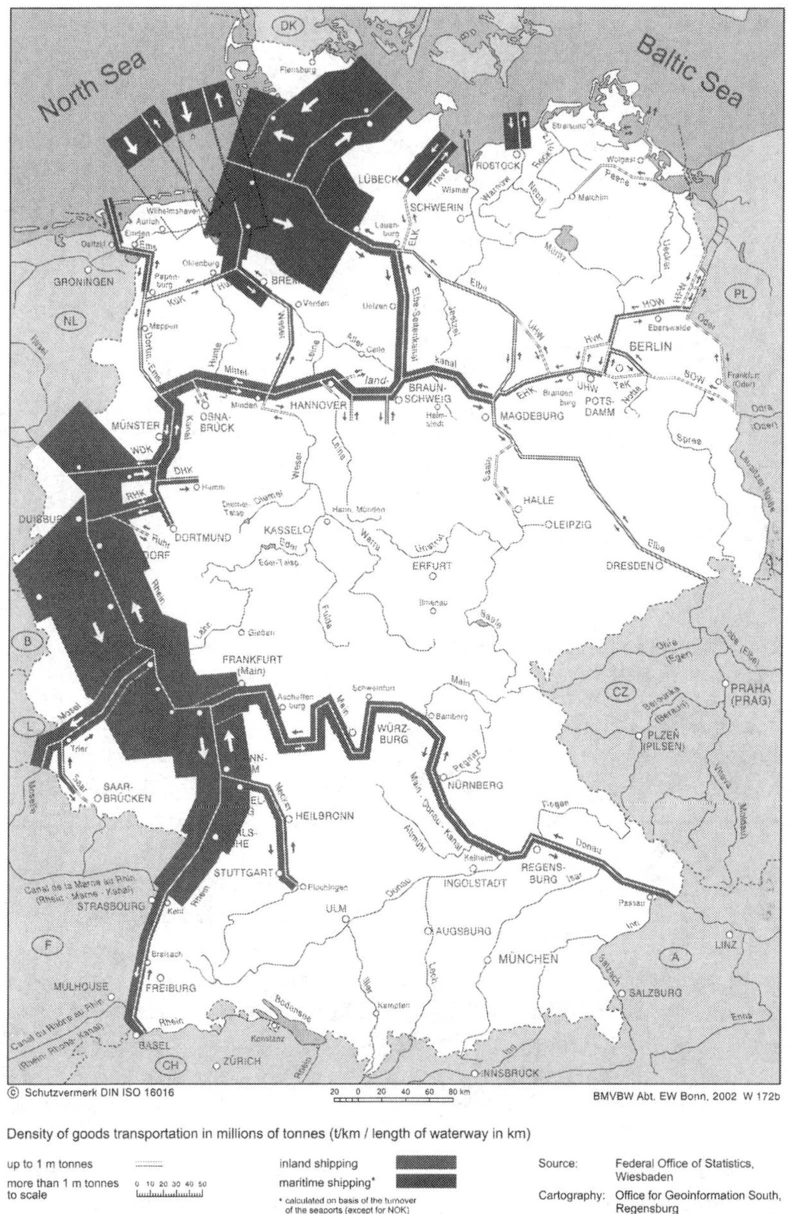

Figure 12.4 Density of goods transportation for maritime and inland shipping along the main network of Germany's federal waterways in the year 2000.

Source: German Waterways and Shipping Administration[13].

simplified in policy debates – and sometimes even in expert debates as well. Debates about expansion plans for the river Saale, for example, continue to be dominated by the mindsets outlined in Section 12.2.3 above relating to environmentally friendly inland shipping, which its proponents wish to promote in order to shift goods from the roads onto the rivers and to give the region an economic boost which, it is hoped, will ultimately create more jobs[11].

However, it is not only the policy debate between the relevant organisations and interest groups that fails to take adequate account of the complexity of the infrastructure system and the multitude of demands that are made of it: the formal 'Federal Transport Infrastructure Planning' institution does the same – even though it is based on a far-reaching and comparatively well-documented method[12]. The plans predicting the needs for various forms of transportation – roads, rail and waterways – are still drawn up largely independently of one another.

In summary, it can be said that the interests, mindsets and patterns of argumentation adopted by the Waterways and Shipping Administration and the representatives of inland shipping as well as the regulations stipulated by nationwide transportation planning lead to a pronounced inertia that stands in the way of any reform of institutions and ultimately of any attempt to examine the fitness for purpose of the waterways network.

12.2.5 Step 6 – The key elements of a sustainable inland shipping policy: concrete sustainability goals

Having analysed the current situation of inland shipping and its predicted trends, we can now summarise the normative demands placed on German inland shipping policy by the general principle of sustainability in terms of the following key elements:

- *Limits to growth*: Goods traffic should not grow unchecked because it does not contribute directly to an increase in well-being but rather serves merely to distribute production materials and consumer goods. In this respect an important sustainability goal consists in decoupling future transportation trends, economic growth and social well-being from one another. Thus one key element would be the goal postulated by the German government in its sustainability strategy (German Federal Government 2002: 111): '… to induce a similar development in the transportation sector as has already been achieved in the energy sector, i.e. to decouple economic performance from transport capacity. Towards this end we seek to achieve a reduction in transport intensity [i.e. tonne kilometres or passenger kilometres per GDP] by around 5% in goods transportation and 20% in personal transportation by 2020 as against 1999 levels'. This means likewise limiting the amount of area taken up by transportation routes.
- *An efficient infrastructure geared towards needs*: The enormous sums spent on maintaining and investing in the waterways infrastructure should be justified on economic grounds[14]. Currently it is doubtful whether some of Germany's

waterways are economically efficient when one sets the costs of maintenance against the transportation benefits. This makes it appropriate to examine economic efficiency not only in relation to investment in expansion projects but also in relation to maintenance measures.

- *Balancing interests fairly*: A comprehensive process of deliberation will take account not only of the interests of businesses in inexpensive goods transportation but also of the interests of current and future generations in access to a healthy natural environment and life-enhancing landscapes. The species diversity that exists in river meadows is a major reason why they require even greater protection than other natural habitats. (BMU 2007). In particular it is important to note that there is currently a largely irresolvable conflict at the local level between waterways expansion for shipping and the goal of preserving a near-natural structure of Germany's waterways.
- *Institutional development of the German Waterways and Shipping Administration*: With regard to its organisational structures the WSV needs to be reformed in such a way that not only the interests of inland shipping – to ensure that shipping conditions are as beneficial as possible – but also the opposing interests regarding maintaining near-natural conditions for water bodies are systematically taken into account.
- *Integrative planning*: Roads, railways and rivers and the modes of transportation they support are interconnected and, to an extent, act as substitutes for one another. The predicted needs set out in nationwide transportation plans have so far given insufficient consideration to this fact. The methods used by Federal Transport Infrastructure Planning (according to which the plans for road, rail and waterways projects are drawn up largely independently of one another) ought in the future to be geared towards drawing up systematic, integrated plans for all the transportation networks.

12.2.6 Step 7 – Define the sustainability problem and outline the need for action

The task at this point is to place the key elements of a sustainable inland shipping policy (Step 6) in relation to the current situation (Steps 3, 4 and 5) in order to identify where and how it is appropriate to intervene in the transportation system.

12.2.6.1 Examine the federal waterways network in terms of economic efficiency and formulate priorities for use

The Rhine as well as several other canals and rivers are used intensively for goods transportation and therefore play an important role on the macroeconomic scale. At the same time, river meadows are the most species rich habitats in central Europe. Looking at Germany as a whole it seems sensible not to treat all water bodies in the same way. Instead, it makes sense to distinguish between rivers whose use as inland shipping routes is of prime importance (as will certainly be the case with the Rhine) and rivers whose near-natural status is primary. At this time the last remaining near-natural rivers and floodplains in Germany are threatened by planned improvement projects and by the impacts of current building activities. This is especially the case on the middle and upper stretches of the Elbe and the Oder, where maintenance activities have been intensified, and on the Danube, where there are plans for improvements at Straubing-Vilshofen.

A large part of the current national waterways network is not (or no longer) used intensively for the transportation of goods. Classifying these water bodies as national waterways generates constant pressure to improve or maintain them, even though the effort and expense involved is not matched by any significant benefit to the country's economy. If a waterway maintains its status as a national waterway but is allocated a lower waterway classification, this in itself can lead to lower spend on maintenance. Beyond this, those rivers and water bodies which are not in intensive use should no longer be classified as national waterways, with responsibility for their upkeep transferred to the federal state in which they are located. This seems sensible not only for the purpose of reducing maintenance costs but also because it would make it easier administratively to implement the European Water Framework Directive for which the individual federal states are responsible. It may well be that the federal states will agree to this reclassification from the national to the regional level of responsibility only if they receive at least some transitional compensatory funding for taking on the burden of maintaining the water bodies in question. To sum up:

- Sustainable inland shipping should continue above all on those rivers that have already been improved for this purpose. There should be no further improvements and very little further maintenance undertaken on rivers which are unimportant economically or of special ecological value.
- The network of waterways in Germany as a whole should be examined in order potentially to reclassify individual waterways.

At this point we would like to mention an initiative currently being undertaken by the German transport ministry which actually does contain some of the key demands just mentioned. In 2012 the ministry wrote on its website:

> [The initiative] is based on a categorisation of the network of national waterways underpinned by expert reports, which sets clear priorities for infrastructure financing and the intensity of waterways operation and maintenance. Within this network structure a distinction will be made between those waterways with high transport capacity and those with little or no role in goods transportation. Category A is the highest category: these are inland waterways with more than 5 million tonnes of goods traffic each year. Category B waterways have between 3 and 5 million tonnes, Category C less than 3 million tonnes and 'others' have no goods traffic[15].

What this means in practice is that low-traffic waterways – such as the Elbe south of Magdeburg and the Saale – are not to be improved at all but only maintained.

However, the ministers for transport of the federal states of Saxony-Anhalt and Brandenburg are up in arms about this classification of the Elbe and the Saale. In response to them, the Federal Ministry of Transport argues as follows on the same website:

> We deploy resources according to need, not according to state boundaries. Our planning is based on realities – the conditions and facts of nature in Germany. 85% of inland shipping in Germany takes place on the Rhine and its tributaries – the same amount in a single week as takes place on all the other waterways combined in a year. [...] The optimistic predictions of growth in shipping for the new [former East] German states made in the 1990s have not come to pass. Further improvements are therefore neither necessary nor financially feasible in the foreseeable future.

12.2.6.2 Reform Germany's Federal Waterways and Shipping Administration

The WSV has enormous capacity in terms of staff and expertise. In the past, however, this has been directed mainly at creating the best possible conditions for shipping, whereas other tasks such as achieving the ecological objectives of the WFD have not been tackled adequately (cf. BMVBS 2010: 290). In structural terms one point of critique is that the WSV combines planning, implementation and approval in a single organisation. The aim of modern waterways legislation ought to be to make the planning of new waterways projects and of improvements to existing waterways subject to monitoring by the legislative authorities. Coordination and consultation regarding work carried out by the WSV and work carried out by other authorities at the national and federal state level that are responsible, among other things, for flood protection, implementing the WFD at water catchment level and nature conservation should be further improved (Möckel 2009). To sum up:

- It is imperative to examine the tasks and competencies of the WSV, to redefine them and, in the process, to adapt the structures of all relevant agencies and authorities accordingly.
- Processes of consultation among the WSV and other national- and federal state–level authorities should be optimised and waterways legislation adopted accordingly.

Here too it should be noted that reform of the WSV is already underway and that, for example, the regional shipping directorates have been combined into a single general directorate based in Bonn. The Federal Ministry of Transport states in this regard (on the website referenced in note 16):

> The structure and tasks of the Waterways and Shipping Administration – especially its representation in the regions – will be based on this network structure. This will involve, for example, pooling resources in agencies that specialise in specific tasks (e.g. expansion, nature conservation).

12.2.6.3 Advance the methodological development of Federal Transport Infrastructure Planning

We do not wish to go into much detail regarding the need for action regarding Federal Transport Infrastructure Planning, as this would go beyond the focus of our analysis. Instead, we will simply state the following:

- Federal Transport Infrastructure Planning should be based on a concept of sustainable transportation and logistics and should be developed further into a planning instrument that includes and integrates all modes of transportation.
- The aim of decoupling economic development from the development of transportation should lead to specific measures aimed at limiting goods traffic.

12.2.6.4 Kairos: the right time to act

To what extent does this analysis of stocks and of their (inherent) dynamics enable us to discern the right time to act? The data on trends in transportation tell us that the general rule 'the sooner, the better' applies to all the above-mentioned needs for action. The areas where a need for action has been identified essentially relate to plans which, by their very nature, are only able to affect the environment in the long term. The analysis of stocks, however, shows that there are no fundamental obstacles to acting right away. The only question is whether or not the political will exists to do so.

The government coalition treaty of 2009, mentioned at the start of this chapter, indicates that in some areas there is indeed the will to undertake a reform of inland shipping policy. In particular, the treaty mentions the restructuring of the WSV. This intention is backed up additionally by the above-mentioned reform of the WSV put forward by the Federal Ministry of Transport in spring 2011 and its associated procedure for prioritising investments in improvements in which the network of inland waterways is divided up into primary waterways, major waterways and subsidiary waterways (*Vorrang-, Haupt- und Nebenwasserstraßen*). This new categorisation of the waterways network makes it feasible to reduce the size of the waterways network and to re-dedicate largely unused stretches of waterway. This in turn would enable regulations to be devised that are beneficial to both the federal government and the federal states while not significantly harming shipping and yet serving nature conservation and the protection of water bodies. Despite this, there is (still) likely to be resistance on the part of the WSV (because its scope of influence is being reduced) as well as the inland shipping organisations (because the reduction of the waterways network can be seen as a sign that policy is shifting away from an increase in inland shipping – even if the stretches of waterway in question are ones that are more or less irrelevant to current and future waterway traffic). Additionally, though, a number of federal states in eastern Germany – supported by lobbyists – are putting up massive resistance because they fear they will be at a disadvantage in the distribution of investment funds by the federal government. Nonetheless a window of opportunity for new arrangements is currently available in this regard, and those in positions of responsibility seem to be taking advantage of it.

A new Federal Transport Infrastructure Plan is currently being devised. In this respect, too, the time would be right to introduce demands for planning that include greater consideration of all modes of transportation taken together in any review of methods. It may be that it is too late for this, however. With the update of the Water Management Act, responsibility for ensuring the passability of barrage facilities along the country's inland waterways was transferred to the WSV. As a result, the window of opportunity for drawing up more extensive regulations around the coordination of transport, water management and nature conservation planning appears to have closed for now.

12.3 Reflection

In the foregoing pages we have applied the heuristic developed in Chapter 11 to the policy field of inland shipping. We have followed the steps set out in the heuristic and have taken account of its guidelines and rules wherever relevant. The kind of information evaluated was essentially that which is readily accessible in statistics or reports. One characteristic feature of our approach is that both quantitative and qualitative information as well as information about physical infrastructures and organisational arrangements – i.e. material and immaterial stocks – were evaluated in conjunction with one another. The very co-presentation of these different kinds of information makes it possible to discern linkages and interconnecting factors which may be surprising. By placing the analytic description in relation to sustainability goals it then becomes possible to work out what the need for action is. In other words, it was possible to generate contextual and practical knowledge.

To summarise, then: the heuristic takes as its point of departure both factual knowledge and knowledge of rules. How these separate pieces of information are selected, weighted and linked together, however, depends on the considerations, judgements and opinions applied to them – and that is the domain of the faculty of judgement. When people use knowledge to underpin the decisions they make about how to act, this knowledge is typified by interweaving facts and judgements. The contextual and practical knowledge created by applying the heuristic is thus a synthesis of factual knowledge and knowledge of rules on the one hand and of experience, judgements and evaluative assessments on the other. To this extent the case study has illustrated how the concept of stocks and the heuristic derived from it can be understood as a bridging principle for purposes of judgement.

Notes

1 This chapter is based on an unpublished study by Klauer and Gunkel (2009) produced as an input for the German government's Council for Sustainable Development. The study made use of a preliminary version of the heuristic developed in Chapter 11 above.

2 Further information about the problems and potential of inland waterways transportation with a specific focus on the River Elbe can be found in Petschow and Wlodarski (2009). Part II of the book by Petry and Klauer (2005) contains a detailed case study relating to the controversy over the usefulness of inland shipping on the River Saale. These two studies form the main source of the case study in this chapter.

3 www.wsv.de/wasserstrassen/index.html, 2.3.2014.

4 www.bgl-ev.de/image/daten/verkehr/transportleistung_tabelle.pdf, 11.11.2010.

5 www.bgl-ev.de/image/daten/verkehr/transportleistung_tabelle.pdf, 11.11.2010.

6 www.wsv.de, 13.05.2009.

7 Water morphology denotes structural features of water bodies such as riverbank features (composition, vegetation, construction etc.), the course of the river (e.g. meandering, winding, straightened), the composition of the riverbed (e.g. banks, deep and shallow zones), differences in current and substrata, etc.

8 Cf. Law governing the revision of water bodies legislation (*Gesetz zur Neuregelung des Wasserrechts*), 31.07.2009.

9 Frankfurter Allgemeine Zeitung, 18.09.2010.

10 Sources: www.wsv.de, www.wsv.de/Schifffahrt/Statistik/index.html, www.wasserblick.net. Additional sources appear in the text.

11 In a brochure produced by the association for increasing shipping on the Saale (*Verein zur Hebung der Saaleschifffahrt*), former Saxony-Anhalt transport minister Daehre is quoted as saying: 'We want to use the Elbe and the Saale for ecological transportation in order to take the strain off the roads and to cope with the constant increase in traffic'. The writers of the brochure also state: 'In this way [inland shipping on the Saale] will become an important driver for continuing positive entrepreneurial development in the region and will offer new opportunities for further local investment. This means that existing jobs are safeguarded and new ones created, giving people in the region positive future prospects, an increase in quality of life and greater purchasing power'. (*Verein zur Hebung der Saaleschifffahrt*: Binnenschifffahrt auf der Saale – Ein Gewinn für alle! [Inland shipping on the Saale – A boon for us all!] www.saaleverein.de; 8.12.2009).

12 The basic features of this method are presented in BMVBW (2002). A key concern of Petry and Klauer (2005) is to offer a critique of the method and consider options for improvement.

13 www.wsv.de/service/karten_geoinformationen/bundeseinheitlich/pdf/w172b_Gueterverkehrsdichte2000.pdf, 19.5.2016.

14 In the past there have been a number of investments made – not least in the waterways sector – whose impacts in terms of capacity have fallen far short of expectations. One example is the expansion of the harbour at Halle on the river Saale, which cost more than 30 m € and made it into a modern, trimodal goods transfer centre, where to this day no significant water-borne transhipment occurs (Petschow and Wlodarski 2009: 279–280).

15 www.nok21.de/wp-content/uploads/2012/06/Fragen-und-Antworten.pdf, 19.5.2016.

13 Stocks: a schooling in long-term thinking

13.1 Begin with things as they are

The idea of sustainability ultimately calls for action in society, politics and academia. Sustainability demands that we take precautionary action to ensure the well-being of future generations, that we dismantle existing conditions of injustice between the rich and the poor and that we treat the natural environment with care. These demands are extremely demanding both ethically and intellectually:

- From an ethical perspective, each person, society as a whole and above all those who represent certain groups of people politically are called upon to take action against unjust conditions. This means striving to live life in such a way that it does not endanger the natural environment upon which human survival or indeed nature as a whole depends. When doing so, each person needs to ask themselves whether what they are doing right now is beneficial in the long term as well. In other words they need to put all the things they do in their everyday lives to this test. In doing so they will probably discover that many of their actions – if not most of them – do not do justice to the demands of sustainability. Unlike ordinary citizens, politicians have an additional responsibility for collective action.
- Intellectually speaking, sustainability demands that we are aware at all times of what is beneficial and how it can be achieved. Furthermore, any decisions that are made need to prove their worth over very long periods of time.

Demands of this kind can easily become overwhelming which, rather than stimulating action, threatens to stifle it. It is not uncommon for them to be clothed in quasi-religious rhetoric accompanied by an appeal to the authority of science. This is often followed by the demand for immediate change – a fundamental, rapid transformation of our modes of production and consumption and of our way of life – because it is only this, so it is said, which can avert the disastrous consequences of climate change (to name an especially pressing sustainability problem). What we identify in such utterances is an over-exaggerated trust in academia, i.e. a lack of appreciation for its limitations, as well as an inflated estimation of the potential of our actions. On this basis, all attempts to solve serious problems of sustainability are doomed to failure from the start. The reality is too far removed from the ideal of a 'sustainable world' to be able to bridge the gap within a short space of time.

The stocks framework developed in the course of this book is intended to provide a realistic, accessible way of approaching sustainability problems. It does not think in terms of goals that really ought to be achieved straight away. From the stocks perspective, sustainable action starts out not from a position of *what ought to be* – i.e. from an initially unachievable ideal – but from what a position of *what is*. It is from here that it strives to achieve what is possible and within reach.

Of course even this kind of sustainability goal is guided by an ideal, which is why the countless academic and non-academic articles that seek to unpack that normative ideal of sustainability and identify its constituent parts are necessary and valuable. Nevertheless our own focus is not on ideas about what should or could be but rather on things as they are. This involves first honouring the present and the past as the initial conditions for action before looking at the future and what we want to achieve. The stocks framework illustrates clearly that although we may be able to achieve little in the short term, in the long term we can achieve a great deal. In this way it prevents us from lurching between overinflated optimism and doleful resignation.

13.2 A focus on 'time'

The stocks framework starts out from the way things are in two respects: first, it is aimed at making existing knowledge – including imprecise, uncertain or subjective knowledge – as fully available as possible so that it can be used by those called upon to act. Second, reality is looked at in such a way that genuine options for action remain in focus. In this way, reality comes to be perceived as changing and changeable over the course of time. This approach complements those sustainability strategies which study issues of justice in particular, because it stresses the aspects of time and the long term which, although they are essential to achieving sustainability, are at the same time especially hard to handle.

One essential feature of the stocks framework is that three different meanings of time are used which, at first glance, may appear to have little in common with one another but which, when placed in relation to one another, open up new perspectives. When we look at stocks in nature and society we need to understand time, on the one hand, in the way we usually do: as an objective entity measurable in terms of seconds, years or centuries. We have named this conception of time *chronos*. We assume that this conception of time is relevant when it comes to durable structures – *stocks* – and their dynamics.

Within the stocks framework, though, the 'way things are' appears at once as a limit to action as well as a space in which options for action exist. Therefore, in addition to the measurable time of *chronos* we also consider time in the sense of the 'right moment' or the right temporal structure for action – that is, as 'time to do …' something or as 'time for …' this or that action. The right time to act – which we call *kairos* – needs to be perceived by those called upon to act, and the opportunity to do so has to be grasped by someone who recognises it. Unlike *chronos*, this kind of time is not value-neutral, homogenous and quantitative in nature but rather qualitative: the right moment is, as it were, the window of opportunity which opens up at certain prominent points during the course of ordinary clock time – for those who look and are able to see it. This understanding of time is subjective, because *kairos* depends on the purposes pursued by the person concerned.

We come to recognise *kairos* by looking at the third form of time, namely, the *inherent time* and *inherent dynamics* of stocks. By this we mean the typical dynamics and processes by which material and immaterial things around us develop and which therefore exert a powerful influence on our options for action. By setting our knowledge regarding the natural course of things alongside our awareness of the inertia of structures, with a little good fortune on the one hand and a practised eye for what is essential on the other we are able to spot the early signs of an upcoming window of opportunity.

The stocks framework is a good way of creating an overview of diffuse situations so that the dimension of time can be viewed systematically. The aim is not so much to create new knowledge as to gain better access to existing knowledge and to make use of it. Working with the stocks framework may therefore often involve going back to existing, generally available sources of information whose knowledge is then integrated into an overall picture. Statistics and, above all, time series are important sources of this kind. They provide information about material stocks and their trends over time. In many cases it is also possible to derive information from them about immaterial stocks such as patterns of behaviour or preferences. Other important sources of information are the study of history – not only political history but above all economic, social, legal and environmental history. The history of institutions in particular offers important insights into both the inertia and the transformation of the broader setting in which action is taken. The stocks framework makes it possible to draw on so-called soft forms of knowledge – practical knowledge, experiences and intuition.

13.3 Judgement and developing a 'sense of what is essential'

The possibilities for sustainable action in the face of the fundamental incompleteness of knowledge and human inadequacies are referred to in the context of our stocks framework in terms of the faculty of *judgement*. Judgement is the human ability to place specific situations and general principles, rules or features in relation to one another. It is needed, on the one hand, to bridge the gap between the fundamental ethical requirements of sustainability and specific conditions for action. It also serves, on the other hand, to apply general knowledge to concrete states of affairs and situations. Judgement comprises the ability to define problems appropriately, to distinguish what is important from what is unimportant and what is conducive from what is misleading, and to integrate diverse elements into an overall picture. On top of this, one of the tasks of judgement is to perceive where there is a lack of knowledge and to deal with it in an appropriate way. It becomes apparent at this point that ignorance, or lack of knowledge, not only indicates the limited nature of our knowledge but also facilitates a certain open-endedness to our actions.

The role of the stocks framework is to provide guidelines for our faculty of judgement in respect of sustainability. We have developed it into a guide for action – a heuristic – which is intended to help decision makers to grasp sustainability problems in terms of their temporal dimension. The heuristic is intended to provide a degree of guidance to them on the complex terrain of sustainability policy and to find paths leading towards successful policies.

13.4 The art of long-term thinking

Given that the purpose of the stocks framework is to provide guidance for sustainable action, obviously it does not constitute a separate academic theory of nature and society aimed at illuminating any regularities or causalities in relation to sustainability. While the stocks framework regularly draws on the findings of such theories and feeds them into the overall picture of a given situation and its dynamics, it is not designed to contribute new insights to expert debates in these fields.

Even if the stocks framework is to be used as a heuristic, this does not mean that it can serve as a kind of recipe that can be followed without critical thought yet with the expectation of ending up with reliable practical solutions. Equally it cannot be used as a scientific instrument for conducting impact assessments. It is not a solution algorithm that could be used to programme a computer. Rather, the stocks framework constitutes a particular *perspective* on sustainability problems. It is intended to be attractive to decision makers who are capable of handling it in a free and playful way. Perhaps the framework is best understood as a *lesson in long-term thinking.*

Anyone who has learned to work skilfully with the stocks perspective will acquire the ability to look at the world in a particular way – one in which the interplay of temporal structures in all the relevant spheres becomes visible and thus forms an overall picture. In the course of this, the stocks perspective proves particularly useful in enabling developments which are very probably *not* sustainable to be identified surprisingly quickly.

Viewed in this way, then, the stocks framework exists at the boundary between theory and practice. It takes everything from theory that is important in relation to a given sustainability problem and processes that knowledge and information in such a way that a kind of 'information handout' for practitioners emerges. As such it provides a basis for conceptualising sustainable action. What is taught above all in this 'lesson in thinking' is how to adopt a free and unencumbered perspective on the problem at hand and on the options for action. What is taught is not a science, then, so much as an *art* – a faculty that enables timely, sustainable action. This is *the art of long-term thinking.*

Bibliography

Akademie der Wissenschaften zu Berlin (Arbeitsgruppe Umweltstandards) (1992): *Umweltstandards: Grundlagen, Tatsachen und Bewertungen am Beispiel des Strahlenrisikos* [*Environmental standards: Basics, Facts and Assessments Taking the Example of Radiation Risk*]. de Gruyter, Berlin, New York.

Albert, Hans (1985): *Treatise on Critical Reason*. Princeton University Press, Princeton, New Jersey.

Amir, Shmuel (1975): Equilibrium in Ecological Systems. PhD thesis. Hebrew University of Jerusalem.

Amir, Shmuel (1987): Energy Pricing, Biomass Accumulation, and Project Appraisal: A Thermodynamic Approach to the Economics of Ecosystem Management. In: Pillet, Gonzague/Murota, Takeshi (eds.): *Environmental Economics: The Analysis of a Major Interface*. Roland Leimgruber, Genf, 53–108.

Amir, Shmuel (1989): On the Use of Ecological Prices and System-Wide Indicators Derived Therefrom to Quantify Man's Impact on the Ecosystem. *Ecological Economics*, **1**, 203–231.

Anderson, Elizabeth S. (2000): Warum eigentlich Gleichheit? [Why Actually Equality?] In: Krebs, Angelika (ed.): *Gleichheit oder Gerechtigkeit*. 3. ed., Suhrkamp, Frankfurt/M, 117–171.

Aoki, Masahiko (2001): *Towards a Comparative Institutional Analysis*. MIT Press, Cambridge, MA.

Apel, Karl-Otto (1994): Die ökologische Krise als Herausforderung für die Diskursethik [The Ecological Crisis as Challenge for Discourse Ethics]. In: Böhler, Dietrich (ed.): *Ethik für die Zukunft. Im Diskurs mit Hans Jonas*. C.H. Beck, München, 369–406.

Aristotle (1993): *Physics*. Books III and IV. Clarendon Aristotle Series, Clarendon Press, Oxford.

Aristotle (2014): *Nichomachean Ethics*. Hackett Publishing, Indianapolis.

Augustine (1988): *St. Augustine's Confessions*. Vol. II. Harvard University Press, Cambridge, Massachusetts; William Heinemann, London.

Ayres, Clarence E. (1944): *The Theory of Economic Progress*. University of North Carolina Press, Chapel Hill.

Barney, Gerald O. (ed.) (1980): The Global 2000 Report to the President: Entering the Twenty-First Century. Vol. 1. Council of Environmental Quality, U.S. Government Printing Office, Washington, D.C.

Bathe, Frauke (2010): Die Umsetzung der EG-Wasserrahmenrichtlinie in Deutschland – eine vergleichende Analyse der Entwürfe der Bewirtschaftungspläne [The Implementation of the EU Water Framework Directive in Germany – A Comparative Analysis of the Preliminary Management Plans]. UFZ Report 01/2010, Helmholtz Center for Environmental Research – UFZ, Leipzig.

Bathe, Frauke/Klauer, Bernd/Schiller, Johannes (2010): Die Ausweisung künstlicher und erheblich veränderter Gewässer in Deutschland – eine länderübergreifende Analyse

[The Classification of Artificial and Heaviliy Modified Water Bodies in Germany – An Analysis for Germany]. *Wasser und Abfall*, **12**, 40–44.

Bathe, Frauke/Klauer, Bernd/Schiller, Johannes (2011): Wirklich auf dem Weg zu guten Gewässern? [Really on the Way to Good Status of German Water Bodies?] *Wasser und Abfall*, **1–2**, 10–16.

Baumgartner, Frank R./Jones, Bryan D. (2002): *Policy Dynamics*. University of Chicago Press, Chicago.

Baumgärtner, Stefan/Becker, Christian/Frank, Karin/Müller, Birgit/Quaas, Martin (2008): Relating the Philosophy and Practice of Ecological Economics. The Role of Concepts, Models and Case Studies in Inter- and Transdisciplinary Sustainability Research. *Ecological Economics*, **67**(3), 384–393.

Baumgärtner, Stefan/Faber, Malte/Schiller, Johannes (2006): *Joint Production and Responsibility in Ecological Economics – On the Foundation of Environmental Policy*. Edward Elgar, Cheltenham, UK.

Baumgärtner, Stefan/Schiller, Johannes (2001): Kuppelproduktion. Ein Konzept zur Beschreibung der Entstehung von Umweltproblemen [Joint Production. A Concept to Describe the Emergence of Environmental Problems]. In: Beckenbach, Frank/Hampicke, Ulrich/Leipert, Christian/Meran, Georg/Minsch, Jürg/Nutzinger, Hans G./Pfriem, Reinhard/Weimann, Joachim/Wirl, Franz/Witt, Ulrich (eds.): *Jahrbuch Ökologische Ökonomik*. Vol. 2: *Ökonomische Naturbewertung*. Metropolis, Marburg, 353–393.

BBR – Bundesamt für Bauwesen und Raumordnung (2006): Raumordnungsprognose 2020/2050. Bevölkerung, private Haushalte, Erwerbspersonen, Wohnungsmarkt [Predictions for Regional Planning 2020/2050: Population, Private Households, Labour Force, Housing Market]. Bonn.

BBSR – Bundesinstitut für Bau-, Stadt- und Raumforschung (2011): Auf dem Weg, aber noch nicht am Ziel – Trends der Siedlungsflächenentwicklung [On the Way but not yet Arrived – Development Trends of Settlement Areas]. BBSR-Berichte KOMPAKT 10/2011, www.bbsr.bund.de/BBSR/DE/Veroeffentlichungen/Berichte Kompakt/2011/DL_10_2011.pdf?__blob=publicationFile&v=2, 16.3.2015

Behrens, Hermann (2007): Rückblicke auf den Umweltschutz in der DDR seit 1990 [Retrospective: Environmental Protection in the GDR after 1990]. In: Behrens, Hermann/Hoffman, Jens (eds.): *Umweltschutz in der der DDR: Analysen und Zeitzeugenberichte. Vol. 1: Politische und umweltrechtliche Rahmenbedingungen*. Oekom, München, 1–40.

Berger, Peter L./Luckmann, Thomas (1991): *The Social Construction of Reality: A Treatise in the Sociology of Knowledge*. Penguin Books, London et al.

Birnbacher, Dieter (1988): *Verantwortung für zukünftige Generationen* [*Responsibility to Future Generations*]. Phillip Reclam jun., Stuttgart.

Birnbacher, Dieter (2006): Responsibility to Future Generations – Scope and Limits. In: Tremmel, Jörg (ed.): *Handbook of Intergenerational Justice*. Edward Elgar, Cheltenham, 23–38.

Bizer, Kilian/Bunzel, Arno/Cichorowski, Georg/Rottmann, Manuela (2006): *Instrumente und Akteure in der Flächenkreislaufwirtschaft (Expertise)* [*Instruments and Actors of Circular Land Management (Expertise)*]. Bundesamt für Bauwesen und Raumordnung, Bonn.

Bizer, Kilian/Gubaydullina, Zulia (2008): Die umweltökonomische Perspektive [The Perspective of Environmental Economics]. In: Köck, Wolfgang/Bizer, Kilian/Einig, Klaus/Hansjürgens, Bernd/Siedentop, Stefan (eds.): *Handelbare Flächenausweisungsrechte. Anforderungsprofil aus ökonomischer, planerischer und juristischer Sicht*. Nomos, Baden-Baden, 35–37.

BMF – Bundesministerium der Finanzen (2008): Eckdaten zur Entwicklung und Struktur der Kommunalfinanzen 1998 bis 2007 [Basic Parameters of the Structure of Local Government Finances 1998 to 2007]. www.sh-landkreistag.de/media/custom/100_24079_1.PDF, 03.07.2012.

BMU – Bundesministerium für Umwelt, Naturschutz und Reaktorsicherheit (2007): Nationale Strategie zur Biologischen Vielfalt [National Strategy on Biodiversity]. Berlin.

BMU – Bundesministerium für Umwelt, Naturschutz und Reaktorsicherheit (ed.) (2010): Die Wasserrahmenrichtlinie – Ergebnisse der Bewirtschaftungsplanung 2009 in Deutschland [The Water Framework Directive – Results of the Management Plans 2009 in Germany]. Berlin.

BMU/BfN – Bundesministerium für Umwelt, Naturschutz und Reaktorsicherheit/ Bundesamt für Naturschutz (2009): Auenzustandsbericht – Flussauen in Deutschland [Report on the State of Flood Plains – River Meadows in Germany]. Berlin, Bonn.

BMVBS – Bundesministerium für Verkehr, Bau und Stadtentwicklung (2010): *Verkehrsinvestitionsbericht 2009* [*Report on Investments into Traffic Infrastructure 2009*]. Deutscher Bundestag, Drucksache 17/444, 17. Wahlperiode, 14.01.2010.

BMVBW – Bundesministerium für Verkehr, Bau- und Wohnungswesen (2002): *Grundzüge der gesamtwirtschaftlichen Bewertungsmethodik*. Bundesverkehrswegeplan 2003 [*Basic Outline of the National Accounting Methodology*. Federal Transport Plan 2003]. Berlin.

BMVBW – Bundesministerium für Verkehr, Bau und Wohnungswesen (2003): Bundesverkehrswegeplan 2003. Grundlagen für die Mobilität der Zukunft [Federal Transport Plan 2003. Foundations of Future Mobility]. www.bmvi.de/SharedDocs/DE/Anlage/VerkehrUndMobilitaet/Schiene/2003/bundesverkehrswege-plan-2003-beschluss-der-bundesregierung-vom-02-juli-2003.pdf?__blob=publicationFile

Brand, Fridolin (2009): Critical Natural Capital Revisited: Ecological Resilience and Sustainable Development. *Ecological Economics*, **86**, 605–612.

Brohm, Winfried (2002): *Öffentliches Baurecht* [*Public Building Law*]. 3. ed., C.H. Beck, München.

Brown, Gardner M./Johnson, Ralph W. (1984): Pollution Control by Effluent Charges: It Works in the Federal Republic of Germany, Why Not in the U.S.? *Natural Resources Journal*, **22**, 929–966.

Buchanan, James M. (1975): *The Limits of Liberty, Between Anarchy and Leviathan*. Chicago, London.

Buchanan, James M./Tullock, Gordon (1962): The Calculus of Consent. *Logical Foundations of Constitutional Demoracy*. University of Michigan Press, Ann Arbor.

BUND/MISEREOR (eds.) (1996): *Zukunftsfähiges Deutschland: Ein Beitrag zu einer global nachhaltigen Entwicklung* [*Sustainable Germany: A Contribution to Global Sustainable Development*]. Birkhäuser, Basel, Berlin.

Burke, Edmund (1803): *The Works of the Right Honourable Edmund Burke*. London.

Chichilnisky, Graciela (1996): An Axiomatic Approach to Sustainable Development. *Social Choice and Welfare*, **13**, 231–257.

Chichilnisky, Graciela (1997): What is Sustainable Development? *Land Economics*, 79(4), 467–491.

Ciriacy-Wantrup, Siegfried v. (1952): *Resource Conservation: Economics and Policy*. University of California Press, Berkeley.

Coenen, Reinhard/Paschen, Herbert (2000): HGF-Projekt: Untersuchung zu einem integrativen Konzept nachhaltiger Entwicklung: Bestandsaufnahme, Problemanalyse, Weiterentwicklung. Überblick über den Abschlußbericht [HGF-Project: Investigation on an Integrative Concept of Sustainable Development: Inventory, Problem Analysis, Advancement. An Overview]. 19.5.2016.

Cohen, Gerald A. (2001): *Gleichheit ohne Gleichgültigkeit* [*Equality without Indifference*]. Rotbuch, Berlin.

Costanza, Robert (ed.) (1991): *Ecological Economics: The Science and Management of Sustainability*. Columbia University Press, New York.

Daly, Herman E. (1994): Operationalizing Sustainable Development by Investing in Natural Capital. In: Jansson, AnnMari/Hammer, Monica/Folke, Carl/Costanza, Robert (eds.): *Investing in Natural Capital: The Ecological Economics Approach to Sustainability*. Island Press, Washington, D.C., Covelo, CA., 22–37.

Daly, Herman E. (1996): *Beyond Growth. The Economics of Sustainable Development*. Beacon Press, Boston.

Dosch, Fabian (2008): Siedlungsflächenentwicklung und Nutzungskonkurrenzen [Development of Settlement Areas and Competition in Land Use]. *Technikfolgenabschätzung – Theorie und Praxis*, 17(2), 41–51.

Downs, Anthony (1967): *Inside Bureaucracy*. Little, Brown and Co., Boston.

EC – European Communities (2000): Directive 2000/60/EC of the European Parliament and of the Council of 23 October 2000 establishing a framework for the Community action in the field of water policy. http://eur-lex.europa.eu/legal-content/EN/TXT/?uri=celex:32000L0060, 16.03.2015.

EEA – European Environment Agency (2006a): Land accounts for Europe 1990–2000. Towards integrated land and ecosystem accounting. Luxembourg.

EEA – European Environment Agency (2006b): Urban Sprawl in Europe. The ignored challenge. Luxembourg.

Eisenbarth, Siegfried (1995): *Altlastensanierung und Altlastenfinanzierung: Freistellung und Sanierung in den neuen Ländern unter Beteiligung des Bundes* [*Remediation and Financing of Contaminated Sites: Exemption and Decontamination in Eastern Germany by Means of Federal Government Funding*]. Economica, Bonn.

Ekardt, Felix (2011): *Theorie der Nachhaltigkeit. Rechtliche, ethische und politische Zugänge – am Beispiel von Klimawandel, Ressourcenknappheit und Welthandel* [*The Theory of Sustainability. Legal, Ethical and Political Approaches – Taking the Examples of Climate Change, Scarce Resources and World Trade*]. Nomos, Baden-Baden.

Faber, Malte (1986): *Studies in Austrian Capital Theory, Investment and Time*. Springer, Berlin, Heidelberg, New York.

Faber, Malte/Frank, Karin/Klauer, Bernd/Manstetten, Reiner/Schiller, Johannes/ Wissel, Christian (2005a): Grundlagen einer allgemeinen Theorie der Bestände [Foundations of a General Theory of Stocks]. In: Beckenbach, Frank/Hampicke, Ulrich/Leipert, Christian/Meran, Georg/Minsch, Jürg/Nutzinger, Hans G./Pfriem, Reinhard/Weimann, Joachim/Wirl, Franz/Witt, Ulrich (eds.): *Innovationen und Nachhaltigkeit. Jahrbuch Ökologische Ökonomik 4*. Metropolis, Marburg, 251–294.

Faber, Malte/Frank, Karin/Klauer, Bernd/Manstetten, Reiner/Schiller, Johannes/Wissel, Christian (2005b): On the Foundation of a General Theory of Stocks. *Ecological Economics*, **55**, 155–172.

Faber, Malte/Manstetten, Reiner (2003): *Mensch-Natur-Wissen – Grundlagen der Umweltbildung* [*Man-Nature-Knowledge: Foundations of Environmental Education*]. Vandenhoeck und Ruprecht, Göttingen.

Faber, Malte/Manstetten, Reiner (2007): *Was ist Wirtschaft? Von der Politischen Ökonomie zur Ökologischen Ökonomie*. Karl Alber, Freiburg.

Faber, Malte/Manstetten, Reiner/Petersen, Thomas (1997): Homo Oeconomicus and Homo Politicus. Political Economy, Constitutional Interest and Ecological Interest. *Kyklos*, 50(4), 457–483.

Faber, Malte/Manstetten, Reiner/Proops, John L.R. (1996): *Ecological Economics. Concepts and Methods*. Edward Elgar, Cheltenham, UK.

Faber, Malte/Proops, John L.R. (1998): *Evolution, Time, Production and the Environment*. 3. ed., Springer, Berlin, Heidelberg, New York.

Faber, Malte/Proops, John L.R./Speck, Stefan/with Jöst, Frank (1999): *Capital and Time in Ecological Economics. Neo-Austrian Modelling*. Edward Elgar, Cheltenham, UK, Northampton, MA, USA.

Faber, Malte/Stephan, Gunter/Michaelis, Peter (1989): *Umdenken in der Abfallwirtschaft. Vermeiden, Verwerten, Beseitigen* [*Rethinking Waste Management: Avoid, Reuse, Dispose*]. 2. ed., Springer, Berlin, New York, London, Paris, Tokyo, Hong Kong.

Faensen-Thiebes, Andreas/Müller, Wolfgang (2008): Erfolge und Defizite bei der Nachnutzung von Altlastenflächen – Darstellung am Beispiel der Berliner Flächen im Freistellungsverfahren [Success and Deficits in the Reuse of Contaminated Sites – Demonstrated by the Example of Berlin Sites in the Exemption

Procedure]. Senatsverwaltung für Gesundheit, Umwelt und Verbraucherschutz. www.berlin.de/sen/umwelt/bodenschutz/de/nachsorge/download/altlasten2008_9_faensen_mueller.pdf, 05.07.2010.

Fischer, Beate/Jöst, Frank/Manstetten, Reiner (2010): Die Persistenz von Institutionen – Hindernisse auf dem Weg zu einer nachhaltigen Flächennutzungspolitik in Deutschland [The Persistence of Institutions – Obstacles on the Way to a Sustainable Land Use Policy in Germany]. *Zeitschrift für Umweltpolitik & Umweltrecht*, **33**(4), 391–416.

Fischer, Beate/Klauer, Bernd/Schiller, Johannes (2013): Prospects for Sustainable Land-use Policy in Germany: Experimenting with a Sustainability Heuristic. *Ecological Economics*, **95**, 213–220.

Frankfurt, Harry (2000): Gleichheit und Achtung [Equality and Respect]. In: Krebs, Angelika (ed.): *Gleichheit oder Gerechtigkeit. Die Kritik am Egalitarismus*. Frankfurt/M, 38–49.

Gabler's Wirtschaftslexikon [Gabler's Lexicon of Economy] (2001). 15. ed., Gabler, Wiesbaden.

Gabriel, Ingeborg (2005): Grundzüge und Positionen katholischer Sozialethik [Main Features and Positions of Catholic Social Ethics]. In: Gabriel, Ingeborg/Papaderos, Alexandros K./Körtner, Ulrich H.J. (eds.): *Perspektiven ökumenischer Sozialethik: der Auftrag der Kirchen im größeren Europa*. Matthias-Grünewald-Verlag, Mainz, 193–204.

Gadamer, Hans-Georg (1975): *Truth and Method*. Bloomsbury, London.

Gawel, Erik/Köck, Wolfgang/Kern, Katharina/Möckel, Stefan/Holländer, Robert/Fälsch, Marcel/Völkner, Thomas (2011): *Weiterentwicklung von Abwasserabgabe und Wasserentnahmeentgelten zu einer umfassenden Wassernutzungsabgabe*. UBA-Texte 67/2011, Umweltbundesamt, Dessau.

Gawron, Thomas (2007): Recht der Raumordnung [Law in Spacial Planning]. In: Köck, Wolfgang/Bovet, Jana/Gawron, Thomas/Hoffmann, Ekkehard/Möckel, Stefan: *Effektivierung des raumbezogenen Planungsrechts zur Reduzierung der Flächeninanspruchnahme*. Im Auftrag des Umweltbundesamtes. Helmholtz Center for Environmental Research, Leipzig, 79–154.

Gehlen, Arnold (1980): *Man in the Age of Technology*. Columbia University Press, New York.

Gehlen, Arnold (2004a): *Urmensch und Spätkultur. Philosophische Ergebnisse und Aussagen*. Klostermann, Frankfurt/M.

Gehlen, Arnold (2004b): Moral und Hypermoral. *Eine pluralistische Ethik* [*Moral and Hypermoral. A Pluralistic Ethic*]. 6. ed., Klostermann, Frankfurt/M.

Georgescu-Roegen, Nicholas (1971): *The Entropy Law and the Economic Process*. Harvard University Press, Cambridge.

German Federal Government (2002): Perspectives for Germany – Our Strategy for Sustainable Development. www.bundesregierung.de/Content/EN/StatischeSeiten/Schwerpunkte/Nachhaltigkeit/Anlagen/perspektives-for-germany-langfassung.pdf?__blob=publicationFile&v=1, 20.01.2014.

German Federal Government (2008): Progress Report 2008 on the National Strategy for Sustainable Development. For a Sustainable Germany. www.nachhaltigkeitsrat.de/fileadmin/user_upload/English/strategy/2008/German_Govt_NSDS_progress_report_08_E.pdf, 13.03.2014.

Gigerenzer, Gerd (2007): *Gut Feelings: The Intelligence of the Unconscious*. Allen Lane, London.

Glas, Christian (1996): *Wirtschaftsgeographische Neubewertung des Main-Donau-Kanals* [*Economic-geographic Reassessment of the Main-Donau-Channel*]. Münchner Studien zur Sozial- und Wirtschaftsgeographie. Vol. 40. Münchner Universitätsschriften, Verlag Michael Laßleben, Kallmünz, Regensburg.

Gnest, Holger (2008): *Entwicklung der überörtlichen Regionalplanung in der Bundesrepublik von 1975 bis heute* [*Development of the National Regional Planning in Germany from 1975 until Today*]. Akademie für Raumforschung und Landesplanung, Hannover.

Goethe, Johann W. (1912): *Faust, Parts I & II*. J.M. Dent & Sons, London; E.P. Dutton & Co., New York.

Goodland, Robert/Daly, Herman E. (1995): Universal Environmental Sustainability and the Principle of Integrity. In: Westra, Laura/Lemons, John (eds.): *Perspectives on Ecological Integrity*. Springer, Dordrecht, Boston, London.

Greif, Avner (2006): *Institutions and the Path to the Modern Economy*. Cambridge University Press, Cambridge.

Grober, Ulrich (2012): *Sustainability: A Cultural History*. Green Books, Totnes, Devon.

Grundwald, Armin/Kopfmüller, Jürgen (2012): *Nachhaltigkeit* [*Sustainability*]. 2. ed., Campus, Frankfurt/M.

Habermas, Jürgen (1984a): *The Theory of Communicative Action*. Vol. I: Reason and the Rationalization of Society. Beacon Press, Boston.

Habermas, Jürgen (1984b): *Vorstudien und Ergänzungen zur Theorie des kommunikativen Handelns* [*Preliminary Studies and Supplements to the Theory of Communicative Action*]. Suhrkamp, Frankfurt/M.

Habermas, Jürgen (1985): *Philosophical-Political Profiles*. Chapter: Arnold Gehlen: Imitation Substantiality. The MIT Press, Cambridge, MA, London, 101–112.

Habermas, Jürgen (1987): *The Theory of Communicative Action*. Vol. II: Lifeworld and System: A Critique of Functionalist Reason. Beacon Press, Boston.

Habermas, Jürgen (1998): *Between Facts and Norms: Contributions to a Discourse Theory of Law and Democracy*. The MIT Press, Cambridge, MA.

Hannon, Bruce (1973): The Structure of Ecosystems. *Journal of Theoretical Biology*, 41, 535–546.

Hannon, Bruce (1985): World Shogun. *Journal of Social and Biological Structures*, 8, 329–341.

Hannon, Bruce (1995): Input-Output Economics and Ecology. *Structural Change and Economic Dynamics*, 6, 331–333.

Harte, Michael J. (1995): Ecology, Sustainability, and Environmental Capital. *Ecological Economics*, 15(2), 157–164.

Hartwick, John M. (1977): Intergenerational Equity and the Investing of Rents from Exhaustible Resources. *American Economic Review*, 66, 972–974.

Hartwick, John M. (1978a): Substitution Among Exhaustible Resources and Intergenerational Equity. *Review of Economic Studies*, 45, 347–354.

Hartwick, John M. (1978b): Investing Returns from Depleting Renewable Resource Stocks and Intergenerational Equity. *Economic Letters*, 1, 85–88.

Hegel, Georg W.F. (2001): *Philosophy of Right*. Batoche Books, Kitchener, Canada.

Heidbrink, Ludger (2003): *Kritik der Verantwortung. Zu den Grenzen verantwortlichen Handelns in komplexen Kontexten* [*Critique of Responsibility. On the Limits of Responsible Action in Complex Contexts*]. Velbrück Wissenschaft, Weilerswist.

Heidegger, Martin (1950): *Die Technik und die Kehre* [*Technique and Bend*]. Neske, Pfullingen.

Heidegger, Martin (1996): *Being and Time*. A Translation of Sein und Zeit. State University of New York Press, Albany.

Held, Martin/Kümmerer, Klaus (2004): Rhythmen und Resilienz – Nachhaltige Entwicklung in zeitlicher Perspektive [Rhythms and Resilience – Sustainable Development from a Temporal Perspective]. In: Ipsen, Dirk/Schmidt, Jan C. (eds.): *Dynamiken der Nachhaltigkeit*. Metropolis, Marburg, 113–150.

Hennis, Wilhelm (1963): *Politik und praktische Philosophie* [*Politics and Practical Philosophy*]. Luchterhand, Neuwied, Berlin.

Hentrich, Steffen/Walter, Komar/Weisheimer, Martin (2000): Umweltschutz in den neuen Bundesländern: Bilanz im zehnten Jahr deutscher Einheit [Environmental Protection in Eastern Germany – Ten Years after the German Reunification]. Diskussionspapier 128, Institut für Wirtschaftsforschung Halle. www.iwh-halle.de/d/publik/disc/128.pdf, 06.07.2010.

Hinsch, Wilfried (2001): Global Distributive Justice. In: Pogge, Thomas W. (ed.): *Global Justice*. Blackwell, Oxford, 55–75.

Hodgson, Geoffrey M. (2004): *The Evolution of Institutional Economics: Agency, Structure, and Darwinism in American Institutionalism*. Routledge, London, New York.

Höffe, Otfried (2001): *Gerechtigkeit. Eine philosophische Einführung* [*Justice. A Philosophical Introduction*]. C.H. Beck, München.

Houthakker, Hendrik S. (1950): Revealed Preferences and the Utility Function. *Economica*, 17, 159–174.

Hübler, Karl-Hermann (1991): Die Bundesraumordnung von 1965 bis 1989 [Federal Regional Planning 1965 to 1989]. In: ARL – Akademie für Raumforschung und Landesplanung (ed.): *Zur geschichtlichen Entwicklung der Raumordnung, Landes- und Regionalplanung in der Bundesrepublik Deutschland*. Hannover, 32–51.

Ickert, Lutz/Matthes, Ulrike/Rommerskirchen, Stefan/Weyand, Emely/Schlesinger, Michael/Limbers, Jan (2007): Abschätzung der langfristigen Entwicklung des Güterverkehrs in Deutschland bis 2050. Schlussbericht eines Auftrages des Bundesministeriums für Verkehr, Bau und Stadtentwicklung [Assessment of the Long-term Development of Shipping in Germany until 2050. Final Report for the Federal Ministry of Transport, Construction and Urban Development], Projekt-Nr. 26.0185/2006. Basel.

IFU – Institut für Umweltschutz (ed.) (1990): Umweltbericht der DDR. Information zur Analyse der Umweltbedingungen in der DDR und zu weiteren Maßnahmen [Environmental Report of the GDR. Information on the Analysis of Environmental Conditions in the GDR and Future Measures]. Berlin.

Intraplan Consult (2007): Prognose der deutschlandweiten Verkehrsverflechtungen 2025. Kurzfassung [Prediction of the National Traffic Integration 2025. Short Version]. FE-Vorhaben Nr. 96.0857/2005. www.bmvi.de//SharedDocs/DE/Anlage/VerkehrUnd Mobilitaet/verkehrsprognose-2025-kurzfassung.pdf?__blob=publicationFile.

Jarass, Hans D. (1987): Der rechtliche Stellenwert technischer und wissenschaftlicher Standards [The Legal Status of Technical and Scientific Standards]. *Neue Juristische Wochenschrift*, 40(1/2), 1225–1231.

Jonas, Hans (1984): *Imperative of Responsibility: In Search of an Ethics for the Technological Age*. University of Chicago Press, Chicago.

Kant, Immanuel (1855): *Critique of Pure Reason*. Henry G. Bohn, London.

Kant, Immanuel (1991): On the Common Saying: 'This May Be True in Theory, But it Does Not Apply In Practice'. In: *Political Writings*. Ed. by Hans S. Reiss. Cambridge University Press, Cambridge et al., 61–92.

Kant, Immanuel (2001): Critique of the Power of Judgement. Ed. by Paul Guyer. *The Cambridge Edition of the Works of Immanuel Kant*, Cambridge University Press, Cambridge et al.

KBA – Kraftfahr-Bundesamt (2007): Statistische Mitteilungen. Fahrzeugzulassungen. Bestand Fahrzeugklassen und Aufbauarten am 1. Januar 2007 [Statistical Communications. Vehicle Registrations, Registered Vehicle Classes and Types of Car Bodies on 1 January 2007]. Flensburg.

Kersting, Wolfgang (1997): *Recht, Gerechtigkeit und demokratische Tugend* [*Law, Justice and Democratic Virtue*]. Suhrkamp, Frankfurt/M.

Kieser, Alfred (2006): Entscheiden Manager klug, wenn sie mithilfe von Unternehmensberatern oder Wissenschaftlern entscheiden? [Do Managers Decide Wisely if They are Assisted by Business Consultants and Scientists?] In: Scherzberg, Arno/Betsch, Tilmann/Blanke, Hermann-Josef/Walgenbach, Peter/Waschkuhn, Arno/Wegner, Gerhard (eds.): *Kluges Entscheiden. Disziplinäre Grundlagen und interdisziplinäre Verknüpfungen*. Mohr Siebeck, Tübingen, 51–73.

Kingston, Christopher/Caballero, Gonzalo (2009): Comparing Theories of Institutional Change. *Journal of Institutional Economics*, 5(2), 151–180.

Klaasen, Ger A.J./Opschoor, Johannes B. (1991): Economics of Sustainability or the Sustainability of Economics: Different Paradigms. *Ecological Economics*, 4, 93–115.

Klauer, Bernd (1998): *Nachhaltigkeit und Naturbewertung. Welchen Beitrag kann das ökonomische Konzept der Preise zur Operationalisierung von Nachhaltigkeit leisten?* [Sustainability and the Valuation of Nature. Of Which Help can the Economic Concept of Prices be for the Operationalisation of Sustainability?] Reihe Umwelt und Ökonomie, Vol. 25, Physica-Verlag, Heidelberg.

Klauer, Bernd (1999a): Defining and Achieving Sustainable Development. *The International Journal of Sustainable Development and World Ecology*, 6(2), 114–121.

Klauer, Bernd (1999b): Was ist Nachhaltigkeit und wie kann man eine nachhaltige Entwicklung erreichen? [What is Sustainability and How Can We Achieve Sustainable Development?] *Zeitschrift für angewandte Umweltforschung*, 12(1), 86–97.

Klauer, Bernd (2000): Ecosystem Prices: Activity Analysis Applied to Ecosystems. *Ecological Economics*, 33, 473–486.

Klauer, Bernd/Drechsler, Martin/Messner, Frank (2006): Multicriteria Analysis Under Uncertainty with IANUS – Method and Empirical Results. *Environment and Planning C: Government and Policy*, **24**(2), 235–256.

Klauer, Bernd/Gunkel, Stephan (2009): Eckpunkte einer nachhaltigen Binnenschifffahrtspolitik – Entwurf. Unveröffentlichtes Manuskript [Key Points of a Sustainable Inland-shipping Policy – Draft. Unpublished manuscript].

Klauer, Bernd/Manstetten, Reiner/Petersen, Thomas/Schiller, Johannes (2013): The Art of Long-term Thinking: A Bridge Between Sustainability Science and Politics. *Ecological Economics*, 93, 79–84.

Klepper, Gernot (1999): Wachstum und Umwelt aus der Sicht der neoklassischen Ökonomie [Growth and Environment from the Perspective of Neoclassical Economics]. In: *Jahrbuch Ökologische Ökonomik*. Vol. 1. Metropolis, Marburg, 291–318.

Köck, Wolfgang/Bovet, Jana (2008): Anforderungen aus rechtlicher Sicht [Requirements from a Legal Perspective]. In: Köck, Wolfgang/Bizer, Kilian/Einig, Klaus/Hansjürgens, Bernd/Siedentop, Stefan (eds.): *Handelbare Flächenausweisungsrechte. Anforderungsprofil aus ökonomischer, planerischer und juristischer Sicht*. Nomos, Baden-Baden, 96–109.

Komar, Walter (1992): Strukturprobleme der Chemischen Industrie im Raum Halle/Merseburg aus ökonomischer, ökologischer und sozialer Sicht [Structural Problems of the Chemical Industrie in the Area of Halle/Leipzig as Seen from an Economic, Ecological and Social Perspective]. In: Arbeitsgruppe Ökologische Wirtschaftspolitik (ed.): *Ökologische Probleme regionaler Strukturpolitik: Probleme und Lösungsmöglichkeiten nach der Vereinigung*. Metropolis, Marburg, 111–133.

Kopfmüller, Jürgen/Brandl, Volker/Jörissen, Juliane/Paetau, Michael/Banse, Gerhard/Coenen, Reinhard/Grunwald, Armin (2001): *Nachhaltige Entwicklung integrativ betrachtet* [*Integrative Analysis of Sustainable Development*]. Edition Sigma, Berlin.

LAF – Landesanstalt für Altlastenfreistellung des Landes Sachsen-Anhalt (2002): *Altlastensanierung in Sachsen-Anhalt* [*Remediation of contaminated sites in Saxony-Anhalt*]. Magdeburg.

LAF – Landesanstalt für Altlastenfreistellung des Landes Sachsen-Anhalt (2010): *10 Jahre Landesanstalt für Altlastenfreistellung des Landes Sachsen-Anhalt. Von Industriebrachen zu attraktiven Wirtschaftsstandorten* [*10 Years State Agency for Exemption from Contamination Liability of the State of Saxony-Anhalt. From Industrial Brownfields to Attractive Business Locations*]. Magdeburg.

Lee-Peuker, Mi-Yong/Klauer, Bernd (2010): Bringing About Institutional Change in Public Brownfield Management – The Case of Saxony-Anhalt (Germany). UFZ Discussion Paper 5/2010, Helmholtz Center for Environmental Research, Leipzig.

Lerch, Achim/Nutzinger, Hans G. (1998): Nachhaltigkeit: Methodische Probleme der Wirtschaftsethik [Sustainability: Methodological Problems of the Ethics of Economics]. *Zeitschrift für Evangelische Ethik*, 42, 208–223.

Luhmann, Niklas (1974): *Grundrechte als Institution* [*Fundamental Rights as an Institution*]. Duncker & Humblot, Berlin.

MacIntyre, Alasdair C. (2013): *After Virtue*. Bloomsbury, London.

Mackie, John (1990): *Ethics. Inventing Right and Wrong*. Penguin Books, London et al.

Manstetten, Reiner (2000): *Das Menschenbild der Ökonomie. Der homo oeconomicus und die Anthropologie von Adam Smith* [The Conception of Man in Economics. The Homo Oeconomicus and the Anthropology of Adam Smith]. Alber, Freiburg, München.

Marx, Karl (1959): *Capital. A Critical Analysis of Capitalist Production.* Vol. I. Foreign Language Publishing House, Moscow.

May, Karl (1962[1892]): *Durch die Wüste* [*Through the Desert*]. Karl-May-Verlag, Bamberg, Wien.

Meadows, Dennis L./Meadows, Donella H./Randers, Jørgen/Behrens, William W. (1972): *The Limits to Growth – A Report for the Club of Rome's Project on the Predicament of Mankind.* Universe Books, New York.

Mieg, Harald A. (2005): Warum wir EINE Umweltwissenschaft brauchen und Interdisziplinarität nur eine (nützliche) Fiktion ist [Why We Need ONE Environmental Science and Why Interdisciplinarity is Just (Useful) Fiction]. In: Baumgärtner, Stefan/Becker, Christian (eds.): *Wissenschaftsphilosophie interdisziplinärer Umweltforschung.* Metropolis, Marburg, 73–86.

Mirowski, Philip (1984): Physics and the Marginalist Revolution. *Cambridge Journal of Economics*, 8, 361–379.

Möckel, Stefan (2009): Bewirtschaftung von Bundeswasserstraßen entsprechend der Wasserrahmenrichtlinie [Management of Federal Water Ways in Accordance With the Water Framework Directive]. Legal opinion written for BUND, unpublished.

Munasinghe, Mohan/Shearer, Walter (eds.) (1995): *Defining and Measuring Sustainability: The Biogeophysical Foundation. World Bank*, Washington, D.C.

Nachbarschaftsverband Mannheim-Heidelberg (ed.) (2006): Flächennutzungsplan 2015/2020. Begründung [Land-use Plan 2015/2020. Justification], Vol. I. Handlungsstrategie, Mannheim.

North, Douglass C. (1990): *Institutions, Institutional Change and Economic Performance.* Cambridge University Press, Cambridge.

Norton, Bryan G./Toman, Michael A. (1997): Sustainability: Ecological and Economic Perspectives. *Land Economics*, 73(4), 553–568.

Nussbaum, Martha C. (1988): *Nature, Function and Capability: Aristotle on Political Distribution. Oxford Studies in Ancient Philosophy* (supplementary volume), 145–184.

Nussbaum, Martha C. (2000): Women and Human Development. *The Capabilities Approach.* Cambridge University Press, Cambridge.

Nussbaum, Martha C. (2006): Frontiers of Justice. *Disability, Nationality, Species Membership.* Belknap Press of Harvard University Press, Cambridge, London.

Oakeshott, Michael (1991): *Rationalism in Politics and other Essays. New and Expanded Edition*, Liberty Fund, Indianapolis.

Odum, Eugene P. (1975): Fundamentals of Ecology. *Teaching-Learning Guide.* Saunders, Philadelphia, London.

Olsson, Per/Gunderson, Lance H./Carpenter, Steve R./Ryan, Paul/Lebel, Louis/Folke, Carl/Holling, Crawford S. (2006): Shooting the Rapids. Navigating Transitions to Adaptive Governance of Social-Ecological Systems. *Ecology and Society*, 11(1), 18.

Ortmann, Günther (2006): Kür und Willkür. Jenseits der Unentscheidbarkeit [Election and Arbitrariness: Beyond Undecidability]. In: Scherzberg, Arno/Betsch, Tilmann/Blanke, Hermann-Josef/Walgenbach, Peter/Waschkuhn, Arno/Wegner, Gerhard (eds.): *Kluges Entscheiden. Disziplinäre Grundlagen und interdisziplinäre Verknüpfungen.* Mohr Siebeck, Tübingen, 167–194.

Ostrom, Elinor (1990): Governing the Commons. *The Evolution of Institutions for Collective Action.* Cambridge University Press, Cambridge.

Ott, Konrad (2004): Essential Components of Future Ethics. In: Döring, Ralf/ Rühs, Michael (eds.): *Ökonomische Rationalität und praktische Vernunft. Festschrift für Ulrich Hampicke.* Königshausen und Neumann, Würzburg, 83–108.

Ott, Konrad (2009): Zur Begründung der Konzeption starker Nachhaltigkeit [On the Justification of the Concept of Strong Sustainability]. In: Koch, Hans-Joachim/Hey, Christian (eds.): *Zwischen Wissenschaft und Politik – 35 Jahre Gutachten des Sachverständigenrates für Umweltfragen*. Schmidt, Berlin, 63–87.

Ott, Konrad (2010): *Umweltethik zur Einführung* [*Environmental Ethics – An Introduction*]. Junius, Hamburg.

Ott, Konrad/Döring, Ralf (2006): Grundlinien einer Theorie 'starker' Nachhaltigkeit [Outline of a Theory of 'Strong' Sustainability]. In: Köchy, Kristian/Norwig, Martin (eds.): *Umwelt-Handeln. Zum Zusammenhang von Naturphilosophie und Umweltethik*. Vol. 2. Karl Alber, Freiburg, 89–127.

Ott, Konrad/Döring, Ralf (2008): *Theorie und Praxis starker Nachhaltigkeit* [Theory and Practice of Strong Sustainability]. Metropolis, Marburg.

Pearce, David W./Barbier, Edward/Markandya, Anil (1990): *Sustainable Development: Economics and Environment in the Third World*. Edward Elgar, Hants, GB, Brookfield, VT.

Pearce, David W./Turner, R. Kerry (1990): *Economics of Natural Resources and the Environment*. Johns Hopkins University Press, New York et al.

Penn-Bressel, Gertrude (2005): Begrenzung der Landschaftszerschneidung bei der Planung von Verkehrswegen [Limiting Landscape Fragmentation in the Planning of Traffic Routes]. *GAIA*, 14(2), 130–134.

Petersen, Thomas (1996): *Individuelle Freiheit und allgemeiner Wille. James Buchanans politische Ökonomie und die politische Philosophie* [*Individual Freedom and General Will. James Buchanan's Political Economy and Political Philosophy*]. Mohr Siebeck, Tübingen.

Petersen, Thomas (2005a): Phronesis und Urteilskraft – Antike und zeitgenössische Philosophie. In: von Sivers, Gabriele/Diehl, Ulrich (eds.): *Wege zur politischen Philosophie. Festschrift für Martin Sattler*. Königshausen & Neumann, Würzburg, 119–133.

Petersen, Thomas (2005b): Phronesis, Urteilskraft und Interdisziplinarität [Phronesis, Power of Judgement and Interdisciplinarity]. In: Baumgärtner, Stefan/Becker, Christian (eds.): *Wissenschaftsphilosophie interdisziplinärer Umweltforschung*. Metropolis, Marburg, 25–39.

Petersen, Thomas/Faber, Malte (2000): Bedingungen erfolgreicher Umweltpolitik im deutschen Föderalismus. Der Ministerialbeamte als Homo politicus [Conditions of Successful Environmental Policy in the German Federal System. The Ministry Official as Homo Politicus]. *Zeitschrift für Politikwissenschaft*, **1/00**, 5–41.

Petersen, Thomas/Faber, Malte (2005): Verantwortung und das Problem der Kuppelproduktion. Reflexionen über die Grundlagen der Umweltpolitik [Responsibility and the Problem of Joint Production. Reflections on the Foundations of Environmental Politics]. *Zeitschrift für Politikwissenschaft*, 1/05, 35–59.

Petersen, Thomas/Klauer, Bernd (2012): Staatliche Verantwortung für Umweltqualitätsstandards. Governance im Kontext der EG-Wasserrahmenrichtlinie [The State's Responsibility for Environmental Quality Standards. Governance in the Context of the EU Water Framework Directive]. *GAIA*, 21(1), 48–54.

Petersen, Thomas/Schiller, Johannes (2011): Politische Verantwortung für Nachhaltigkeit und Konsumentensouveränität [Political Responsibility for Sustainability and Consumer Sovereignty]. *GAIA*, 20(3), 157–161.

Petry, Daniel/Klauer, Bernd (2005): *Umweltbewertung und politische Praxis in der Bundesverkehrswegeplanung – Eine Methodenkritik illustriert am Beispiel des geplanten Ausbaus der Saale* [*Environmental Assessment and Political Practice in Federal Transport Planning – A Critique of Methods using the Example of the Projected expansion of the River Saale*]. Metropolis, Marburg.

Petschow, Ulrich/Wlodarski, Wojciech (2009): Stand und Potenziale der Elbe-Binnenschifffahrt und deren wirtschaftliche Wirkungen auf die Elbe-Region [Situation and Potentials of Inland Shipping on the River Elbe and its Economic Effects on the Elbe Region]. Schriftenreihe des IÖW 194/09, Inst. für ökolog. Wirtschaftsforschung, Berlin.

Pezzey, John C.V. (1992): *Sustainable Development Concepts: An Economic Analysis*. World Bank Environment Paper No. 2, Washington, D.C.

PIK – Potsdam-Institut für Klimafolgenforschung (2009): Memorandum zu den Folgen von Klimaänderungen und globalem Wandel im [Memorandum: Consequences of Climate Change and Global Change in the Elbe Region]. 11.10.2009. https://www.pik-potsdam.de/glowa/pdf/glowaiii/elbe_memorandum.pdf.

Pogge, Thomas W. (2001): Priorities of Global Justice. In: Pogge, Thomas W. (ed.): *Global Justice*. Blackwell, Oxford, 6–23.

Popper, Karl R. (1944): The Poverty of Historicism, II. A Criticism of Historicist Methods. *Economica, New Series*, **11**(43), 119–137.

Popper, Karl R. (1974): Replies to My Critics. In: Schilpp, Paul Arthur (ed.): The Philosophy of Karl Popper. Vol. II. *The Library of Living Philosophers*. Vol. XIV, Book II. Open Court, La Salle, Illinois, 961–1197.

Popper, Karl R. (2005): *The Logic of Scientific Discovery*. Taylor & Francis e-Library, Routledge, London, New York.

Prechtl, Peter/Burkhard, Franz P. (1999): *Metzler Philosophie Lexikon* [*Metzler Lexicon of Philosophy*]. 2. ed., Metzlersche J.B., Stuttgart, Weimar.

Preuschoff, Christian (2000): Vorbild mit Schwächen: Eine kritische Analyse der ökologischen Modernisierung in Ostdeutschland [Model with Weak Points: Critiqual Analysis of the Ecological Modernisation in Eastern Germany]. *Ökologisches Wirtschaften*, 2, 29–30.

Prognos AG (2001): Erarbeitung von Entwürfen alternativer verkehrspolitischer Szenarien zur Verkehrsprognose 2015 [Development of Drafts for Alternative Transport – political Scenarios for the 2015 Traffic Prediction]. FE-Vorhaben 96.579/1999, im Auftrag des Bundesministeriums für Verkehr, Bau und Wohnungswesen. Basel.

Radnitzky, Gerard/Bernholz, Peter (1987): *Economic Imperialism. The Economic Method Applied Outside the Field of Economics*. Paragon House Publishers, New York.

Rahner, Karl (1978): *Foundations of Christian Faith. An Introduction to the Idea of Christianity*. Darton Longman & Todd, London.

Rawls, John (1973): *A Theory of Justice*. Oxford University Press, Oxford et al.

Rawls, John (1999): *The Law of Peoples*. Harvard University Press, Cambridge, MA.

Redford, Kent H./Robinson, John G. (1995): Sustainability of Wildlife and Natural Areas. In: Munasinghe, Mohan/Shearer, Walter (eds.): *Defining and Measuring Sustainability: The Biogeophysical Foundations*. UN University, World Bank, Washington D.C., Tokyo, 401–406.

Rehberg, K.-S. (1990): Eine Grundlagentheorie der Institutionen: Arnold Gehlen. Mit systematischen Schlußfolgerungen für eine kritische Institutionentheorie [A Fundamental Theory of Institutions: Arnold Gehlen. With Systematic Conclusions for a Critical Theory of Institutions]. In: Göhler, Gerhard/Lenk, Kurt/Schmalz-Bruns, Rainer (eds.): *Die Rationalität politischer Institutionen*. Nomos, Baden-Baden, 115–144.

Remmert, Hermann (1980): *Ecology: A Textbook*. Springer, Berlin, Heidelberg, New York.

Renn, Ortwin/Deuschle, Jürgen/Jäger, Alexander/Weimer-Jehle, Wolfgang (2007): *Leitbild Nachhaltigkeit – Eine normativ-funktionale Konzeption und ihre Umsetzung* [*Sustainability as Guiding Principle – A Normative-functional Conception and its Implementation*]. VS-Verlag, Wiesbaden.

Repetto, Robert C. (1986): *World Enough and Time: The Findings of the Global Possible Project*. Yale University Press, New Haven, London.

Richter, Rudolf/Furubotn, Eirik G. (1998): *Institutions and Economic Theory. The Contribution of the New Institutional Economics*. The University of Michigan Press, Ann Arbor.

Ritschl, Albrecht (1995): Aufstieg und Niedergang der Wirtschaft der DDR: Ein Zahlenbild 1945–1989 [The Rise and Downfall of GDR's Economy in Numbers 1945–1989]. *Jahrbuch für Wirtschaftsgeschichte*, 2, 11–46.

Robbins, Lionel (1932): *An Essay on the Nature and Significance of Economic Science.* Macmillan & Co., London.

Sabatier, Paul A. (1988): An Advocacy Coalition Model of Policy Change and the Role of Policy-Oriented Learning Therein. *Policy Sciences*, 21, 129–168.

Schelsky, Helmut (1970): Zur soziologischen Theorie der Institution [On the Sociological Theory of Institutions]. In: Schelsky, Helmut (ed.): *Zur Theorie der Institution.* Bertelsmann, Düsseldorf, 9–26.

Schiller, Johannes (2002): *Umweltprobleme und Zeit. Bestände als konzeptionelle Grundlage ökologischer Ökonomik [Environmental Problems and Time. Stocks as a Conceptional Basis of Ecological Economics]*. Metropolis, Marburg.

Schiller, Johannes/Manstetten, Reiner/Klauer, Bernd/Steuer, Philipp/Unnerstall, Herwig/Wittmer, Heidi/Hansjürgens, Bernd (2006): *Herausforderung Programmforschung – Konzeption, Organisation und Evaluation problemorientierter Umweltforschung [The Challenge of Program-based Research – Conception, Organisation and Evaluation of Problem Oriented Environmental Research]*. Metropolis, Marburg.

Schmidt-Bleek, Friedrich/Klüting, Rainer (1994): *Wieviel Umwelt braucht der Mensch? MIPS – Das Maß für ökologisches Wirtschaften* [How Much Environment Does Man Need? MIPS – The Measure for Sustainable Management]. Birkhäuser, Berlin.

Schmitz, Stefan/Paulini, Inge (1999): Bewertung in Ökobilanzen – Methode des Umweltbundesamtes zur Normierung von Wirkungsindikatoren, Ordnung (Rangbildung) von Wirkungskategorien und zur Auswertung nach ISO 14042 und 14043 [Assessment in Ecological Balances – The Method of the Federal Environmental Agency for the Nomination of Impact Indicators, Ranking of Impact Categories and Evaluation in Accordance with ISO 14042 and 14043]. UBA Texte 92/1999, Umweltbundesamt, Dessau.

Schröder, Meinhard/Claussen, Martin/Grunwald, Armin/Hense, Andreas/Klepper, Gernot/Lingner, Stephan/Ott, Konrad/Schmitt, Dieter/Sprinz, Detlef (2002): *Klimavorhersage und Klimavorsorge [Climate Prediction and Climate Protection]*. Springer, Berlin, Heidelberg.

Seibel, Wolfgang (2005): *Verwaltete Illusionen. Die Privatisierung der DDR-Wirtschaft durch die Treuhandanstalt und ihre Nachfolger 1990–2000.* 2. ed, Campus, Frankfurt, New York.

Sen, Amartya (1979): Utilitarianism and Welfarism. *The Journal of Philosophy*, LXXVI, 463–489.

Sen, Amartya (1985): *Commodities and Capabilities*. Elsevier Science Ltd, North-Holland, Amsterdam.

Sen, Amartya (1987): *The Standard of Living*. Cambridge University Press, Cambridge.

Sen, Amartya (2009): *The Idea of Justice*. Allen Lane, London.

Sen, Amartya/Nussbaum, Martha (eds.) (1993): *The Quality of Life*. Clarendon Press, Oxford.

Siedentop, Stefan (2008): Siedlungspolitischer Kontext des 30-Hektar-Ziels [The Settlement-policy Context of the 30 Hectare Target]. In: Köck, Wolfgang/Bizer, Kilian/Einig, Klaus/Hansjürgens, Bernd/Siedentop, Stefan (eds.): *Handelbare Flächenausweisungsrechte. Anforderungsprofil aus ökonomischer, planerischer und juristischer Sicht*. Nomos, Baden-Baden, 21–35.

Sigel, Katja/Klauer, Bernd/Pahl-Wostl, Claudia (2010): Conceptualising Uncertainty in Environmental Decision-making: The Example of the EU Water Framework Directive. *Ecological Economics*, 69, 502–510.

Simon, Herbert A. (1959): Theory of Decision Making in Economics and Behavioural Science. *American Economic Review*, 49(3), 253–283.

Smith, Adam (1977): An Inquiry into the Nature and Causes of the Wealth of Nation. *Encyclopaedia Britannica*, Chicago et al.

Smith, Adam (2002): *The Theory of Moral Sentiments*. Ed. by Knut Haakonssen. The Cambridge University Press, Cambridge.

Smith, Adam (2004): *Selected Philosophical Writings*. Ed. by James R. Otteson. Imprint Academic, Exeter, UK.

Solow, Robert M. (1974a): Intergenerational Equity and Exhaustible Resources. *Review of Economic Studies*, 14 (Symposium Exhaustible Resource), 29–45.

Solow, Robert M. (1974b): The Economics of Resources or the Resources of Economics. *American Economic Review*, 64, 1–14.

Solow, Robert M. (1986): On the Intergenerational Allocation of Natural Resources. *Scandinavian Journal of Economics*, 88, 141–149.

Solow, Robert M. (1992): *An Almost Practical Step Towards Sustainability. An Invited Lecture on the Occasion of the Fortieth Anniversary of Resources of the Future. Oct 8, 1992*. Resources for the Future, Washington, D.C.

Spaemann, Robert/Löw, Reinhard (1985): *Die Frage Wozu? Geschichte und Wiederentdeckung des teleologischen Denkens* [*The Question "What for?" – History and Rediscovery of Teleological Thinking*]. Piper, München.

SRU – Rat von Sachverständigen für Umweltfragen (1989): *Altlasten. Sondergutachten Dezember 1989* [Contaminated Sites. Special Report December 1989]. Metzler-Poeschel, Stuttgart.

SRU – Rat von Sachverständigen für Umweltfragen (1994): *Für eine dauerhaft umweltgerechte Entwicklung. Umweltgutachten 1994* [*For a Sustainable Development. Environmental Report 1994*]. Metzler-Poeschel, Stuttgart.

SRU – Rat von Sachverständigen für Umweltfragen (1996a): *Umweltgutachten 1996* [*Environmental Report 1996*]. Metzler-Poeschel, Stuttgart.

SRU – Rat von Sachverständigen für Umweltfragen (1996b): Ein Mehrstufenmodell zur Festlegung von Umweltstandards. Zur Umsetzung einer dauerhaft-umweltgerechten Entwicklung [A Multi-step Model for the Determination of Environmental Standards. For the Implementation of Sustainable Development.]. *Zeitschrift für angewandte Umweltforschung*, 9, 166–172.

SRU – Rat von Sachverständigen für Umweltfragen (2002): Umweltgutachten 2002. Für eine neue Vorreiterrolle [Environmental Report 2002. Towards a New Leading Role]. Stuttgart. Summary in English: www.umweltrat.de/EN/Reports/EnvironmentalReports/environmentalreports_node.html, 16.03.2015

SRU – Rat von Sachverständigen für Umweltfragen (2004): Umweltgutachten 2004. Umweltpolitische Handlungsfähigkeit sichern [Environmental Report 2004: Ensuring Environmental Protection Capacity]. Nomos, Berlin. Summary in English: www.umweltrat.de/EN/Reports/EnvironmentalReports/environmentalreports_node.html, 16.03.2015

SRU – Sachverständigenrat für Umweltfragen (2008): Umweltpolitik im Zeichen des Klimawandels. Umweltgutachten [Environmental protection in the shadow of climate change. Environmental Report]. E. Schmidt, Berlin. Selected chapters in English: www.umweltrat.de/EN/Reports/EnvironmentalReports/environmentalreports_node.html, 16.03.2015

StaBA – Statistisches Bundesamt (2006): Verkehr in Deutschland [Traffic in Germany]. Wiesbaden.

StaBA – Statistisches Bundesamt (2008a): Flächenstatistik [Land Use Statistics]. Personal information (e-mail), Uwe Scherhag (uwe.scherhag@destatis.de), 11.01.2008.

StaBA – Statistisches Bundesamt (2008b): Flächenstatistik. Personal information (e-mail), Uwe Scherhag (uwe.scherhag@destatis.de), 20.10.2008.

StaBA – Statistisches Bundesamt (2008c): Wohnstatistik [Residence Statistics]. Personal information (e-mail), D. Sedmihradsky (wohnsituation@destatis.de), 24.01.2008.

StaBA – Statistisches Bundesamt (2008d): Umweltnutzung und Wirtschaft. Tabellen zu den umweltökonomischen Gesamtrechnungen 2008, Teil 10: Flächennutzung [Natural Resource Consumption and Economy. Tables Showing the Ecological-economic Balances 2008, Part 10: Land Use].

StaBA – Statistisches Bundesamt (2009a): Bevölkerung Deutschlands bis 2060. 12. koordinierte Bevölkerungsvorausberechnung [Germany's Population until 2060. 12th Coordinated Population Prognosis]. Wiesbaden.

StaBA – Statistisches Bundesamt (2009b): Pressemitteilung Nr. 426 vom 11.11.2009. Zunahme der Siedlungs- und Verkehrsfläche 104 Hektar pro Tag [Press release No. 426, 11.11.2009. Increase of Settlement and Traffic Area 104 Hectares per Day].

Suchanek, Andreas (1993): Der homo oeconomicus als Heuristik. Diskussionsbeiträge der wirtschaftswissenschaftlichen Fakultät Ingolstadt und der Katholischen Universität Eichstätt [The homo oeconomicus as heuristic. Discussion Papers of the Faculty of Economics Ingolstadt and the Catholic University Eichstätt], Nr. 38. KUE, WFI, Ingolstadt.

Suchanek, Andreas (2001): *Ökonomische Ethik* [Economic Ethics]. Mohr Siebeck, Tübingen.

Tolstoy, Leo (1952): War and Peace. William Benton, *Encyclopaedia Britannica*, Chicago, London, Toronto.

Tugendhat, Ernst (1992): Die sprachanalytische Kritik der Ontologie [The Critique of Ontology by Linguistic Analysis]. In: *Philosophische Aufsätze.* Suhrkamp, Frankfurt/M., 21–35.

UN – United Nations (1992): Sustainable Development. United Nations Conference on Environment & Development, Rio de Janerio, Brazil, 3–14 June 1992, AGENDA 21. http://sustainabledevelopment.un.org/content/documents/Agenda21.pdf, 29.09.2014.

Unnerstall, Herwig (1999): *Rechte zukünftiger Generationen* [*Rights of Future Generations*]. Königshausen und Neumann, Würzburg.

van der Brugge, Rutger/Rotmans, Jan/Loorbach, Derk (2005): The Transition in Dutch Water Management. *Regional Environmental Change*, 5(4), 164–176.

Veblen, Thorstein (1899): *The Theory of the Leisure Class: An Economic Study of Institutions.* Macmillan, New York.

Verwaltungsgemeinschaft Flöha (2006): Flächennutzungsplan. Erläuterungsbericht [Land Use Plan. Explanatory Report]. Büro für Städtebau GmbH, Chemnitz.

Verwaltungsgemeinschaft Friedrichshafen-Immenstaad (ed.) (2006): Flächennutzungsplan 2015. Erläuterungsbericht [Land Use Plan 2015. Explanatory Report]. Friedrichshafen-Immenstaad.

Waldhoff, Christian (2006): § 2 Entwicklung der kommunalen Finanz- und Haushaltswirtschaft in historischer Perspektive [Development of the Municipal Financial and Fiscal Economy in a Historical Perspective]. In: Henneke, Hans-Günter/Pünder, Hermann/Waldhoff, Christian/Albers, Heinrich (eds.): *Recht der Kommunalfinanzen. Abgaben, Haushalt, Finanzausgleich.* C.H. Beck, München, 24–33.

Walzer, Michael (1983): *Spheres of Justice: A Defense of Pluralism and Equality.* Robertson, Oxford.

WCED – World Commission on Environment and Development (1987): *Our Common Future.* Oxford University Press, Oxford, New York.

Weber, Max (1968): Economy and Society. *An Outline of Interpretive Sociology.* Vol. 1. Ed. by Guenther Roth and Claus Wittich. Bedminster Press, New York.

Werner, Jan (2008): *Das deutsche Gemeindefinanzsystem. Reformvorschläge im Kontext der unterschiedlichen Einnahmeautonomie der lokalen Gebietskörperschaften in Europa* [*The German System of Municipal Finances. Suggestions for a Reform in the Context of the Varying Revenue Autonomies of the Regional Authorities in Europe*]. Peter Lang, Frankfurt/M.

Wieland, Wolfgang (1999): *Platon und die Formen des Wissens* [*Platon and the Forms of Knowledge*]. 2. ed., Vandenhoeck & Ruprecht, Göttingen.

Wieland, Wolfgang (2001): *Urteil und Gefühl. Kants Theorie der Urteilskraft* [*Judgement and Feeling. Kant's Theory of the Power of Judgement*]. Vandenhoeck & Ruprecht, Göttingen.

Williamson, Oliver E. (2000): The New Institutional Economics: Taking Stock, Looking Ahead. *Journal of Economic Literature*, XXXVIII, 595–613.

Winkler, Ralph (2003): *Zeitverzögerte Dynamik von Kapital – und Schadstoffbeständen. Eine österreichische Perspektive* [*Delayed Dynamics of Capital – and Pollutant Stocks. An Austrian Perspective*]. Metropolis, Marburg.

Wodopia, Franz-Josef (1986): Time and Production. Period Versus Continuous Analysis. In: Faber, Malte (ed.): *Studies in Austrian Capital Theory, Investment in Time*. Springer, Berlin, Heidelberg et al.

Wolf, Margareta (2003): Entstehung und Entwicklung der ökologischen Altlasten-Großprojekte in den neuen Bundesländern. Einschätzung der Altlastensituation aus der Position des BMU [Formation and Development of the Large-Scale Projects Dealing with Contaminated Sites in Eastern Germany. Assessment of the Situation of Contaminated Sites from the BMU's Perspective]. Speech by Margareta Wolf (Parliamentary State Secretary), Festkolloquium "10 Jahre Altlastenprojekt Saxonia", Freiberg/Sachsen, 01.09.2003. www.bmu.de/reden/archiv/15/wolf/doc/pdf/4507.pdf, 05.07.2010.

Index

Persons index